DENISE LEVERTOV IN COMPANY

• DENISE LEVERTOV IN COMPANY •

Essays by Her Students, Colleagues, and Fellow Writers

Edited by
Donna Krolik Hollenberg

The University of South Carolina Press

Published by the University of South Carolina Press
Columbia, South Carolina 29208

www.sc.edu/uscpress

Manufactured in the United States of America

26 25 24 23 22 21 20 19 18
10 9 8 7 6 5 4 3 2 1

Library of Congress Cataloging-in-Publication Data
can be found at http://catalog.loc.gov/.

ISBN: 978-1-61117-872-2 (cloth)
ISBN: 978-1-61117-873-9 (ebook)

CONTENTS

ACKNOWLEDGMENTS

I'd like to thank all of the contributors for the energy and effort they put into their essays, as well as, in some cases, permission to quote from their poems. I'd also like to thank Jim Denton and Linda Haines Fogle at the University of South Carolina Press for their support. Special thanks, also, to my husband, Leonard M. Rubin, for his helpful technical advice.

Permission to quote from unpublished material is granted by the Denise Levertov Trust, Paul A. Lacy and Valerie Trueblood Rapport, Co-Trustees.

Grateful acknowledgment is given to the following people and institutions for permission to quote from published sources:

New Directions Publishing Corporation for permission to quote from *Collected Poems of Denise Levertov,* © 2013 by Denise Levertov and the Estate of Denise Levertov, Reprinted by permission of New Directions Publishing Corp.

Emily Warn, "Beyond" (Part II) from *The Novice Insomniac.* © 1996 by Emily Warn. Reprinted with the permission of The Permissions Company, Inc., on behalf of Copper Canyon Press, www.coppercanyonpress.org. Benjamin Alire Sáenz, excerpt from "The Ninth Dream: War (in the City in Which I Live)," from *Dreaming the End of War.* © 2006 by Benjamin Alire Sáenz. Reprinted with the permission of The Permission Company, Inc. on behalf of Copper Canyon Press, www.coppercanyonpress.org.

Bruce Weigl, "One Lie" and "Quiet Fountain," from *The Abundance of Nothing.* © 2012 by Bruce Weigl. Published 2012 by Northwestern University Psress. All rights reserved.

"Ascension" and excerpts from "Land of the Living" and "Housekeeping" from *Little Girls in Church,* by Kathleen Norris, © 1995. Reprinted by permission of the University of Pittsburgh Press.

Excerpt from "Body and Blood" from *Journey: New and Selected Poems, 1969–1999,* by Kathleen Norris, © 2001. Reprinted by permission of the University of Pittsburgh Press.

Excerpt from "Urn Burial" from *Money Shot,* by Rae Armantrout © 2011. Reprinted by permission of Wesleyan University Press.

Excerpts from "Getting Warm" and from "View," both from *Veil: New and Selected Poems,* by Rae Armantrout © 2001. Reprinted by permission of Wesleyan University Press.

"Endings." © 1982 by Eavan Boland, "The Journey." Copyright © 1987 by Eavan Boland, from *Outside History: Selected Poems 1980–1990* by Eavan Boland. Used by permission of W.W. Norton and Co. and by Caracanet Press in the United Kingdom.

Anglo-American poet Denise Levertov (1923–1997) was the author of more than thirty books of poetry, prose, and translations and is acknowledged as an important figure in the literary and social history of the second half of the twentieth century. She grew up in England during a period of increasing fascism and approaching war, the youngest daughter in a family that was actively involved in rescuing Jewish refugees from Adolf Hitler's Germany. Her father, Paul Levertoff, was an Anglican priest who converted from Judaism; her mother, Beatrice Spooner-Jones Levertoff, a pious Welsh schoolteacher. A precocious child, Levertov began to publish poems as a teenager, and by 1946, when her first book appeared, she was noted as a promising British neo-Romantic poet. She moved to the United States after World War II and soon gained further recognition as a member of the Black Mountain school of poets, practitioners of poetry in "open" forms influenced by American modernists Ezra Pound, H.D., and William Carlos Williams. The poetry and presence of Williams became crucial in this regard, as did the support of such contemporaries as Cid Corman, Lawrence Ferlinghetti, Jonathan Williams, Robert Creeley, and Robert Duncan, poets who were her first publishers and critics.

Levertov's friendships with Creeley and Duncan were particularly important. In her transition from England to the United States, Creeley helped her to adjust to the differences in usage and stress in American speech, and, through him Levertov learned about Charles Olson's concept of composition by field, although her tie with Olson was weaker than that with Creeley. As her correspondence with Duncan shows, Levertov's close friendship with him, already complicated because of religious and political differences, was irreparably damaged over the Vietnam War and their different views of the role of the poet in politics. Levertov also benefited from the moral support of women friends who, though less recognized by the literary world, were equally committed to creative vocations, including art, ballet, and photography, as well as writing. Perhaps the most important of these was Muriel Rukeyser, who was like an older sister to Levertov.

In the 1960s, 1970s, and 1980s, Levertov participated passionately as a poet/activist in the peace movement, the antinuclear movement, and the environmentalist movement and in controversies surrounding poetry and politics, even as she taught at several American universities, mostly on the East and West Coasts. In her later years, a journey toward Christian faith, inspired by liberation theology, culminated in her conversion to Roman Catholicism. In this period her poetry was reanimated by religious fervor.

Levertov's work is included in all the major anthologies of twentieth-century poetry. A recent bibliography lists two pages of books or dissertations entirely or partially devoted to her work, and there are two earlier book-length bibliographies of primary and secondary sources. Since her death book-length editions of her letters have appeared, testifying further to her importance in literary history. Her correspondence with William Carlos Williams, edited by Christopher MacGowan, was published by New Directions (1998), and her correspondence with Robert Duncan, edited by Albert Gelpi and Robert Bertholf, was published by Stanford University Press (2004). It is worth noting, as a related primary source, that Vine of David Press recently published Paul Levertoff's *Love and the Messianic Age* (2009) as part of their Messianic Luminaries Series. Most recently Dana Greene's biography, *Denise Levertov: A Poet's Life,* was published by the University of Illinois Press (2012), and my biography, *A Poet's Revolution: The Life of Denise Levertov,* was published by the University of California Press (2013). New Directions published Levertov's *Collected Poems* in 2013.

In the course of researching my biography of Levertov, I became aware of the many distinguished younger poets whose lives and work she touched as a teacher, mentor, and friend. Yet, although there are scattered tributes and letters, this is the first book to gather and assesses that influence. *Denise Levertov in Company* demonstrates Levertov's impact upon contemporary poetry by including twenty essays, ten by a selection of these poets and ten by other poets and critics, who have written companion essays about the work of each contributor in relation to Levertov's poetry. A dialogue is thus implicit in the structure of the book between two perspectives: first, autobiographical testimony by the selected poets, and second, critical analysis, written by others in a spirit of affiliation with them. I chose the contributors on the basis of their spiritual, intellectual, and political connections with Levertov at different stages of her life in the United States as well as on the basis of their individual distinction. The pairs of essays are organized chronologically. A common motif in many of the companion essays, with one notable exception, is the ways in which Levertov enabled her students to find his or her own voice.

The first five poets became acquainted with Levertov in the 1960s and 1970s. Mark Pawlak and David Shaddock were students of Levertov's at MIT and Berkeley, respectively, when she and they protested against the war in Vietnam in the late 1960s. Pawlak continues to publish books of poetry devoted to peace and justice, and he cofounded Hanging Loose Press, which publishes the work of new writers. His essay, "Wordsmiths in the Idea Factory," discusses what he learned from Levertov during his class with her at MIT. Shaddock, now a poet and a psychotherapist, shared Jewish elements of Levertov's spirituality as well as her counterculture politics. His essay, "God Wrestling in Levertov's Life and Art," stresses the continuity between the artistic, the political, and the spiritual in Levertov's life and work, a continuity that parallels his own journey. The companion essays for these two poets are by Paul Lacey and Peter Dale Scott. Lacey, a literary critic, was also clerk of the American Friends Service Committee's board of directors and is coeditor of Levertov's *Collected Poems*. His essay, "Working Poets," shows both what Pawlak learned from Levertov and how he moves in a new direction in his more recent work. In addition to his many books of poetry and prose, Scott was cofounder of the Peace and Conflict Studies program at Berkeley and of the Coalition on Political Assassinations. His essay, on the "parallel voyages" of Levertov and Shaddock, traces those voyages back to their origin at Berkeley and shows the roots of "God wrestling" to be in political protest. Rae Armantrout, who won the Pulitzer Prize in 2010, was also a member of Levertov's Berkeley class, but she took a different direction from Levertov and became a Language poet. Her essay, "Denise and Me," describes her experience as Levertov's student as well as recent thoughts about Levertov's poetry. Literary critic Romana Huk's companion essay, "Levertov and Armantrout," explores the specifics and limits of their poetic divergence.

Although not a student of Levertov's, the poet Bruce Weigl, a Vietnam veteran, was mentored by her, and she introduced an anthology of antiwar poems he edited. Because Weigl was too ill to write an essay about his relationship with Levertov, I taped an interview with him and include the transcription here. Poet and fiction writer Reginald Gibbons's companion essay, "Generations of Poets," shows how Levertov's view of the social purposes of poetry gave Weigl permission to enact in his poems the inner aftermath that lingers in the psyches of soldiers forever. A leader in the tradeswoman movement as well as a poet, Susan Eisenberg studied with Levertov at Tufts in the 1970s and credits Levertov with encouraging her to explore feminist issues of power and social policy. "The Expansive View," the companion essay by poet Martha Collins, delineates the effect on Eisenberg's poetry of Levertov's insistence on the level of craft necessary to explore the places where the political and the personal intersect.

The next five poets were close to Levertov in the 1980s and 1990s. Several of them respond to aspects of Levertov's religious quest. The poet and memoirist Kathleen Norris was mentored by Levertov in the early stages of Norris's own spiritual journey, and their engagement around religious issues continued after Levertov's conversion to Catholicism. In her essay, "The Integrity of Words," Norris describes what she learned from Levertov in and beyond a religious context. The companion essay, "From Denise Levertov to Kathleen Norris," by literary critic Peggy Rosenthal, shows how Norris not only integrates these lessons but also shares Levertov's awareness of religious mystery. Poet Ben Sáenz, a student of Levertov's at Stanford in the 1980s, shared her interest in liberation theology, as he indicates in his essay, "Fragments of a Memoir," in which he says her interest in his work changed his life. Allison Hawthorne Deming, also a poet, takes a very different tack. Rather than focusing on the poetry of Sáenz and Levertov, she writes about her own, hurtful relationship with Levertov, which she still doesn't understand. Although primarily rooted in African American culture, poet Al Young was a friend during Levertov's years at Stanford who admired the mystical quality of her lyricism. In his essay, "Dear Denise," he shares the things they have in common, from the gaps between their front teeth, to their empathy for the underdog, to their revulsion at much of American foreign policy. In his companion essay, "P.S. Mind the Gap," literary critic Aldon Nielson explores the concept of a "gap" further, arguing at one point that the poetics of Young and Levertov was based on it. An environmentalist poet with a Zen practice, Emily Warn studied with Levertov at Stanford and was instrumental in her move to Seattle at the end of her life. In her essay, "The Almost Wilderness," she discusses the ways in which the landscape of the Pacific Northwest was a presence both in their friendship and in Levertov's sensibility, returning her to the milieu of her childhood in England, which was steeped in nineteenth-century literature and in the eclectic Christianity of her parents. In my companion essay, "Primary Wonder, Primary Joys," I compare the two poets' penchant for spiritual quest, particularly around the classic triangle of God, mind, and nature. Finally the volume includes "Craft and Conscience," an essay by the Irish poet Eavan Boland, whom Levertov recommended to replace her at Stanford when she retired from teaching there. Because of her Anglo-Irish roots, Boland represents a degree of continuity with Levertov's own transatlantic heritage, and in her essay she interrogates Levertov's approach to the civic poem as a communal statement. The literary critic Michael Thurston's companion essay, "Ending in Abandon," offers a new lens with which to approach the political poetry of both of them.

Denise Levertov in Company offers new insights into the range of Levertov's legacy. Its combination of personal witness and critical analysis contributes uniquely to our understanding of the contemporary poetry scene.

• WORDSMITHS IN THE IDEA FACTORY •

Denise Levertov's MIT Poetry Workshop

Mark Pawlak

My hope was that they would feel themselves,
however ephemerally, *a community of poets,* and never
as competitive aspirants for approval.

Denise Levertov, introduction to
"Poems from the MIT Poetry Workshop," in *Hanging Loose* 12

We met one night each week for two and a half hours both semesters in 1969–70. There were about ten of us students in attendance at the first meeting. Over the course of the next few weeks, others joined the class, until we had a full complement of thirteen. The assigned "classroom" was a black-box theater space on the second floor of the Humanities Building. Its track lighting, flat black walls, and absence of windows gave it a cavelike feel.

Denise instructed us to form a circle—some sat on stools, others on the floor; many lit up cigarettes. The atmosphere resembled that of a dimly lit coffeehouse but minus the coffee, café tables, and folk music. Denise made some introductory remarks, then asked us to introduce ourselves by sharing information about what college we attended, what we studied, and more. "Tell us about your inter--est in poetry," she instructed. "How long have you been writing? Which poets do you read?" Then she asked each of us to read aloud one of our poems. In some instances she suggested which one to read from among those we had originally submitted when applying for admission to the class. After someone had finished reading, she asked the rest to comment, but if we hesitated to speak, then she took the lead and talked about what she thought were the strengths of the poem, in this way modeling how she wanted us to lead with positive feedback in responding to the work of our peers.

The first surprise was that many of the others were not MIT students: Margo Taft and Lucy Marx were both Radcliffe students. Ernie Brooks was a Harvard undergrad, and Roger Bohmer a Harvard graduate student. Judy Katz was an undergrad at Simmons College, and Ted Benttinen was an oceanographer, ecology activist, and recent graduate school dropout. MIT undergrads, half of them physics majors like myself, made up the rest of the original group: Vic Elias, Barry Levine, and Arthur Sze, plus Don Krieger, an electrical engineering major; Bill Ratstetter, a chemistry major; and Richard Edelman, a philosophy major. Others joined the class at later points in the semester or during the second semester: Kevin O'Leary, a carpenter, who practiced Yoga and Zen, joined for a time during the winter, as did Paul Callahan, an engineering student at Northeastern University, and Aaron Shurin, who arrived from Berkeley that winter to try out living on the East Coast. (He had been in Denise's Berkeley writing class the previous semester.) The last to join the class, during the spring semester, was Hillarie Capps, an MIT math major and computer programmer.

MIT and Wellesley College had begun an exchange program a year or two earlier, but this class was different, not a formal arrangement between schools but rather a decision Denise made on her own about whom to admit. I had picked her class because of my budding interest in poetry and my curiosity about studying with a practicing artist. I didn't see myself as a poet then, nor did I aspire to become one. (Rather I expected to go on to graduate school, get a PhD, and pursue a career as an experimental physicist.) I suspect most of the other MIT students in the class came to it with a similar attitude. However, I viewed the others differently. They seemed to be passionately committed to writing poems; some aspired to become professional writers. Margo, for example, had a poem published that year in the groundbreaking anthology of women poets *No More Masks*.

On the principle that she would always take part in the activities and exercises that she asked us to do, Denise also read a poem of her own that first night, "Merritt Parkway," from her collection *O Taste and See*. Heads nodded in recognition during her recitation; one or two piped up to say that it was a favorite poem of theirs. This, along with other remarks, indicated to me that many of the other students were already acquainted not just with that poem but with the body of her work. In contrast, poet and poem were new to me. I was embarrassed that I had neglected to follow my normally studious habits for class preparation. It hadn't occurred to me to seek out copies of her books in advance of the first meeting, although I did set out the very next day to purchase one. What I found between the covers of *The Sorrow Dance*, my first Levertov acquisition, were poems unlike any my limited reading had prepared me for. Many were lyrics about common objects, actual events, and the rituals of everyday life, intensely observed, expressed in a sensual language that sometimes verged on the erotic. Other poems were didactic in nature, expressing moral outrage at war and social injustice.

I remember thinking to myself after that first class that I was venturing into foreign territory—also that I was out of my league. It seemed to me that the others were far better read and perfectly comfortable talking about poems, as if they shared a common vocabulary. Thanks to Denise's genial presence, these realizations didn't make me want to run for the door. I trusted in her command of the situation, which assured me that it was OK to be a novice. She had, after all, selected me to join this group for *some* reason. Instead of feeling anxiety, I remember thinking, "This could be interesting. There's a whole new world of things for me to learn here." Not a characteristic response for a seasoned MIT student, where intense competition with one's peers was the norm.

My prior classroom experience at MIT had, for the most part, consisted of attending lectures by prominent scientists, given in yawning halls that seated hundreds of students. I would try my best to listen attentively and comprehend what was being said, while at the same time madly scribbling notes in an effort to get down for later study all the diagrams and mathematical symbols chalked on the blackboards. Room 10-250, the primary lecture hall, could accommodate my entire class of 1970, about nine hundred students. Because the MIT curriculum back then was very rigid, allowing for few electives, we all took the same courses our first couple of years; and so, along with my peers, I took my place in that hall's raked seats that rose row upon row the height of two floors. Humanities courses, with twenty or so students per class, were less formal. Professors, only one of whom was female in my six semesters prior to Denise's class, expounded on their subjects, invited debate, and moderated discussions of the texts; but seated at the front of the room, they were always the focal point of every exchange.

Denise's approach to teaching was in striking contrast to all this, as when she had instructed us that first night to sit in a circle and address one another. If we directed questions or comments to her, she would turn them back to our fellow students for responses. Her aim seemed to be to make us appreciate just how much we might learn from one another. Only after the last student had had her or his say, would she chime in—unless she was bursting with something she absolutely *had* to say, when she simply could not restrain herself. In this way Denise let us know that we should view her as another member of the group—granted, the most worldly, experienced, and, in terms of poetry, knowledgeable one of us, but not always the "authority" expecting deference.

That first night Denise laid down some ground rules, the principal ones being that we should listen attentively to one another's work and offer only constructive comments and suggestions. She made it clear that in order to discuss honestly one another's poems without inhibitions, we needed to respect and value each other's ideas, perceptions, and opinions. The charge she gave to us, which she herself modeled throughout the workshop, was to say first what we liked about any poem under discussion, to point out its strengths and the parts we thought worked, and only then to follow with suggestions about how the author might improve the parts that needed fixing—all of this was to be done in the spirit of "mutual aid," as outlined by the Russian anarchist Prince Kropotkin. Whereas social Darwinists such as Thomas Huxley believed that the wealthy were wealthy because they were most fit to be so and that the poor were by nature suited to that status, Kropotkin disputed such claims. "Those animals which acquire habits of mutual aid . . . ," he wrote, "attain, in their respective classes, the highest development of intelligence and bodily organization."[1] This aspect of her teaching philosophy was something very dear to Denise, as I learned over time, and not something she thought of as just restricted to the classroom. "Mutual aid" was a principle she believed one should live by.

With one or two exceptions, Denise did not give us assignments to be completed outside the classroom, between meetings. She had no expectations, she said, for us to produce a given number of poems or pages of writing from week to week. She treated us all from the start as if we were already poets, regardless of our quite varied experience as writers. It was her firmly held belief that as poets we must have something to say before we put pen to paper. Poems, "true" poems, she told us time and again during the term of the workshop, must arise naturally—organically—out of the need we felt to express and give shape to our experiences, emotions, perceptions, ideas. Denise was of the opinion that classroom exercises of the "write a villanelle" kind all too frequently resulted in artificial poems. She felt that if we had poems in us to write, then we would do so and bring them to class to be shared, read aloud, discussed.

Her manner was always personal, even intimate. Denise frequently shared with us her experiences as a creative artist in the belief that doing so would help us to recognize aspects of our own creativity. This included the possibility, she warned us, that we might go through what she referred to as "fallow periods" when poems just didn't come; but not to worry, she assured us, because it was a perfectly natural occurrence in the life of an artist. If it meant that for weeks at a time any of us did not have new poems to bring to class and share, then that was OK, she told us, as long as this didn't affect our commitment to the group and our ability to respond to the work of the others who *were* regularly presenting new poems. "My hope was not to teach anybody to write poetry," Denise had written about another poetry workshop she had led, her first, some five years earlier in New York, "but to attempt to bring each one to a clearer sense of what his own voice and range might be and to give him some standards by which to evaluate his work."[2] She made it clear to us that something like this was her hope for our workshop, too.

On a night when there were only one or two new poems to discuss, Denise would devise an activity for us. I recall one early class when she asked Lucy, whom she knew to have studied modern dance, to perform for us, improvising movements to a piece of recorded music, after which Denise had us all write down whatever came into our heads. Another time she asked Judy to play her flute as a stimulus to improvisational writing. She didn't expect that these activities would result in finished poems, she explained; rather she hoped they might get our creative juices flowing in an unanticipated direction that, if we later returned to it and followed its course, might eventually result in a poem.

                                                                    Mark Pawlak

While most of these classroom activities struck me as things that Denise had thought up on the spur of the moment, others seemed more purposeful. One that she had us do early in the year laid a foundation of trust in one another for the later sharing of poems of a personal nature, especially ones that might reveal our vulnerabilities. "Paint a self-portrait in words," she instructed. "Draw upon the plant, animal, or mineral world for metaphors that convey characteristics of your inner, private self." Afterward we read aloud what we had written. In every instance Denise wrote alongside us and shared with us what she had produced. Notably, the only sample of this exercise that I preserved, in a folder of materials saved from that class, was Denise's own contribution.

Incomplete Monstrous Self-Portrait (in class)
Like the swan, I waddle clumsily on dry land—the dry land of certain relationships, certain situations. Or like a violently affectionate dog, I frighten some of those upon whom I rush, barking loudly, tearing their silken clothes with heavy paws. Yet in my own element I can glide strongly, regally even—yet less like the white swan than some water-bird of darker plumage that shines in colors. But I am a chameleon too, for among leaf-people I am a leaf, indeed a poplar leaf, never still; or among chair-people I am a chair, even an upholstered chair, and with rocking-chair people I rock well enough. (Yet perhaps long ago my chameleon nature would have taken precedence in the constellation of selves—a pole-star that flickered!—while now it spends its days asleep under a stone.)

I can carry burdens from forest to sea sagaciously as the Thailand elephant, yet I beat on lit windows with the wistful passion of any moth.

(A slightly revised version of this was later anthologized in *Self-Portrait: Book People Picture Themselves,* edited by Burt Britton [1976].)

This kind of activity, however, was the exception rather than the rule. Most days there were poems to discuss, including Denise's own. These she brought to class either as newly finished pieces or as working drafts, poems that later appeared in her collections *To Stay Alive* and *Footprints.* If we gave Denise our new poems far enough in advance of the class meeting, she would have them Xeroxed so that everyone could have a copy when we gathered. Authors' names were always included. There was no attempt at anonymity, no false sense of objectivity when considering one another's work. "A poet," she would often say, "must stand beside his words." More often than not, however, there wasn't time to make copies, and so Denise would ask the author to read her or his poem aloud. Frequently, for the effect of hearing different voices deliver the same poem, she would ask another member of the class to read it aloud also, and then another and then another. There would be long, thoughtful silences afterward, followed by animated discussion, in which we learned to address our responses to one another and not through Denise as mediator.

One of Denise's aims, it became clear to me over time, was to teach us to distinguish between mere self-expression and "real" poetry, that is, poetry that draws upon personal experience but transmutes it through the writer's craft into art. As an object lesson, one night she read aloud a poem by Rod McKuen, who back then was the most popular poet in the United States. She followed it with a poem on the same subject by W. B. Yeats. Afterward she sat back from the discussion and allowed us to name for ourselves what the difference was.

I recall two occasions when she brought to class objects that she instructed us to observe. We were to compose the written equivalent of still life paintings. One night it was a potted plant; the other time a book of photographic portraits. Confessional poetry was ascendant in American poetry in those days. Robert Lowell was teaching down the avenue at Harvard, Anne Sexton was ensconced across the Charles at Boston University, and Sylvia Plath's collection *Ariel* was all the buzz. Counter to this trend, Denise stressed observation and objectivity. Instead of the dominant *I, I, I* of so much of the poetry being written, she encouraged us to use "objective correlatives." As an example of what she meant by objectivity, Denise read us Charles Reznikoff's paraphrase of a Chinese Song dynasty poet's words: "Poetry presents the Thing in order to convey the Feeling. It should be *precise* about the Thing and *reticent* about the Feeling."[3] And, of course, she frequently cited William Carlos Williams's mantra, "No ideas but in things."[4]

The one formal assignment I distinctly recall Denise giving us to do outside of class was to choose a poem written in a foreign language to translate, preferably a language we spoke or had studied. The important thing, she stressed, was to pick a poem that had emotional resonance for us. She told us that she wasn't interested in the strict accuracy of our English rendering so much as in having us bring the essence of the original over into English, that is, to make an English poem based upon the foreign-language original. Since I had had four years of German in high school, I chose a short lyric by Goethe, "Natur und Kunst," "Nature and Art," which despite its brevity proved challenge enough to me.

This exercise, I later learned, was a standard part of Denise's poetry workshop repertoire, assigned intentionally as practice in the craft of poetry. She was still using it when, one day, five or six years later, we sat talking in her office at Tufts University, where, at her invitation, I had just made a guest appearance in her class as a "published poet." (It was Denise's habit to keep in touch with her former students; in many instances we became part of her circle of friends.) She told me that she continued to find this exercise useful. She explained that student writers, undergraduates especially, because of their youth and lack of experience in the world, seldom had anything to say that was very original.

Mark Pawlak

Denise then went on to qualify what she meant. It wasn't that she didn't respect the emotions and experiences of her students—quite the opposite. She valued their intelligence, their perceptions, and the complexity of their feelings; but the feelings of young people are usually a muddle, she said. Added to that, as inexperienced writers they hadn't yet acquired the language tools to convey their emotions clearly and accurately. Choosing a poem from another language, one that resonated with their own experiences, and then rendering it in English was an opportunity for students to practice prosody without getting mixed up in their own subjective content, since the original author supplied the content, ready-made. "I almost always find," Denise added, "that the outcome is a poem of greater technical accomplishment than anything the student has produced on her or his own."

Denise didn't provide us with a syllabus or any written instructions for this class; rather she conveyed her expectations verbally. Just as there were few if any assignments of the kind write X number of poems, produce Y number of pages by next week, try your hand at a poem modeled on Z, or write a sestina, so too Denise assigned us no specific texts to read—unless I count Rainer Maria Rilke's *Letters to a Young Poet,* which although not actually assigned, became the class bible because she referred to it so often. In sum her manner of instruction was what one might call the "inspiration" method.

She often read poems aloud to us by modern masters—Williams, Wallace Stevens, Yeats, Rilke in translation, as well as poems by her American contemporaries. Her choice on any given day was usually suggested to her by a topic we had discussed in class the previous week or by one of our student poems. Frequently the poet or poem she picked as illustration was new to me. When that was the case, I would scribble a note to myself to seek out the poem by way of reflecting on and further absorbing the lesson. The attention we all paid to what she said and our eagerness to absorb what she offered, met, I think, her expectations for this class. We were all industrious, disciplined, self-directed—the kind of students who appealed to her. Most, if not all, of us were, as Judy Katz-Levine recalled in a note to me years later, "intense . . . about drinking in everything and absorbing all [Denise] said." The way Judy remembered it, Denise urged us "to write from the heart and to create intense moving work of high quality, consistently—emphasis on quality."

On several occasions Denise read to us passages from letters or new poems written by one of the many poets with whom she regularly corresponded. I remember one such instance when it was both a letter and poem that Paul Blackburn had sent her. She read these aloud in their entirety then passed them around for us to look over. On another occasion Denise brought to class a copy of *Origin* she had just received. Published in it was a poem of her own, "Novella," one that she had written the summer before. She used this as an occasion to talk about the importance of publication for a poet once one's writing had developed to the stage where it was ready to find an audience. She also talked about the role of small literary journals in encouraging and supporting writers.

The effect this manner of "instruction" had on me—and I know I was not alone—was to kindle a passion for poetry. Denise shared with us not only the associations that came to her mind of poets and poems both past and present, but also her own experience as a working poet. In doing so she showed me that there was a living poetic tradition to which she belonged, one that existed in a spirit of camaraderie and of mutual encouragement among her closest contemporaries (another instance of "mutual aid"). She gave me an understanding of her vision of what it meant to be a poet. It had to do with being a craftsperson who belonged to a guild with something like Masonic or Rosicrucian overtones of mystery. By making us confidantes to dialogues with her contemporaries and by showing us her own freshly minted poems, Denise drew us in to the periphery of that band of poets, that guild chapter she belonged to that included Blackburn, Robert Duncan, Robert Creeley, Galway Kinnell, Muriel Rukeyser, and Hayden Carruth, among others.

Although the poetry workshop had no required texts, Denise nevertheless handed out copies of two essays that she had published: "Some Notes on Organic Form" and "Notebook Pages." With these she hoped to convey to us her ideas and convictions about poetry and her habits as a working poet. The publication of *The Poet in the World,* her collection of essays on poetry and poetics, was still several years off. When it did appear, I recall Denise expressing relief that her students would now have ready access to her essential ideas when they first crossed the threshold of her classroom. She said she felt that in future workshops she could expect a common base of understanding about her ideas on form, sound, and line breaks.

"Notebook Pages" included a letter she had written to a former student and subsequently copied into her notebook. This was the piece that I found most valuable at the time. In it she explained the distinction between what she called "poetry of ideas" and "true" poetry. It not only made a lot of sense, but it helped me to see why some of my own poems didn't work: they were all head and no heart; that is, they were just ideas and didn't incorporate my feelings, experiences, or observations.

Another lesson that Denise imparted to our class—a revelation to me—was how to read as a writer. From her I learned to pay attention to sound, shape, and structure in both prose and poetry. She would draw our attention to the way an idea is presented through the organization of sentences in a paragraph, to the comeliness of a sentence, to an evocative image, to the music of words in a poem and how their sound works in concert with their meaning. She imparted, above all, the pleasure to be derived from savoring a well-wrought paragraph or stanza. All this she conveyed not through cold analytic discussion but through her enthusiasm for the felicitous parts of the text under study, an enthusiasm that was both genuine and inspiring.

Denise always privileged the "orality" of poems: not just reading with the eye but also listening to the sound of each word as well as hearing the rhythm, tone, and melody of a poem as a whole. Toward that end she would frequently ask one student after another to read the same poem aloud until every one of us had done so. Hearing the poem twelve or thirteen times in succession produced a deep intimacy with the text. The interplay of its words, images, and sounds, the way they all came together, gave me a new understanding of how the poem made meaning. Denise emphasized that we had to achieve that kind of understanding through "hearing" the poem first before we began to analyze its components to find out how it achieved its effect.

The key to reading poetry aloud, she told us—and this was something she modeled for us repeatedly—was to read slowly and clearly, articulating each word, filling one's mouth with its sound. If one of us started to recite a poem too rapidly, she would stop him or her and tell the reader to start again but more slowly this time—"feel the words on your tongue." Sound and sense, she told us, go together, they are inseparable in real poetry. To underscore this point, she quoted from her notebooks on one occasion a statement by Boris Pasternak: "The music of the word . . . does not consist of euphony of vowels and consonants taken by themselves, but of the relationship between the meaning and the sound of the words."[5]

However spontaneous her lessons often were, Denise was at the same time methodical in her effort to reproduce her own habits as a working poet whenever we gathered as a class. One way she did this was to share with us her practice of keeping a notebook as a way of "inviting the muse." Use your notebook, she told us, the way she did, as a place to jot down lines from poems you find important to you or passages that you have read that expand or deepen your understanding of what poetry is. If a word or phrase or image comes to you, write it down in your notebook, she said—also snippets of conversation you might have overheard, as well as your observations of people and objects. Denise emphasized the importance of dreams as a source for poems. Dreams, she told us, were worth recording in and of themselves; once written down in your notebook, they might also become the seeds from which poems sprouted.

I took her advice. Keeping a writer's notebook is something I began back then when I was first starting out as a poet and have done ever since. I have also kept a dream journal from time to time. My notebooks have been the place where my own ideas about poetry have evolved, as well as where many of my own poems have gotten their start. One of the first uses to which I put my poetry notebook was to copy into it the stories, colorful phrases, and often tortured syntax of letters my parents sent me in an attempt to recover the language and ethnic speech patterns of my Polish working-class childhood in Buffalo. The poems that began to take shape as a result made up my first collection, *The Buffalo Sequence* (1978).

It was while studying with Denise that I was first exposed to the idea of the notebook or journal as a literary genre, distinct from the journal or workbook. She frequently brought to our class new installments fresh from her typewriter of the poetic journal in progress that she had begun in 1968. By the time she arrived at MIT, this "notebook poem" had become her primary mode of working. She added new parts during the period when I studied with her and completed it the following year. She eventually combined the different parts, including previously published ones, and shaped them into a book-length poem titled "Staying Alive."

Denise invited us to read and discuss these excerpts from her notebook poem, just as we did with one another's work. What I experienced reading her poems was dramatically different from what I felt when reading *The Waste Land,* which I read in another class that semester. There the professor's focus was T. S. Eliot's ideas about poems as carefully worked texts, steeped in classical literary references. Denise, in contrast, demonstrated by example that effective poems could be as fresh and spontaneous as one's response to the day's events. They could be about what you were feeling at the moment or about things you had just observed, overheard, or contemplated.

I learned from Denise, and particularly from "Staying Alive," that a poet can derive strength from the creative tension between her beliefs in the "artist as craftsman . . . engaged in making discrete and autonomous works" and the "artist as explorer in the language of the experience of her life."[6] My own sequential poems and poetic journals have been informed by this kind of tension I first encountered in her notebook poem, where she was working it out as she went along and where her language sometimes reveals the strain of that effort. I learned that it has to do with the push and pull between viewing a poem as "a table or chair with the requisite number of legs so as not to wobble"—a definition of poetic craft that I always thought that Denise had borrowed from Ezra Pound, though I have never found the source—versus the poem as field notes of a naturalist in the uncharted wilderness of experience.

At the conclusion of the poetry workshop's third or fourth meeting, Denise suggested a change of venue. It was a sign that we had begun to coalesce as a group that we all eagerly agreed to the move. Our assigned classroom just wasn't conducive to the kind of relaxed, intimate conversation Denise encouraged, and so for the remainder of the semester and the whole of the next one, we abandoned that black box to seek out more suitable places.

One time we gathered in a lounge in the MIT student center, where there were couches, stuffed chairs, and wall-to-wall carpeting. Another time we met in the old graveyard in Harvard Square. On several occasions we met at the apartment that Denise and her husband, Mitch Goodman, rented across the harbor in East Boston; and one weekend Denise arranged for the class to go away together to the Cape Cod house of one of her friends so that we might enjoy extended, uninterrupted time together and further bond. But mostly we met in one another's apartments or dormitory rooms.

One class meeting that stands out took place in a basement apartment on Newbury Street in the Back Bay, on a block full of head shops, health food stores, and organic restaurants, long since replaced by expensive boutiques, art galleries, upscale antique stores, and pricey restaurants and cafés. Denise was unusually voluble and excited that night, because her publisher, James Laughlin, had sent her an advance copy of *Relearning the Alphabet,* her new poetry collection, which she had brought along to show us.

After several student poems were read and discussed, the evening turned into an impromptu celebration of her new book—actually a double celebration, because a photograph snapped by our fellow student Margo had been used on the book's cover. Denise capped off the evening by treating us to a private reading of selections from it. In addition to the title poem, she read "Tenebrae," "Dance Memories," and "From a Notebook: October '68 – May '69." This last, she explained, was really the first installment of the notebook poem she was then still writing, parts of which she brought to class as work in progress for us to discuss. The night concluded with her reading "A Tree Telling of Orpheus," which, in the parlance of the times, simply blew me away.

The final class meeting of the year was a potluck dinner at Denise's apartment. By then we had evolved into a tightly knit group of friends, novice poets, campus radicals, and antiwar activists—a "community of poets," as Denise had intended from the start. When we had finished eating and talking, Denise announced that she wanted to read to us a long poem by Galway Kinnell that she was very excited about. She told us that he had been sending her drafts of the poem as it evolved for her comment and that now he had sent her a complete final draft to review and critique.

We were all familiar with Kinnell's poetry. Many of us had the sound of his voice in our heads from the poetry reading he'd given on campus earlier in the year, so we were eager to hear this new book-length poem. I had all but memorized several poems from his previous book, *Body Rags,* and I thought his poem "Avenue C" was a masterpiece. I remember feeling a conspiratorial excitement at sharing in the intimacy between these two masters of the poet's craft. We listened rapt as Denise read *A Book of Nightmares* in its entirety without pause. After a long, meditative silence, one or two spoke. I remember feeling deeply moved by its scope and by the richness of its language and imagery.

That evening brought closure to our class, but it had greater significance of a ritualistic kind for me and perhaps for others. I think that for Denise it represented the culmination of her ambitions as a teacher of poetry, which she reflected upon in "The Untaught Teacher," the essay she was writing at the time: "[to] generate, and ferment among the students, enough passion and drama to produce a *collective* epiphany; and this not for its own sake . . . so much as for the sake of its function as gateway, portal, to new levels of feeling, to a greater openness after passing through it, and the sense of comradeship than can develop even among quite a large number of people who have been together in a time of crisis or revelation."[7] Although I still had many years ahead of me in my poetry apprenticeship, I left Denise's apartment that night and walked back to the T station, feeling that I was no longer just a student of poetry but was now an initiate into the fellowship of poets.

Mark Pawlak

• WORKING POETS •

Denise Levertov and Mark Pawlak

Paul Lacey

This essay reflects on Mark Pawlak's poetry and on journal keeping as he learned it from his chief mentor, the poet Denise Levertov; it also considers his experience in the transformative writing course that Levertov taught in 1969–70 at MIT, the "Idea Factory" of science, and to trace out the implications for Pawlak of becoming part of a "community of poets" in terms of poetic craft and political activism in a dark period of the American war in Vietnam.

Pawlak entered Levertov's course intending to get a PhD and then follow a career in scientific research. But a major consequence of his studying with her was a changed view of MIT, radicalized politics, and the conviction that he could not ethically pursue science tainted by war research. He turned to teaching, first in experimental elementary education, and today he is director of academic support programs and teaches mathematics at the University of Massachusetts Boston. He also continues to practice the crafts of poet, anthologist, and editor.

Pawlak met Levertov at perhaps the most pivotal time in her own artistic, political, and personal life, about which she was generously open. She became his whole university, his "Deniversity"—Pawlak's recalling of James Laughlin's "Ezra-veristy," his word for his education under Ezra Pound. Levertov taught Pawlak how to read and write poetry, how to keep and use a journal as an aid to his creativity, and perhaps most profoundly, how the dedication of a life of art requires a commensurate political commitment, a fidelity to peace and social justice, even to revolution.

She read aloud some of her own work in progress and invited student response to the deliberately fragmentary "From a Notebook: October "68 – May "69," which documents the daily life of preparing for Mitch Goodman's trial and conviction for advocating draft resistance. "From a Notebook" appeared in *Relearning the Alphabet* (1970), and the extended and completed notebook poem, now called "Staying Alive," appeared in *To Stay Alive* (1971). The titles of both books underline her struggle to start again—to relearn the most fundamental building blocks of poetry, to sharpen one's observation of the world, and to affirm the desperate need to hold on to life itself. From her example Pawlak adopted journal keeping as a daily activity and became a faithful practitioner in preparing for what Levertov termed "inviting the muse." To Pawlak and the other participants in the MIT workshop, Levertov was a generous mentor who modeled what it could mean to belong to a fellowship and guild of writers. As she asked of her students, she read her own current poems aloud for their critique.

Pawlak recalls that Levertov helped her students become writers by studying good models and learning to recognize what she always called ""true" poetry. The students' aim was not to imitate the models but to be inspired by them to find what they themselves had to say. Levertov asserted that poets must have something to say before putting pen to paper, but the essence of "open poetry" would seem to be that the writer discerns through an interplay of form and content what the poem is to become. How does an apprentice writer experiment in order to discover through trial and error what is waiting to be said?

Pawlak says that Levertov stressed creating intense, moving work of high quality and technical accomplishment. Her essays on organic form and the importance of line breaks were available to the MIT class and helped define how they could assess one another's work, but they are not mechanical "how to" instructions to those ends. In her criticism Levertov regularly drew on a small store of powerful, evocative modernist critical terms, including *inscape* and *instress*, learned from Gerard Manley Hopkins, and *objective correlative* from T. S. Eliot.

The import of such terms is to require readers to attend to the details of a poem, to observe closely and enumerate ways that a poem's sounds and images support one another by repetition or variation or help to set up useful tensions or ironies. They are technical terms only broadly speaking, though not empirically objective. Instead they are useful shorthand terms readers learn to use with one another in order to help throw light on what they have noticed. What one reader discerns as an effective inscape another may not see at all, but through discussion the term may help them come to an understanding. "Oh, I see what you are saying" does not mean critical assent. But helpful conversation about making art is an aid to its greater enjoyment.

As a context for discussing Pawlak's adaptations of Levertov's journal form, it is worthwhile to discuss the benefits and limitations of poetry in traditional forms versus some limitations of poetry in open form, Levertov's preferred way of writing. Poetry in traditional forms can give readers a common beginning vocabulary or typology. Look at this compact, tightly rhymed poem: Could it be a sonnet? Does it conform to the sonnet template or a specific "type"? If it is not a traditional sonnet, does the poem conform to any other named rhyme scheme or pattern? Typology can give readers some shortcuts for identifying the poem and evaluating it as a sonnet, for example, whether religious, personal, political, philosophical, or satirical. Gathering information on how the poem works as an artifact, how technically adept it is, and how deeply rooted in feelings it is, readers may begin to

                                                         Paul Lacey

observe the poem's effect on them. They may enjoy it or lose interest as they read. There is a world of technically smooth but boring closed-form poems, as there is a world of dry, flat, uninteresting open-form ones. Levertov's dictum was "form is never more than a revelation of content" ("Some Notes on Organic Form," *The Poet in the World*, 7).

Poetry in traditional form—that is, regular rhyme patterns and meter capable of being scanned—may allow an apprentice poet to learn technique more quickly. But a traditional or closed form may also betray its stereotypical qualities more readily than in open form. In *Pendennis*, William Makepeace Thackeray says that someone looking for a rhyme for *sorrow* besides *borrow* and *tomorrow* is already more on the mend than he thinks.[1] Levertov sometimes dismissed contemporary poetry written in rhyme as anachronistic, but she loved the poetry of George Herbert, John Keats, Emily Dickinson, and other poets who wrote in traditional forms. There are examples of rhyme and regular meter in some of Levertov's early poetry, and the poet carefully used traditional forms here and there in her later work.

Getting free of restraining conventions, finding loosened forms for a present time, privileging the ear over the eye in creating or enjoying poetry: for Levertov, William Carlos Williams was the great exemplar of a poet freed from convention and conceiving of poetic lines not in fixed meter but as notations like measures in a musical score. Williams offered fresh analogies between poetry and music or painting, writing still lifes and poetic equivalents to Brueghel paintings. His critics made fun of his three-step poems and his discussion of the "variable foot," but his practice encouraged something beyond scansion or noting rhyme schemes for talking about poetic technique.

Cary Nelson argues that *To Stay Alive* reflects the limits of an open form associated with "an adamic, childlike, innocent perceptiveness."[2] While he acknowledges that "Levertov's sense of the war's human cost for us is precise and telling," he complains that, "brutal and accurate as these lines may be, they are essentially clichés of violent war . . . violence verbalized at a distance."[3] He finds that for "Staying Alive," "the patchwork form suggested to her by Williams' *Paterson*, including journals, letters, conversations, newspaper reports," is inadequate to the material. "These poems are made of personal defeat," Nelson continues, "but she does not pursue her depression far enough" (159, 17). The final word has not been spoken on Levertov's poetry of the Vietnam War era, but the argument that open forms essentially embody a hopeful vision that may not suffice for addressing the brutality of war has special relevance for contemporary U.S. readers, with the United States engaged in more recent unwinnable wars.

In his chapter in *Writers and Their Notebooks*, Pawlak describes how essential journal keeping has been to his life as a poet, allowing him to hold on to perceptions and insights and describe things that matter to him, especially since his daily work demands that his attention be focused elsewhere.[4] Levertov recommended keeping what in an earlier time would have been called a "daybook," not a diary but a place to write down quotations from books and articles. She also kept notebooks of self-reflective work, drafts of poems and essays, and occasional dream journals. Pawlak has followed her example in all these ways, as well as using the journal form to explore his interest in found language and found poems. He writes in his journals almost every day, including during family vacations on the coast of Maine. His entries include things he noticed as he sat reading on the porch or when he was walking, objects, place-names, fragments of overheard conversations, and words and phrases from signs and newspapers.

Mining this mix of materials, he developed his "Hart's Neck Haibun," a five-part poetic journal adapting a form best known from Bashō's *Narrow Road to the Deep North and Other Travel Sketches*. These haibun make up the backbone of Pawlak's 2006 collection, *Official Versions*. Following Henry David Thoreau as well as Levertov, he identifies the poetic journal as a literary genre distinct from the journal as a workbook. Pawlak has begun to publish works that derive from his journals, notably *Quoddy Journals* from four years of Maine vacations and the manuscript "Inbound/Outbound," in which he records things he observes and reflections on his daily commute to and from work. He speaks of his journals as "artifacts," which is a useful reminder that even those journals that seem to be unguarded first drafts are probably being aesthetically and consciously shaped. Even when people attempt something like automatic writing, the reader who comes along subsequently may discern marks of a shaping consciousness, like footprints across new snow; one word triggers the memory of another, strings of words become sequences of ideas.

It is no disparagement of Levertov's "From a Notebook," and the subsequent enlarging and remodeling of that material into a longer poem sequence, to observe that she never suggests that any part of the work springs unmediated from notebook entries. She typically gave a secretary handwritten material, reworked it in typescript, and continued that back-and-forth process until she was satisfied with the work. Pawlak wants to advance the journal as a literary artifact in its own right, and a goodly number of writers and artists have published their own notebooks and journals. William Stafford's lifelong practice of daily, early morning freewriting had the same effect as the notebooks of others. May Sarton deliberately turned to producing journals with the intent of publication. In most cases there is little chance to examine the raw notes of a poet's notebooks, the work in process in comparison with the printed version. The rough draft can be interesting to a scholar, but only the heightened effect of a consciously shaped work will attract a general audience.

Pawlak has published three volumes of poems: *The Buffalo Sequence* (1977), *Special Handling* (1993) and *Official Versions* (2006).[5] A consideration of these

Paul Lacey

books shows the ways in which he adapts Levertov's notebook form to create something entirely his own.

A dominant feature of *The Buffalo Sequence*, fifteen poems of varying lengths, is Pawlak's affirmation of his childhood experiences and tender recovery and embrace of the language spoken by his family and the friends he grew up with. This was not always "correct" or Standard English but rather a rich blend of American English and his grandparents' Eastern European speech patterns. The poet describes these patterns as meals "stewed with the bones of happier days" (25). As good cooks know, the best-tasting stews are made from the toughest cuts of meat, tangy "aromatics," and root vegetables, all seasoned and cooked together a long time in a little water over low heat. Eating a stew seems a fair analogy for how readers experience *The Buffalo Sequence*.

The first poem begins "never again," a phrase recurring twelve more times in two pages. That poignant negation powerfully inflects everything being recollected, whether as lament or benediction. "Joey the cross eyed," who sentenced ants to death with a magnifying glass: "never again." The nuns who "threw us against the walls. . . . / till we learned to be good: never again. never again."[6] The poem memorializes the fifteen-year-old girl who had to get married, and her father, "such a good man"—"no, never again." The companion in street fights, the best friend who became a neighborhood bully, a black friend whose death remains tangled in newspaper stories: "never again." There is a shift, signaled by the word "meanwhile" midway through the poem, to a time frame ten years before and ten years after. Meanwhile the man who left never to return comes back with a lesson plan in his hand, and the poem arrives at "right now."

This first poem shapes the whole work, though the fourteen that follow do not seem to be sequential, in the sense that they lead in only a single direction. Instead they are impressionistic, fragmented, and overlapping narratives of a past lived in a tough, working-class urban neighborhood, viewed without self-pity. "Meanwhile" in the first poem leads to "ten years ago and ten years after and / never again. Never again." Echoing "never again," the seventh poem begins: "there is no going back, / and after all that's been said, now this: / mom, who doesn't understand, and / dad, who don't want to hear about it, / fingering their prayer strings of little wooden doubts, / and varnished opinions / which fell as crumbs from the table / where childhoods drown in the spilled milks of love."

Recurring references to mom and dad act like musical motifs for how each parent deals with life. Does the mother not understand because of language barriers? Is the father's way to avoid the worst news? The poems do not tell. "Oh, but their voices always return." Other repeated words and phrases also help shape the poem: "On a day like today. You know you've begun to die"; "And after death, are we really born again?" Spliced into these story fragments is the present time, when the son comes home to teach radical working-class American history, prison letters, and songs about Nicola Sacco and Bartolomeo Vanzetti, intertwined with the signature phrase, "mom, who doesn't understand, and dad, who don't want to hear about it."

The eighth poem captures the tone of a letter from mother to child, not one of complaint so much as sad commentary, the letter carrying all the burden of correspondence for the husband who never writes: "today there is no letter from her boys / and her son's mother is sad. / her son's father is sad too / —they know how he misses his boys; / and couldn't they show a little more appreciation?" The father is getting older and has health problems, "digesting over and over / the meal stewed once again / with the bones of happier days / her sons know their father is a good man."

Other poems in *The Buffalo Sequence* narrate family reunions, recollections of grandparents, bits of song, "tunes they sang when we were little," recipes inherited from grandmothers, and third-grade classroom instruction that intensified the poet's distancing from his family's native Polish: "write the letter A perfectly, with no accent." There are exhortations to get ahead, right out of the Andrew Carnegie myth of success: "we should apply ourselves, / and the smartest may even get a scholarship to college; / and become a professional something-or-other.—god knows!" This poem continues, "now we should go over the homework / there are a few stories, but for grammar and spelling, / would have gotten A's." That forecasts the arc of the poet's life, from going away to college and returning to teach.

A Polish peasant's saying that puns on the poet's first name leads readers into the final two poems in the sequence: "Marek na jarmarek," "Mark going to market." The saying, used as an epigraph to the penultimate poem, is the sort of nonsense parents use to puzzle their children. It is in the language of the Old Country and so carries with it a sense of being out of touch with some past history. (Consider a similarly uninformative saying of my Irish American urban childhood: when asked where you had been, you answered, "Up Mike's and down Jake's, where they make potato cakes." No one knew what that was about, either.) The Polish saying sends the poet back to recall the wooden scooter he did not want to admit was made by his father, the cardboard globe of the world, pointed out by a nun's finger, "washed by the soap of chastity." Memories simply arise: the things his father did for him, the fact that his life revolved around his father. "Marek na jarmerek."

The final poem cancels out "never again," beginning "then let this / be the city, now I will call home." The poet walks through the city, seeing workmen on scaffolds and a square where old men cluster around a newsstand. He overhears snatches of conversation about old politicians, complaints about poor men having to borrow from their death-insurance to pay for food. He recalls his grandpa, "with the other men, / like himself, retired from the railroad: / grandpa, every fifteen minutes pulling his gold watch out by the chain."

                                                              Paul Lacey

The poet now claims the city he wanted to get away from; the poem's last image is of the retirement gold watch, the traditional gift of thanks for a lifetime of work, in this case a means of marking time that the old railroaders no longer need to keep track of. The poem sequence has traced the marking of time, the soundtrack of a lifetime of monologues and conversations, elegies and obituaries: his friends got married, a friend died in Vietnam, another got a good job. There are unhealed hurts and reproaches—"you could be a better example to your brothers"—but with the passing of time comes an understanding of the ways that time can be well used for human work and duty and family.

Special Handling is largely shaped by Pawlak's attention to political concerns and to the contemporary documents such as newspaper stories that fuel his responses. The title suggests careful, trustworthy transmission of something valuable, as for example a piece of mail or a package for which the sender pays extra and the recipient needs to confirm its receipt. It is also a way of telling readers to pay attention to the stories they are hearing.

"VFW Bar Talk" exactly catches the tone of the battered old patriot/victim, the fall guy who always fights Americans' wars for them.[7] Maybe he is remembering his service in the rosy glow of a few beers he and the other vets have had down at the VFW lodge, and maybe they are all trying to impress one another with who they were, but there is a genuine simplicity in the words. The reader believes this worn-out old vet would go fight again, if he could, and feels sad for how easily patriotism can be manipulated.

"A Merry Band" offers a snapshot of eccentrics—a man who lives in a cave and takes long, barefoot walks for charity, a woman with four grand pianos in her top-floor flat, the man from Nottingham who legally changed his name to Robin Hood and wears only Lincoln green—who "think it is the world that is / out of step with them." They are the sort of people one can expect to find on a nearby barstool.

Dispatches from the Falklands War remind reader how trivial that war was and how passionately the crowds in both countries cared about the outcome. And how "after the cheering has subsided / the returning heroes exchange their battle helmets. . . . / then resume their place on street comers / and in the queues outside the unemployment offices."

In "Newsbriefs, 1984" Pawlak intersperses news flashes about the Guatemalan Civil War with reports of how happy businessmen are at the new freedoms that will come. "Firsts" and "Marks to Beat," such as watermelon seed, cherry pit, and tobacco spitting contests and competition for "Watermelon Thump Queen," are presented to the reader. Pawlak does not intend to entertain with these events; his tone is not quite savage humor, but the Guatemala context heightens the vulgarity of the contests until they seem almost evil. Human rights violations jostle with magazine advertisements and reports that, for example, the economy has made Ivy League cafeterias shift from linen to paper napkins. Pentagon generals "now wipe duck sauce from their lips / with paper napkins." Newspapers often run human interest stories; Pawlak's found poems might well be called inhuman interest stories. Contemporary accounts from El Salvador and Cambodia play off historical accounts of Treblinka and the Holocaust. Notes at the end of the book scrupulously point readers to the testimonies from which the poems have been drawn.

The title *Special Handling* prepares readers for evidence of duplicity in the documents and strong, bitter ironies in what Pawlak has found. These are not the simple ironies of saying one thing and meaning another, or accidentally telling the truth while trying to lie; these ironies are traps to make readers complicit in the falsehoods hidden behind the surface stories. They instill both deep distrust of authority and a heated moral outrage. The poems' cumulative effect is lacerating.

The title *Official Versions* is a tip-off to the reader to be on guard. Almost by definition the official version of an event asserts its trustworthiness as information. The opening poem of the book, "Credible Information, 1999–2003," provides alternating accounts of the doctoring of an official photograph from the 1999 wedding of Prince Edward of Great Britain and Sophie Rhys in which his nephew Prince William does not appear euphoric enough; the controversy over whether the twenty-first century began on January 1 of 2000 or 2001; the creation of a federal Office of Strategic Influence in the wake of the September 11, 2001, attacks; and President George W. Bush's actions on 9/11. In the sections about Y2K celebrations, a science reporter asserts that "too many people have come to believe *everything*—even a historical fact—is a matter of opinion."[8] A spokesman at the Center for Millennial Studies, meanwhile, argues that "people who are selfappointed experts / on timekeeping and chronology and calendars . . . should shut the hell up / and let people have their party" (15). The sections about the Office of Strategic Influence recount that it was created "to use foreign news media and the internet to tell the American side of the story" (14) in the face of fears that the United States was losing support overseas. The poem also includes a "coda" that offers the Bush administration's explanation of the president's "Mission Accomplished" appearance on the aircraft carrier *Abraham Lincoln*.

A playful subsection of the book, "All Shook Up," offers some "do's and don'ts" for writing poetry.

> Precision and economy of language
> are virtues this author (me) recommends
> when writing poems,
> but finds difficult
> to put into practice.

The found poem "Tips" offers many uses for petroleum jelly; another poem pairs imaginary movie double features such as *The Deer Hunter* and *Dances with*

Wolves; a list poem features song titles that include the word *Baby;* and "All Shook Up" riffs on rock and roll phrases and titles, as, for example, "Next Time You See Me / Mustang Sally / Laugh Laugh." "Alley Oop" strings together four pages of nonsense refrains: "Ching Chong / Choo Choo Ch'Boogie / Chug-a-Lug / Da Doo Ron Ron." For anyone of a certain age, the effect is to generate memories of the whole songs; "Tutti Frutti," for example, instantly recalls additional lyrics "oh rutti" and "wop-bop-a-loo-bop a lop-bam-boom." Since this is all primarily in the oral tradition, a level of irony is added to the concept of official versions.

The most emotionally and aesthetically engaging sections in *Official Versions* are the five books of "Hart's Neck Haibun." These works are open, serious, and unironic, mixing prose and poetry, intense observation, front-porch journal entries, and short lyrics, on the model of Bashō's travel journals. The *haibun* is a form Pawlak has used extensively in his later work. *Official Versions* and *Special Handling* are experimental and risk taking. The found poem seems to contradict the notion of the well-made poem and only rarely seems even to aspire to Levertov's standards of beauty or technical excellence. Just as a strong line in a drawing loses some of its strength if it is repeated too often in the same piece, so found poems must have greater vigor of insight and language not to lose strength. Gathered in a collection, they tend to flatten out the effect of any single poem, since part of the pleasure of the form is discovering something waiting to be carved out of the prose matrix, as a sculptor conceives of a form waiting to be freed by the carving away of material.

Not only is Pawlak Levertov's student in these poems, he moves confidently beyond her into another poetic genre.

• THE SUDDEN ANGEL AFFRIGHTED ME •

God Wrestling in Denise Levertov's Life and Art

David Shaddock

A number of years ago, I gave a reading at Eliot Bay Books in Seattle in support of my book of Jewish-themed poems, *In This Place Where* Something's Missing *Lives*. When I had finished my reading, my friend and teacher Denise Levertov stood up from the audience and proceeded to instruct the attendees (and me as well) on exactly what she saw was going on in these poems. "These are poems of God wrestling—it's a long-established tradition in both Judaism and Christianity. Rather than just accept or receive faith, one carries on an ongoing argument with God." She then described Jacob's battle with the angel of God in Genesis. "It's not a placid or intellectually lazy faith, you see"—perhaps goading the West Coast laxity of the audience a bit. Then, to my shock, she asked for a copy of my book and gave one of the poems a sharp, prophetic reading, her gap-toothed, English-accented voice hissing with assonance and flaring the consonants.

I took her instruction seriously, as always. At first I thought she was chastising my natural reticence, telling me to be more committed, more demonstrative. Slowly I realized that she was not so much telling me not to hide my light under a bushel as she was telling me it was not really my light at all—that my words, once written, took their place in a larger context of man's passionate, loving, and vexing dialogue with God. That dialogue requires the engagement of our whole being. Denise's faith life, her artistic life, and her political life were all of a piece, and all were informed with the kind of passion that keeps a man up all night wrestling with angels, demanding a new name for himself.

In modern theology the term *God wrestling* has come to mean a creative, dynamic, and, above all, personal relationship with God, the Bible, and religious tradition. Rabbi Arthur Waskow, one of the founders of the Jewish Renewal movement, writes, "What went before we turn and turn like a kaleidoscope; with every turn there appears new beauty, new complexity, new simplicity."[1]

God wrestling implies a hermeneutic theology, inherently fallible. An absolute knowledge of God's will is impossible; what meaning we can glean emerges from our active engagement and interpretation. Borrowing a term from contemporary psychoanalysis, I would describe the God wrestler as having an *intersubjective* relationship with the deity. Contemporary psychoanalysis, drawing from such disparate sources as the hermeneutics of Hans-Georg Gadamer, Edmund Husserl's phenomenology, and contemporary child development research, describes meaning in psychoanalysis as an emergent property of the encounter between two differently organized subjective worlds—those of the analyst and the patient. By extension I am suggesting that for the God wrestler, religious faith emerges from the encounter between our subjective world and a God who is himself a subject, a feeling, fallible being who moment to moment is in an intimate relationship with us.

That God is a subject is a radical enough idea to a fundamentalist sensibility that privileges his objective judgments. But the Bible is full of God's feeling: he is vexed, prideful, and remorseful, all in varying measures.

In order to encounter fully the divine, we need to develop what Martin Buber famously called an "I / Thou" relationship with him. Buber drew on the legacy of Hasidism for his notion of an intersubjective relationship with God, just as Denise, from her earliest poetry, drew on the Hasidic tradition of her father, who, though a convert to Christianity, was the heir to a line of Hasidic rabbis. One of the earliest Hasids, Rabbi Levi Yitzchok of Berditchev, developed a religious practice that was a kind of divine psychoanalysis. He would go to a deserted place in the countryside and pour out his stream of consciousness to God.

In this essay I will draw on Denise's writings, on our many conversations on religion and spirituality, and on understanding gleaned from my own, parallel journey from a rather diffuse spirituality to one based, however idiosyncratically, in organized religion, in order to trace Denise's "slow movement from agnosticism to faith."[2]

To suggest that the term *God wrestling* means a spiritual path of angst and struggle would be a serious mischaracterization. Denise and I might have a long and serious conversation on the nature of evil or the future of our planet, but then we would take a walk by my house and the all-too-familiar scene would, through her eyes, reveal wonders. She would see an iris bloom sticking through a broken fence and break into an improvised ballet step in response. As her friend and Stanford colleague Al Gelpi notes, "Her early poetry shimmered with the almost sacramental mystery of each perceived object."[3] Underlying this poetry was her father's Hasidic tradition of the Shekinah, the indwelling presence of the divine in all creation. The response to her perception of this "sacramental mystery" was praise, which Denise called "the irresistible impulse of the soul."[4] The mystical perception of imminent divinity and the concomitant impulse to praise creation form a constant thread through her work, from her earliest poems written in England to her last, mortality-infused verse.

But to perceive Levertov as merely a mystic is to miss her engaged, iconoclastic, and prophetic side—a side wherein faith and passionate argument lived, however uneasily at times, in the same person. One can surely trace the roots of her wrestling with God to the example set by her "Jewish Christian" father, who, as she writes in *Tesserae,* as a young student experienced "a profound and shaking new conviction. This Jesus of Nazareth, 'despised and rejected of men' had indeed been the messiah!" He did not see himself as leaving the Jewish faith but as extending it, offering his own insights and struggles to the tradition of interpreters and God wrestlers who came before him. As Denise writes, "but it was not to be absorbed into a Gentile world that he had broken, in sorrow, with his mother and father, but to be, as he believed, more fully a Jew."[5] The lesson that faith was based on personal experience and might lead one in a direction that completely defies the expectations of one's friends and family was not lost on Denise.

Wrestling as Surrender

> She in whose lipservice
> I passed my time,
> whose name I knew, but not her face
> came upon me where I lay in lie castle!
> Flung me across the room, and
> room after room (hitting the walls re-
> bounding—to the last
> sticky wall—wrenching away from it
> pulled hair out!)
> till I lay
> outside the outer walls!
> ("The Goddess")

As Jacob wrestled the angel of God to a draw and won his name, he was wounded in the thigh. The wrestler with God (or goddess) will often come away both enlightened and vanquished. Though the questioning, prophetic voice is mostly absent from Denise's early poems, the sense of being ravished or vanquished by an outside power does occur. "Drown us, lose us, / rain, let us loose / so to lose ourselves," she writes in "The Way Through" from *Here and Now,* her second book. In "The Goddess" the key word is *lipservice.* The poem seems a rather violent admonition against spiritual trifling.

In "Caedmon," (1984), one of the poems in which Denise announced her conversion to Catholicism, the story of the first English poet becomes a tale in which the subject is overwhelmed by a spiritual force with less violence but no less power than the Goddess: "the sudden angel affrighted me—light effacing / my feeble beam, / a forest of torches, feathers of flame, sparks upflying." These powers are

David Shaddock

not enemies. One constant thread through Denise's entire career is that, despite the violence of the encounter, the antagonist is not God but untruth and self-delusion. Every poem of Denise's is an attempt to spring readers (and herself) from "lie castle."

The fierceness of the angel was matched by Denise's own fierce spirit. Whether rather cattily complaining about a certain poet's lack of integrity or shouting "Oh, do shut up!" to an off-key street musician interrupting our outdoor dinner in Palo Alto, Denise could be a scathing adversary. In her finest poems, she turned her blowtorch ire to a fine flame of political outrage or spiritual courage. But she would never spare herself from the same scrutiny. As she wrote in "Flickering Mind": "Lord, not you / it is I who am absent." This voice reaches its apogee in poems written during the Vietnam War.

> Vietnam: Despair, Prophecy and Faith
>
> While the war drags on, always worse
> the soul dwindles to an ant
> rapid upon a cracked surface;
>
> lightly, grimly, incessantly
> the unfathomed cliffs where despair
> seethes hot and black
> ("Prologue: An Interim")

I met Denise as a student in her poetry seminar at Berkeley in 1969. Her husband, Mitch, was under indictment in New Haven along with the pediatrician Benjamin Spock and others for having urged young men to defy the selective service draft. Our class met at students' apartments to honor a campus-wide strike for a third world studies department.

The horror of war was immediate and visceral for Denise, who had worked as a nurse tending to the wounded in London during World War II, and it appeared early in her poems as well, most prominently in "During the Eichmann Trial" from *The Jacob's Ladder* (1961), which ends with the poet's description of Adolf Eichmann shooting a Jewish boy who had stolen one of his beloved peaches: "there is more blood than / sweet juice / always more blood."[6]

But this was our war, the blood was on our hands, the lies told to justify it were our lies—for those of us who, like Denise, were caught up in the movement to stop it, it is difficult to convey, at a distance of forty years and more untold bloodletting, the way the war dominated our every waking thought. As Denise wrote in "Statement for a Television Program," published in *The Poet in the World:* "The spring sunshine, the new leaves: we still see them, still love them: but in what poignant contrast is their beauty and simple goodness to the evil we are conscious of day and night."[7]

Denise's increasing stridency in her poems and her willingness to spout somewhat uncritically the revolutionary rhetoric of the New Left was seen by some, including the poet Robert Duncan, as leading to a diminishment of her poetic power. Duncan's criticism of her political stance and her antiwar poems (though he himself was strongly opposed to the war) led to a permanent break in their friendship.[8]

Though some of the antiwar poetry seems, in retrospect, woodenly rhetorical (as in the refrain "revolution or death" from "Staying Alive"), I do not see them as a diminishment. Denise's antiwar and political poems are acts of great courage, the courage to let her outrage speak, to carry her poetic vision as deeply into the fallen world as humanly possible in an effort to enact poetically the resurrection of the human spirit from despair.

In her essay "Poetry, Prophecy and Survival," Denise wrote that "a poetry articulating the dreads and horrors of our time" should be accompanied by "a willingness on the part of those who write it to take additional action toward stopping the great miseries that they record."[9] There is an Isaiah-like feel to this admonishment against words unmatched by actions. In this essay she goes on to say that the poet and the prophet "may exceed their own capacities." The prophetic voice that Denise developed in her antiwar poems led her to exceed her own capacities—the unflinching witness they bore helped carry Denise from a kind of diffuse quasi-agnostic spirituality into her life as a committed Catholic.

The early antiwar poem "Advent 1966" chronicles and foreshadows the inner dialogue between her voice of witness and the redemptive promise of Christianity:

> Because in Vietnam the vision of a Burning Babe
> is multiplied, multiplied,
>   the flesh on fire
> not Christ's as Southwell saw it, prefiguring
> the Passion upon the Eve of Christmas
>
> but wholly human and repeated, repeated,
> infant after infant, their names forgotten
> their sex unknown in the ashes,
> set alight, flaming but not vanishing,
> not vanishing as his vision but lingering,
>
> cinders upon the earth or living on
> moaning and stinking in hospitals three abed;

because of this my strong sight,
my clear caressive sight, my poet's sight I was given
that it might stir me to song,
is blurred.

In the complex rhetoric of this poem, it is not only the poet's spiritual vision that is effaced by the horror of Vietnam, blocking her from seeing the "unique Holy Infant / burning sublimely, an imagination of redemption," but also her ability to turn her poetic vision to the task of bearing witness to the carnage of war in its particular detail, other than to be transfixed into a kind of insect-like consciousness by the endless iterations of carnage. The poem continues, speaking of a "cataract" filming over the "inner eyes" of the speaker, which see "not the unique Holy Infant / burning sublimely, an imagination of redemption," but rather "senseless figures aflame":

And this insect (who is not there—
it is my own eyes do my seeing, the insect
is not there, what I see is there)
will not permit me to look elsewhere,

or, if I look, to see except dulled and unfocused
the delicate, firm whole flesh of the still unburned.

The implicit wish here is to be granted a clear vision not of the redeemer but of a single Vietnamese child. If there is a promise of redemption in this poem, it is not in the suffering of Christ but in the poet's bearing witness to the suffering of the Vietnamese people and to the fragile humanness of the individual. This moral, prophetic voice, speaking through her political poems, led Denise to her transcendent, Christian vision, a vision that, in characteristic fashion, announced itself in a poem.

The Lamb of God

Come rag of pungent
        quiverings,
        dim star.
Let's try
        if something human still
        can shield you,
        spark
        of remote light.
("Mass for the Day of St. Thomas Didymus")

Denise read me "Mass for the Day of St. Thomas Didymus" soon after she had finished it. I do not usually have a very vivid visual memory, but I can still picture where she sat in the living room of her Stanford apartment and how she seemed both humble and transported. I can feel the late afternoon winter light and the hush in the room. When she finished the Agnus Dei section, I blurted, "Oh, Denise, that's your masterpiece." She shyly nodded and said, "I think it may be; I'm very pleased with how it came out."

I do not recall that Denise made a point of the poem's announcing a religious conversion, as she later made explicit in her essay "Work That Enfaiths." Her first acknowledgment to me of her newfound Catholic faith came later in an offhand comment that she had found the Anglican service lacking in passion and so had begun attending Catholic services. Denise had an inimitable way of assuming that I already knew the things she knew, including the basic form of the Catholic Mass. That Denise had appropriated this form for her poem was of poetic interest to me; I considered it an important development in the ongoing dialogue in her work between received or traditional form and the "organic form" that arose intrinsically from the material.

What we did discuss that day, as on most of our visits, was our ongoing concern for the fate of the world and our personal struggle to do something about it. In the years that followed the end of the Vietnam War, Denise's political and poetic life became more and more concerned not just for the survival of an oppressed group of people (though such events as the civil wars in Central America occupied her attention) but with the survival of all people and the planet that we live on, threatened as we are by the twin plagues of nuclear war and ecological holocaust. In "Urgent Whisper" she writes of the earth itself shuddering like "a beaten child or captive animal." As a poet writing about nature, she is driven not just to write poems of "pure celebration," but also "inevitably to lament, to anger, and to the expression of dread."[10]

Although she was often her old, ebullient self, my sense is that the confrontation with the twin possibilities of nuclear and ecological annihilation darkened Denise's outlook considerably. Personal issues such as the end of her marriage to Mitch Goodman and her ongoing concerns for her son, Nikolai, who seemed rather adrift, played a part in this. But more and more our conversations concerned man's role in the fate of the planet. Denise began to talk about evil as an active force in the world, trying at every opportunity to corrupt and destroy God's work. At first I thought that she was speaking metaphorically, but I came to conclude that Denise had adopted a dualistic worldview, with its concomitant requirement that humanity's role was to oppose actively the corrupting work of the dark one. With regard to such questions as why the church should have so often in history been on the side of the oppressors, Denise replied that it was the devil's way to insinuate himself into good institutions and corrupt them.

David Shaddock

The dualistic view of good and evil was not entirely new to Denise; it had led her on many occasions to take political stands with absolute moral conviction. It was this tendency that led Robert Duncan to warn her, in one of the first salvos of what became a relationship-breaking argument, that "the poet's role is not to oppose evil, but to imagine it."[11] Increasingly, though, Denise's opposition to the point of view represented in Duncan's more nuanced, if not exactly apolitical, position, was based in her religious convictions. Influenced as she was by the radical tenets of Liberation Philosophy, which located the battle between good and evil not in our souls but in the struggle of poor people against oppression, Denise now was wrestling not with God, but for him.

At this point in her ongoing intersubjective relationship with God, Denise had moved from an immanent god revealed in all creation to one that requires our moral witness to evil to one that gave us free will but who requires us to oppose actively the force of evil in the world. In "Agnus Dei," though, her relationship to God takes one last step: God himself requires our love and protection. This final step in her conversion to Catholicism involved a sense not of being overwhelmed by a blinding force, as had happened in her earlier poems, but of being struck with the profound sense of God's vulnerability and need for *us.*

In "Agnus Dei" she takes the metaphorical notion of God's radical innocence quite literally: he is an "infant sheep," "having neither rage nor claws," wholly dependent on human kindness for his survival. And our relationship with this God-being is completely reversed. Rather than depending on God for any salvation or intervention, we must care for and nurture his radical innocence. If this is what the salvation of the world rests on, it is a dicey proposition—we humans have "icy hearts" and are "shamefaced" in our passive wish to be rescued, and the innocence of God is a "dim star."[12] But on this remote possibility Denise bases her religious conversion, one that entails not just an I/thou relationship with a God who will listen to our pleas and arguments, but a relationship like a mother feels for her infant—a total, protective commitment to this young and helpless life.

In the Jewish mystical tradition in which Denise was steeped, there is an important antecedent to the notion of God's need for our intervention. According to the Kabalistic creation myth of the sixteenth-century Jewish mystic Isaac Luria, it was God's loneliness and longing that led him to create the world, which he did by first withdrawing to create a void, then filling that void with his divine love. The vessels into which he poured his divine love could not contain the force of that love, however; they broke, and sparks of love were scattered throughout the universe. It is mankind's job to liberate and reunite these sparks through love and ethical action, a process that can be begun only by us, without regard to the ultimate endpoint of redemption. Denise and I both were moved by this myth with its story of a vulnerable God and His need for our help to reclaim His creation, as well as its implicit understanding that whatever sparks we could liberate from matter would never be enough to complete the task but were nonetheless vitally important.

Even as we touched on these many topics in our ongoing conversations, I can recall no moment when Denise called attention to her having become a practicing Catholic. Her conversion was a process, not an epiphany. There are many parallels here to Denise's notion of organic form in poetry: the Catholic Church had evolved or been "discovered" to be the form that fit the emerging content of her religious life. This is more than an analogy—Denise wrote in an essay, "Work That Enfaiths," that her poetry led the way in her religious life and that her faith in God may be wavering but that she has an ongoing faith in what she calls, quoting John Keats, "the truth of the imagination."[13]

Journey of Art . . . Journey of Faith

> We must feel
> the pulse in the wound
> to believe
>   that "with God
> all things
>   are possible"
> taste
> bread at Emmaus
> that warm hands
> broke and blessed.
> ("On Belief in the Physical Resurrection of Jesus")[14]

Once, when asked to contribute to an anthology of spiritual poetry, Denise replied that she wouldn't know what to send, since all poetry, by virtue of its existence, is spiritual. When she told me this story, I wondered to myself if this wasn't another of Denise's ongoing fights against being pigeonholed or stereotyped into being a certain kind of poet, since I knew she loathed being called a Beat or a Black Mountain poet and didn't want to be known primarily as a woman or feminist. But as she continued, I realized she was being completely ingenuous. When she consented to anthologizing her specifically religious poems in *The Stream and the Sapphire,* she took pains to insist that she was doing so "as a convenience to readers."[15]

In her slow movement from agnosticism to faith, one thread remains constant: a reverent belief in the primacy of the poetic imagination. Denise's faith life was inextricable from her writing life, and writing on any subject from nature to art to politics to Catholic doctrine was for her a profoundly spiritual act. The primacy of the act of discovery in her poems—both of the content and the form—sheds

David Shaddock

light on her faith life as well. Belief becomes an act of imagination, as in "Passage,"
where the poet envisions:

> The grasses, numberless, bowing and rising, silently
> cry Hosanna as the spirit
> moves them and moves burnishing
>
> over and again upon mountain pastures
> a day of spring, a needle's eye
> space and time are passing through like a swath of silk.[16]

This openness to discovery was accompanied by rigorous attention to detail and an
almost fanatical demand for lucidity in her poems. I can remember, at the beginning of our friendship, when I was still primarily in the student role, debating for
an hour the placement of a single comma in one of my poems. Here too is a key to
her faith life and to her eventual conversion to Catholicism. No slop in her poems,
and no vague or universal spirituality in her church.

The rigor that Denise brought to her art informed her faith life in another
way as well. Hers would not be an intellectual exercise, divorced from sensual,
immediate experience. The idea that the rituals and teachings of the church were
just myths, ciphers of a deeper, psychological truth, held little or no interest to her.
In "On Belief in the Physical Resurrection of Jesus," she calls herself, quoting Mari-
anne Moore, a "literalist of the imagination." She is not, like an epiphyte, "nour-
ished on air," nor can she "subsist on the light, / on the half / of metaphor that's
not // grounded in dust, grit / heavy / carnal clay."[17] Here she expands William
Carlos Williams's famous "No ideas but in things" from an artistic to a spiritual
dictum. The blood of Christ's wounds must be real to the imagination's apprehension and not some mere symbol of human suffering.

Denise is not aligning herself here with a fundamentalist belief in the literal
truth of God's word in the Bible. It is not an absolute belief she is after but a poet's
imagination of a miracle. She is bringing a poet's aesthetic to the religious experience. She wants, paraphrasing Moore, to have imaginary gardens with real miracles
in them. The critic Northrop Frye wrote that "literature always assumes, in its metaphors, a relation between human consciousness and its natural environment that
passes beyond—in fact outrages and violates—the ordinary common sense based
on a permanent separation of subject and object."[18] To cut the metaphor in half
and savor only the subject, as the purveyors of religion as mythology do, is no less
a diminishment than the fundamentalist's trying to savor only the objective truth.
The real miracle, Denise is arguing, takes place in the field of the poem, where
the subject is completely penetrated by the physical world and the physical world,
while not losing a drop of its heft and feel, is lifted up, reborn from its inertness.

Faith and Doubt: A Spiritual Friendship

> Waiting
> for who comes at last
> late, lost, the forever
> longed-for, walking
> not my road but crossing
> the corner where I wait.
> ("Waiting")[19]

In writing this essay, I have had the pleasure of rereading a great deal of Denise's poetry and prose. I have reread letters and heard her voice anew in them. But my understanding of her spiritual odyssey comes largely from our long talks and from my own life of God wrestling that those talks inspired and sustained. Despite the fact that Denise became Catholic and I am Jewish, there grew between us a deep, almost intuitive affinity.

Though Denise's earliest gifts to me as a teacher centered around her demand for rigor and clarity, the gift that emerged from our spiritual discussions was permission: permission to believe and doubt in equal (or unequal) measure; permission to have as idiosyncratic or literal a relationship with the teachings of organized religion as I needed; and most important, permission to trust, as Denise surely did, my own religious instincts. Although there were many times where our views on religion and the world diverged, I can feel in this moment the way Denise was for me the author of the permission that informs my religious life.

In the last half of the 1980s, I encountered two very difficult experiences—my wife and I failed in our attempts to conceive a child, and my mother was killed by medical malpractice. Denise was very supportive and consoling to me. She listened with interest and compassion as I recalled my mother's life. She helped my wife and me through the ups and downs of infertility and then through the adoption and early years of our son. She also confided in me when Nikolai had to undergo surgery for a brain tumor, from which he never fully recovered.

From our ongoing dialogue and the life experiences we shared, there emerged for me a realization that faith did not require a moment of blinding understanding or enlightenment but merely a commitment to be fully present to the experience of living and particularly to allow oneself to surrender to suffering, doubt, and longing.[20] My long poem *In This Place Where* Something's Missing *Lives* elaborates an idea from the Kabbalah: that each thought is a husk that contains within it a spark of God's original light. By extension the longing for God to exist, or even one's sadness at being unable to believe that he exists, marks the presence of a divine spark. When I discussed this with Denise, she explained that ideas of this sort have a long and honored history in theology, mentioning in particular

David Shaddock

Thomas Aquinas. I began to feel that it was indeed possible to found belief on the *presence* of absence.

Doubt and uncertainty for Denise often took the form of questioning a God who could allow so much suffering and injustice in the world. Her St. Thomas Didymus describes seeing the father's spiritual agony over his son's suffering and feeling closer to him then. The poem returns, almost as a refrain, to Christ's cry, "Lord I believe, help thou my unbelief." But faith does not alleviate affliction. Even her Julian of Norwich, after "God for a moment in our history / placed in that five-fingered / human nest / the macrocosmic egg, sublime paradox / brown hazel-nut of all that is," says, "*deeds are done so evil, injuries inflicted / so great, it seems to us impossible any good / can come from them*" (emphasis in original).

In terms of actual practice, our faith lives did not much overlap. I attended Midnight Mass on several Christmas Eves with Denise, and on a retreat for spiritual directors, she met and connected with my beloved rabbi and teacher, Burt Jacobson. She participated in an interfaith protest at the Nevada nuclear test site, and I participated in two memorable Passover Seders that were held outside the entry gate of that facility. I know that Denise prayed and observed Catholic rituals, but these never seemed to be a big part of her religious life. When I became interested in Jewish meditation practices, she remarked that she had always worried that meditation might interfere with her writing life. It seemed to me that the truest expressions of Denise's Catholic faith were her poetry and her participation in political actions and protests. It was in our annual exchange of poems, either at Stanford or my home in Berkeley, that the news of our religious lives was exchanged.

There was one time, though, that our wrestling with God might have come close to wrestling with each other. I was noting, perhaps with a touch of envy, the increasing presence of the literal figure of Christ in her poems. I said something to the effect that your religion has its messiah, while mine is still waiting for him. She turned to me, very seriously, and said, "Well, David, do you want me to convert you?" She was completely in earnest. I was tense and defensive for a moment, as Jews often are in the face of such Christian "good will." Then I realized that I was in the presence of something very old and intimate in Denise's experience: she seemed to be channeling her father, a man who, as I had learned from her, was made of equal parts zeal and tenderness. This intimacy diffused the tension. I was in fact a bit tempted, but in the end I demurred, and the subject did not come up again.

As Denise settled into her new home in Seattle, she delighted in the access that she, a nondriver, had to nature: the shores of sea-and-migratory-bird-filled Lake Washington and the views of fourteen-thousand-foot Mount Rainier. In her series "Lake, Moon Mountain" from *Evening Train,* Denise's view of the mountain, emerging and receding from the cloud cover, becomes a symbol of a faith life built around absence and presence. As she wrote in "Effacement" of Mount Rainier:

majestic presence become
one cloud among others,
humble vapor,
barely discernible,

like the archangel walking
with Tobias on dusty roads.

This sense of living at peace with the angel of God was perhaps most apparent to me when she came for a visit after a weeklong retreat with Brother David Steindl-Rast in Big Sur. There was a light in her eyes and a sense of ease in her body. It seemed to me then that she had found on that retreat a deep peace and an abiding sense of the presence of the divine, as she would express in her poem "Primary Wonder" from *Sands in the Well,* the last book she published in her lifetime:

once more the quiet mystery
is present to me, the throng's clamor
recedes: the mystery
that there is anything, anything at all
let alone cosmos, joy, memory, everything,
rather than void, and that O Lord,
Creator, Hallowed One, You still,
hour by hour sustain it.[21]

Denise died on December 20, 1997, the winter solstice, after a long struggle with non-Hodgkin's lymphoma. Although I was present when she died, our last real visit was a few months before when I came to Seattle and followed her up to Port Townsend, where she gave a reading. Though I had seen her latest work the previous summer, I was astonished at the number of new poems she read. These poems were tinged with mortality but not with despair.

In my poem "The Certainty of Return," which uses as an epigraph Denise's lines "The certainty of return / cannot be assured," I wrote "Your life in me . . . has been a trellis that my own life has grown on." Writing this essay has made me think again of that trellis and of the thirteen years since she died. Despite the intervening years (during which I have often thought it was a blessing she was spared living through 9/11 and George W. Bush's wars of choice), I can still feel the structure-giving presence I meant to evoke with the trellis image. If she were alive, she would be not surrendering to despair but urging a tendril of spirit to lift off the top rung, into the wind, poised between purchase and uncertainty.

                                                                    David Shaddock

• ENGAGEMENT, INQUIRY, FAITH •

The Parallel Voyages of Denise Levertov and David Shaddock

Peter Dale Scott

David Shaddock was Denise Levertov's student in 1969 when she taught at Berkeley. After that they continued as friends, particularly after 1979 when, at Denise's invitation, David assisted her in teaching poetry at Centrum's Port Townsend Writers' Conference, organized by Sam Hamill.

David's importance to Denise is attested to by two explicit references to him in her *New and Selected Essays,* plus a third more important reference where he is not named, to which we will return.[1] The first reference is in the important opening essay, "Some Affinities of Content" (1991), in which Denise records a shift, realized "in the fall of 1990," in her poetic development: she was moving away from the formal considerations of her earlier, William Carlos Williams–dominated, so-called Black Mountain period to a poetry that was a "spiritual quest" for a deeper level of being. She now recognized a personal affinity with two related kinds of poetry: poems from the American Northwest about the mysteries of nature (for example a heron poem by Hamill) and poems "concerned more or less with matters of religious faith."

Among the latter she singled out David's just-published second book of poems, *In This Place Where* Something's Missing *Lives:* "A number of David Shaddock's poems take up the ancient Jewish tradition which Arthur Waskow . . . has called 'God-wrestling.'"[2] She proceeds to quote two passages from the book for more than a page, which is more space in the essay than is devoted to newer friend Czesław Miłosz, whom in correspondence she liked to address as "my Master."

For the two decades between their first meeting and the appearance of David's book in the fall of 1990, both poets had traveled on parallel but interconnected paths from political engagement to spiritual commitment: David as a founding member of a Jewish Renewal synagogue and Denise (after November 18, 1990) as a communicant in the Roman Catholic Church. Their two paths involved no dramatic reversals (like that of Paul on the road to Damascus) but rather a gradual emergence and deepening of tendencies latent in each of their respective origins.

Each poet has applied the term *God wrestling* to the other's work. But it is most applicable to their poems in the 1980s and could hardly have been predicted in Denise's poems set in Berkeley. On the surface God had little or nothing to do with her description of the sense of community, of fellowship, experienced in the People's Park in Berkeley in 1969. As she put it in her poem, "Staying Alive," in a passage dated "May 14th, 1969—Berkeley": "Went *with some of my students* to work in the People's Park. There seemed to be plenty of digging and gardening help so we decided, as Jeff had his truck available, to shovel up the garbage that had been thrown into the west part of the lot and take it out to the city dump." There was however a hint of the apocalyptic in what she called the "place, locus, of what could be our New World even now, our revolution"—even though, just one day later, that possibility ended:

> *Thursday, May 15th*
> At 6 a.m. the ominous zooming, war-sound, of helicopters . . .
> Bulldozers have moved in . . .
> all shall know
> this day, and the days that follow:
> now, the clubs, the gas,
> bayonets, bullets. The War
> comes home to us.[3]

David was one of those students with Denise at the park and later reported that on the day of bayonets and tear gas, "I was arrested and badly mistreated by the Alameda. . . . Denise bailed me out. . . . and spent a morning helping me overcome the trauma."[4]

In retrospect Denise's euphoria at People's Park seems like a brief and heady infatuation. But many people looking for a better society, if not an earthly paradise, shared it at that time. My own idealized view of the park was more complicated than Denise's. I knew the chief organizers and was aware that some of them had ambitions of a violent challenge to authority that was in my view very unlikely to produce a "New World." Nevertheless, in the spirit of curbing the war-making establishment of that era, I defended People's Park in the Berkeley Academic Senate, much to the disapproval of erstwhile friends such as Miłosz. I too tended to idealize certain moments. My friend John Reed, a landscape architect, covered a block of a Berkeley street with sod, where we danced barefoot, watched by expressionless uniformed teenagers with bayonets on their rifles. Of course the euphoria did not last long, but many Americans recall spending the next decades, inspired by that heady sense that change is possible, in a search for some kind of alternative to the status quo.

Denise's initial antiwar involvement had been with protesters who were mostly secular, such as the Boston Five, of whom her then-husband, Mitchell Goodman, was one. After 1971 Denise spent more and more time with religious activists,

Peter Dale Scott

some of whom she met at poetry readings in support of nonviolent protesters such as Dan Berrigan, the Catonsville Nine, and the Milwaukee Fourteen. In this way she befriended one of the Milwaukee Fourteen: Jim Forest of the *Catholic Worker,* Catholic Peace Fellowship, and Fellowship of Reconciliation, a lay disciple and later biographer of Dorothy Day and Thomas Merton. She dedicated to Forest her poem "The Old King" (a poem about aging and isolation). We can see in the poem's ending a presentiment of the direction toward which her own life was returning:

> The multitude gone, labyrinths
> crumbling.
>   To go down
> back into the known hole.

Developments in both Denise's and David's lives drove them toward a deeper and more tragic introspection. Both of their mothers died—Denise's in 1977 and David's in 1986. Denise's marriage was disintegrating in the early 1970s, leading to her divorce in 1974. David in contrast was married in 1975, at a ceremony in which Denise read "Prayer for Revolutionary Love." As David has written, however, the 1980s were for him a time of difficult experiences, during which Denise was again supportive and consoling.

In these two decades, David shared Denise's growing preference for nonviolent spiritual activism. Though their protest communities were of different denominations, they were able to talk about both spirituality and nonviolence in the course of their usual discussions of poetry. By 1990 both were deeply settled in the religious ambience of their childhoods. Though Denise had become a Roman Catholic and David had joined a Jewish Renewal neo-Hasidic temple, their two developments were closely intertwined.

After the end of the Vietnam War, Denise returned to her earlier interest in protesting nuclear weapons. This was a preoccupation at the time of the U.S. Conference of Catholic Bishops, which in 1983 put out a pastoral letter, "The Challenge of Peace," calling for a "no first use" declaration by the United States. As a consequence Denise was in the company of Roman Catholic priests and bishops at a number of protests. She wrote two poems about her presence in March 1991 at the nuclear test site in Nevada, when the Brazilian archbishop Dom Hélder Camara was arrested there. She wrote of this experience in her late poem "Dom Helder Camara at the Nuclear Test Site":

> After hours of waiting,
> penned into two wire-fenced enclosures, sun
> climbing to cloudless zenith, till everyone

has been processed, booked, released to trudge
one by one up the slope to the boundary line
back to a freedom that's not so free,
we are all reassembled. We form
two circles, one contained in the other, to dance,
clockwise and counterclockwise
like children in Duncan's vision.
But not to the song of ashes, of falling:
we dance in the unity that brought us here,
instinct pulls us into the ancient
rotation, symbol of continuance.
Light and persistent as tumbleweed,
but not adrift, Dom Helder, too,
faithful pilgrim, dances,
dances at the turning core.[5]

Here the word *unity* is best understood as neither political not spiritual but the two together.

In the late 1980s, David repeatedly attended the nuclear test site protests as well, but he celebrated a Seder there, while Denise communed at Mass. David attended with members of the Berkeley Jewish Renewal temple Kehilla, which he had joined when it was founded in 1984. Under the leadership of its rabbi, Burt Jacobson, it included a core group of people who had first met in political activity but moved on to worship together as well. The Judaism of Rabbi Jacobson, a student of Rabbi Abraham Heschel, was shaped by the Hasidic rabbi Israel Baal Shem Tov, the eighteenth-century mystic who also inspired Denise's ancestor Schneour Zalman.[6] David's religious community also led to his being introduced to Arthur Waskow, the Jewish Renewal social activist who contributed an afterword to David's first book and whose book *Godwrestling* supplied the term Denise used to refer to David's work. In this milieu David intensified his own study of kabbalah and Hasidic mysticism. This enabled him in discussions with Denise to intensify her own interest, derived initially from her father but also reinforced in the 1950s by her reading Martin Buber's *Tales of the Hasidim*.[7]

The "God-wrestling" poems that emerged from these dialogues in both poets' work reflect these changes that had occurred in their friendship over two decades. In Denise's work the change from *To Stay Alive* (1971) to *The Door in the Hive* (1989) is easier to see than the total integrity of experience that underlies both books. A brief digression about this quality in the much-maligned *To Stay Alive* is relevant to David's poetry as well.

For four decades it has been fashionable for tenure-minded academic critics to regret the expansion of Denise's poetry in the Vietnam era to include revolutionary

Peter Dale Scott

politics. Even defenders of her poetry after *The Sorrow Dance* (1967) see in it a "disjunction between political anguish and poetic affirmation."[8] In contrast I see in her poetry of this era, particularly *To Stay Alive* (1971), a vital widening and deepening of her work. *To Stay Alive* is the first explicit example of what might be called the recapitulative technique in her later work. "The Olga Poems," first published in *The Sorrow Dance,* are reintroduced in *To Stay Alive,* reflecting an inscape in which Olga's political anger, to which Denise as a child was an observer, has now been internalized into Denise's own poetic field.

Denise explained her motive for the inclusion in her introduction.

It happens at times that the poet becomes aware of the relationships that exist between poem and poem; is conscious, after the act, of one poem, one line or stanza, having been the precursor of another. . . . The justification, then, of including in a new volume poems which are available in other collections, is esthetic—it assimilates separated parts of a whole. And I am given courage to do so by the hope of that whole being seen as having some value not as mere "confessional" autobiography, but as a document of some historical value, a record of one person's inner/outer experience in America during the '60's and the beginnings of the '70's, an experience which is shared by so many and which transcends the peculiar details of each life, though it can only be expressed in and through such details.[9]

Because of her collage inclusion of documents from the People's Park era, *To Stay Alive* has been compared to Williams's long poem *Paterson.* An even better comparison might be to *Paterson*'s model: Ezra Pound's *Pisan Cantos,* another diary-like poem "including history," that was also a poem of recollection and pentimento, in which organic form dissolved to become organic process. Denise, writing about Pound in 1972, described how she belatedly came to appreciate the balance of lyric and antilyric in the larger mosaic of the Cantos. Quoting from Pound's *Guide to Kulchur* ("I haven't just dropped one thread to pick up another . . . . I need more than one string for a fabric"), Denise adds, "I begin to apprehend the poetry of history, that flickers both in the olive leaves and in the voices speaking of trade; in the ant and the lynx, the sensuous imagination and the dry implications of document, in legislation and song and all the fabric of news that stays news."[10]

All of this serves as a precursor to the laudatory introduction Denise wrote to David's first book of poems, *Dreams Are Another Set of Muscles:* "He is a poet who doesn't glance at an experience and skip on to the next one but, in the course of making the poem or poems that come of it, follows it through as far as it will take him—through years of honing a single poem or into linked sequences of exploration. Years of love and labor in the service of poetry. As a result, his themes . . . interconnect, whether he's writing of dolphins or of children, of a beloved woman or of the threatened earth. There's an osmosis between the sections, as between separate poems; they present, though diverse in tone and structure, an ensemble, a spiritual ecology."[11]

Even the titles of David's poems—"Dolphin to the Author," "Bomb as Jesus"—corroborate the osmosis of which Denise speaks. The poems themselves carry echoes of diverse authors, but some are clearly influenced by Denise's reportages in *To Stay Alive,* for example, "The White Train":

> The white [weapons] train is crossing the mile-wide Mississippi
>   near Memphis,
> On the Tennessee side eight Catholic protesters
> kneel on the tracks in prayer.
> The train slows to thirty-five on the bridge;
> the engineer sees the kneeling figures; wheels
> lock and screech as he hits the brakes.
> Seven jump away, Sister Dobrowolski stays
> still, praying in the name of Jesus for peace.
> The train stops two yards from her.
> The others walk back in front of the white train and are arrested.[12]

I see no traces of "God-wrestling" in David's first book of poems. However by 1987 his discussions with Denise had begun to move his poetry more and more into a mystical vein, one that had already been explored by Denise in *The Jacob's Ladder* (1961). Thus as they continued to meet in the late 1980s, their interests and poetics were converging. Denise had already written the poem "Sparks":

> A letter . . .
> discloses, in words and between them,
> a life opening, fearful, fearless,
> thousand-eyed, a field
> of sparks that move swiftly in darkness, to and from
> a center. He is beginning
> to live.[13]

As Joan Hallisey has written, this poem recalls the Hasidic belief that "in the primeval creation preceding the creation of our world, the divine light-substance burst and 'sparks' fell into the lower depths, filling the 'shells' of the things and creatures of our world."[14]

Peter Dale Scott

The second of David's "God-wrestling" poems, addressed directly to God, displays more clearly these kabbalistic sources:

> I envision a light source
> spiraling from a single point
> out through the galaxies of the Universe,
>
> but always it is stopped
> by the opaque wall
> of my skin.
>
> What do you want of me
> with Your talk of the Holy Sparks
> in each particular thought?
>
> Why do You keep after me
> asking this emptiness
> to procreate?[15]

David's struggle with the separation between self and God had been famously depicted by Denise in her seminal poem "The Jacob's Ladder":

> . . . and a man climbing
> must scrape his knees, and bring
> the grip of his hands into play. The cut stone
> consoles his groping feet. Wings brush past him.
> The poem ascends.[16]

In "Flickering Mind," as in David's poems, the addressee is God, but the complaint is about the poet's own deficiencies:

> Lord, not you, it is I who am absent.
> At first
> belief was a joy I kept in secret,
> Stealing alone
> into sacred places;
> a quick glance, and away—and back,
> circling.
> I have long since uttered your name
> but now
> I elude your presence.[17]

David, in the same period, wrote verses such as

> I did not know then
> that I would not find You
> in prayer, or vision, or even
> as consolation to my great sorrow.

> I did not know then that this yearning
> was visitation, nor that the exhaustion of all my hope
> of finding something Holy
> was nothing but a step
> toward pride's renunciation.[18]

In both kabbalistic and Christian theology, this awareness of emptiness in the nearness of God, the *ein-sof,* is part of the path to insight and commitment. What makes these poems Hasidic in tone is the address directly to God. As David notes in his essay in this volume, the early Hasid Rabbi Levi Yitzchok of Berditchev poured out his stream of consciousness to God, not holding anything back.

I do not know whether Denise or David was the first to address God in this way: their poems cited here are roughly contemporaneous. One of David's poems is dated 5748 (1987). I am unaware of any earlier Levertov poems in which the addressee is God; one does not find this format in *Oblique Prayers* (1984). There are five examples in the last section of *The Sands of the Well* (1998), but these are not God wrestling poems: they deal not with God's distance but with his presence. In his essay in this volume, David explains that, to Denise, the term "God wrestling" did not suggest a "spiritual path of angst and struggle." Rather, in the course of walking with him by his house, she might turn from a "long and serious conversation on the nature of evil or the future of our planet" to the "wonders" revealed by the "all-to-familiar scene" of an "iris bloom sticking through a broken fence and break into an improvised ballet step in response."

Denise also had a chance to clarify that for her God wrestling was not to be seen as a struggle with God. Shortly before she died in 1997, Denise was interviewed by Gary Pacernik for a book about Jewish poets, and she went to great lengths to explain that she was (whatever rabbis might think) indeed Jewish and also a poet but not a specifically Jewish poet (any more than a Catholic poet, a political poet, or a feminist poet, although all of these labels have been attached to her work). She referred to David's God wrestling poems again as part of an effort the distinction:

> *GP* • You refer many times to Jacob's ladder (Gen 28:15) as well as Jacob's
> wrestling with the stranger (Gen. 32:28) after which he is known

Peter Dale Scott

as Israel (For you have striven with God and with men, and have prevailed). Your epigraph re the ladder quotes Buber: "Even the ascent and descent of the angels depends on my deed." How do you interpret your fascination with Jacob? Is this not evidence of your Jewishness?

DL • Many non-Jewish people have been fascinated by the story of Jacob and the Angel! So I don't think my interest constitutes "evidence of Jewishness" at all! I do think arguing with God (or "God wrestling") is a (delightful) Jewish characteristic—but though I have poems expressive of doubt or the sense of disconnection, I'm not, I think, particularly apt to argue with God. My friend David Shaddock wrote a wonderful series of "God-wrestling" poems a few years back, for which Arthur Waskow wrote an introduction (unfortunately the book was only published in a very limited edition . . .).[19]

David, however, does at times explicitly argue with God, as many Jews have, since the Shoah and also before:

> How can I beg You not to go,
> to stay here and comfort me,
> when we haven't finished our argument? . . .
>
> What were the terms of our argument?
> I wanted a sign, some knowledge
> that You exist, separate from my needing You.
> You wanted prayer, a miming of belief.[20]

Denise also beautifully described, in words that might speak by analogy for both poets, how the writing of poetry was essential to her path beyond belief to faith, and in her case her reception into the community of the Roman Catholic Church. As David put it in his essay here, her poetry led the way in her religious life and, though her faith in God might waver, she had an ongoing faith in what she called, quoting Keats, "the truth of the imagination."

She wrote in particular how the experience of writing "Mass for the Day of St. Thomas Didymus" (*Candles in Babylon,* 1982), which she first undertook when "I still considered myself an agnostic," became by the end "also a conversion process." One can indeed see a development in the course of the poem, from the undefined Lord as "deep unknown" in the opening Kyrie to the doctrinal and incarnate Lamb of God in the concluding Agnus Dei. Undoubtedly she is more intimately engaged with specific Christian doctrine at the end of the poem than at the beginning.

Yet if the term *conversion* implies a turning from an old to a different life, it may be more appropriate to see the process Denise describes as one of fulfillment and *t'shuvah,* or return—the completion of a preordained process or journey—rather than as conversion to something new. In 1984, which is to say after writing this poem but before her commentary on it, she wrote, with great self-awareness, "All that has taken place in my life since [childhood]—all, that is, that has any bearing on my life as a poet—was in some way *foreshadowed then*" (emphasis added). She continues, "My father's Hasidic ancestry, his being steeped in Jewish and Christian scholarship and mysticism, his fervor and eloquence as a preacher, were factors built into my cells even though I rarely paid conscious heed to what, as a child, I mostly felt were parts of the embarrassing adult world, and which during my adolescence I rejected as restrictive."

Hasidic influence had been apparent in her poetry since, after reading Buber, she published "The Jacob's Ladder" in 1960. But in the 1980s, she completed the unfolding of her Jewish Christian roots by converting, much as her father had done before her. It is easy to believe that her friendship with David, more steeped than she in Hasidism, strengthened her in this return. As David writes here, Denise read him her "Mass" poem soon after she completed it, and he can still picture her looking both "humble and transported" as she read it to him. He also remembers her shy agreement with his statement that this poem was her masterpiece.

In "Work That Enfaiths," Denise refers to the importance of this transdenominational validation: "It could not fail to occur to me that, once these poems of religious quest were published, I was likely to lose some of my readers. This proved not to be true. . . . My Jewish readers, for instance—while not subscribing, of course, to whatever is specifically Christian in the poems—responded to them without hostility, and with solidarity in the basic interfaith assumption of belief in God."[21] Likewise David's familiarity and ease with Hasidic faith may have helped Denise imagine the certainty in her father's Hasidic heart, a certainty that led paradoxically away from Hasidism to his Anglican conversion. As she wrote in her poem "Wings in the Pedlar's Pack":

> The *certainty of wings:* a child's bold heart,
> not, good little Schul-boy, Torah or Talmud
> gave it to you, a practical vision:
> *wings were needed,* why should people
> plod forever on foot, not glide like herons
> through the blue and white
> promise unfolding
> over their heads, over
> the river's thawing?

Peter Dale Scott

> Later, *ochetz moy,* when you discovered
> wings for your soul, the same bold heart
> empowered you.[22]

In this beautiful poem, which recapitulates her own earlier work and progress, Denise describes how the wings that brushed by the man in "The Jacob's Ladder" were then yearned for by the poet herself. In "The Standoff," she writes,

> Our *shoulders ache.* The abyss
> gapes at us.
>
> When shall we
> dare to fly?[23]

These wings were easily possessed by her father's childlike heart. In this way her father became a role model, not just for her, but for all of us: "Invisible wings are given to us too, by which, if we would dare to acknowledge and use them, we might transcend the dualities of time and matter—might be upheld to walk on water. Instead, we humans persistently say no, and persistently experience our wings only as a dragging weight on our backs, "Levertov writes in "Work That Enfaiths."[24] The intimacy with which she speaks to her father in Slavic (*ochetz moy* means "my father") reflects the gradual change in her life and practice. For some time she had been attending church services at the Emmanuel Episcopal Church in Boston, because of both its inspiring liturgies and its commitment to peace and justice issues. (Only later, when she found Episcopalian services too tepid, did she shift to the Roman Catholic Church.)

The pastor of the Emmanuel Church "'practically commissioned' her to write her poem 'Annunciation' for an Advent service there."[25] Whether the poem was commissioned or not, Denise was able to use the Virgin's experience to formulate the challenge in her own life, which was then at the point of reception into a different, more demanding version of her father's Anglo-Catholicism:

> Bravest of all humans,
> > consent illumined her.
> The room filled with its light,
> the lily glowed in it,
> > and the iridescent wings.
> Consent,
> > courage unparalleled,
> opened her utterly.[26]

In her essay "Work That Enfaiths," Denise compares "the sheer *daring* of the Virgin Mary" with "the state of mind of St. Thomas"—"whose entire being had knotted itself / into the one tight-drawn question"—after his touching the wounds of the resurrected Christ "frees him at last." In a poem included in the essay, she does not feel "scalding pain" or "shame" but rather "light, light streaming" into her.[27]

After 1990, with Denise's reception finally achieved and David's book honored with Waskow's afterword, we cease to see evidence of God wrestling in either poet. Critics have commented on the serenity of Denise's late poems in *Sands of the Well* and *The Great Unknowing*. At the same time I still see in her last recapitulative work traces of her characteristic self-questioning and negative capability, after her reception as a Roman Catholic as well as before. As she writes in "For Those Whom the Gods Love Less,"

> When you discover
> your new work travels the ground you had traversed
> decades ago, you wonder, panicked,
> 'Have I outlived my vocation? Said already
> all that was mine to say?'
> There's a remedy—
> only one—for the paralysis seizing your throat to mute you,
> numbing your hands: Remember the great ones, remember Cezanne
> doggedly *sur le motif,* his mountain
> a tireless noonday angel he grappled like Jacob,
> demanding reluctant blessing.

God (like Mount Rainier shrouded in cumulus) remains as remote and mysterious as the glimpse of distant Snowdon Denise recalled seeing with her mother a half century before:

> The mountain's daily speech is silence.
> Profound as the Great Silence
> between the last Office and the first.
> Uninterrupted as the silence God maintains
> throughout the layered centuries.

Rainier represents a Godhead securely present but never familiarized. As she puts it in her poem "Effacement," the mountain "is cloud . . . barely discernible."[28]

David continued to see Denise regularly until her death (he was one of three former students at her deathbed), and he describes a Denise who in real life was much more doctrinally dogmatic than in her poems. Like the theologians Thomas Merton, Jim Douglass, and David Ray Griffin, she worried about the presence of

Peter Dale Scott

the demonic in contemporary life and suggested that the devil might explain the malign influence of American Christian fundamentalists. I was surprised, and at first a little shocked, to hear that in the course of one of their endless religious discussions, Denise suddenly addressed David and said, "Do you want me to convert you?" My first reaction as a North American Protestant was to find this distastefully invasive, believing that David, like everyone else in Micah's vision, should be left under his own fig tree. Later I came to see the episode quite differently: that she, still wholeheartedly enthusiastic in her maturity, saw in David a Hasidic Jew like her father. And she wanted him to experience what she saw as her father's liberating conversion, just as she herself had done.

Since Denise's death, David, while preserving and deepening his own Jewish roots, has continued, both as a critic and as a poet, to enhance her legacy. In an era when postmodern critics still tend to remember her as part of a Black Mountain countertradition and Catholic critics tend to focus on her later poems that are about "the quest for or the encounter with God," as she writes in "Some Affinities of Content," David's prose appreciations of Denise have struck a sound middle ground, seeing her as both "steeped in the English literary tradition" and also influenced by Williams and Robert Creeley and thus never feeling the "necessity of choosing between the raw and the cooked in American poetry."[29] This is well said, and a welcome corrective to the tendency of postmodern poet-critics such as Michael Palmer first to locate Denise in a marginal countertradition and then marginalize her within that "alternative to the traditional discourses of power and mystification."[30] Denise is clearly outside the crowd of postmodern outsiders, because, as David noted, of her fidelity to the mainstream English tradition of Keats, Gerard Manley Hopkins, and Thomas Hardy.

David's mature poetry has continued to be faithful to Denise's legacy while also honoring his own Jewish roots. A fine example is "A Great Blue Heron in Boynton Beach," reminiscent of Denise's heron poem "The Great Black Heron" while osmotically blending political with religious perspectives.

> A great blue heron in Boynton Beach
> Camrys in the lantana shade,
> pock of yellow balls on green courts,
> splash of water aerobics,
> talk of total knees and hips replaced,
> the blind psychiatrist working his way
> past the gauntlet of kibitzers to his favorite chaise:
> all this is pleasing to the higher orders,
> who would themselves like soon to retire,
> *Tif'eret*, compassion, *Binah*, the womb of the world,
> are worn out at the end of a bloody century.

A great blue heron's six-foot wings
cast a shadow over the pool,
granting a moment's respite from the sun
for the second generation furriers and insurance men
whose five-year-old granddaughters in pink-frilled two-pieces
swim like a fish, their red-polished nails breaking the surface.

A *machaia,* really, to be ever so briefly in shade,
to stop thinking about all that is lost
and believe, along with the Kabalists,
that the Eternal One's thirst is slaked by our pleasure.[31]

In conclusion I believe David's familiarity with his spiritual Hasidic roots helped Denise to become increasingly at ease in returning to her own early influences. As a result her poetry represents a unique fusion of modernist American technique with the mainstream of English spiritual poetry. There is, however, a slight difference between the two poets. David, as a Jew in post-Christian America, is an outsider but hardly alone. Denise, even after converting to a religion significantly not part of her rich genealogical heritage, was to the end on her own path: an outsider, but also one in conversation with the great outsider visionaries of the past.

• DENISE AND ME •

Rae Armantrout

first came across Denise Levertov's poetry while browsing in a bookstore in 1967 or 1968 when I was twenty years old. It rang a bell for me, I think, probably because it was—and I don't know if anyone ever says this—very much in tune with that now distant time. I read the poem "Overland to the Islands" in some anthology, and pretty soon I was collecting her books. "Overland" is a very characteristic Levertov poem. It begins, "Let's go—much as that dog goes, intently haphazard," and ends (in single quotes) "'every step an arrival.'" Levertov admires the dog's adventurous spirit and its apparent purposefulness, its boundless interest and openness, its lack of "disdain." The poem celebrates the senses and represents the opposite of xenophobia. I had (so many of us had) been raised by parents scarred by the Depression, deeply cautious, and afraid of outsiders (communists, immigrants, etc.). What Levertov articulated here and in books such as *O Taste and See* seemed like an antidote to my upbringing. As a generation we were ready to travel overland to the islands, if necessary, and also to break on through to the other side. (It was especially thrilling to me that this message was being delivered by a woman.)

Although Denise was my professor for one quarter in 1969, I have never actually listed her among my main influences. As I got older, I found I had some reservations about her work. I resisted its didacticism. Even here, in this early poem, she is telling us how we should behave, she is prescribing joy. I came to resist that—both because I don't think joy can be mandated and because I think she often underestimates the perversity of human nature. I also came to feel that her poems end with too definite a closure—like a door slamming shut. (I still want to remove that last unattributed quote from the end of "Overland.") Now, writing this essay, though, I see that whether or not she was a direct influence on me, I *do* write as she suggested, very much in the way "that dog goes." In my approach to a poem I am "intently haphazard." I believe that whatever appears to my senses should be able to enter my work; none of it should be disdained.

I transferred from San Diego State to Berkeley in 1968 and soon learned that Denise was teaching a poetry workshop in the winter of 1969. Only one place was available in the class because all of her fall students except one had signed up with her again, and they took precedence. She was going to hold interviews for the single available spot. I showed up early. In fact I was the first person in what turned out to be a long line. Eventually I saw Denise, for the first time, striding down the hall in a miniskirt. She was still a relatively young woman. She opened the door and asked me to come in and show her a poem I had written. I showed her something. It wasn't great. I don't recall the title. Lying, I said I had come expressly to study with her. She went to the door and told the line of aspiring poets that she had "found her student." I don't know whether that was because she saw something in my work or because of my flattering lie. I was very surprised. I thought she would interview everyone in line and forget about me somewhere along the way. I'm still not sure whether to admire her decisiveness or to think she was careless. I am pretty sure, though, that many of the good things that have happened to me since stem from her decision.

This class coincided with the People's Park demonstrations at Cal and with the American bombing of Cambodia, which led to a student boycott of the campus. To facilitate this boycott, Denise held our class in her apartment. As I recall, her responses to poems were as immediate and intuitive, as was the way she admitted me to the course in the first place. She encouraged me to think about my line breaks. Like many, if not most, young poets, I hadn't given them much thought. She also encouraged me to read Robert Creeley, a poet whose unpredictable swerves made an immediate impact on my work. It was in Denise's class, too, that I met the poets David Melnick and Rochelle Naneroff. Rochelle was then married to Ron Silliman, one of the poets who, in a few years, became a language poet. I am still in almost daily contact with Ron.

I think Levertov is, essentially, a poet of celebration. Of course, as the Vietnam War dragged insanely on and on, the didactic streak that was always present in her work grew, understandably, more persistent, focused, some might say shrill. There are great war poets, but I don't think she was one of them. I pretty much stopped reading her somewhere along the way. Having agreed to write this essay, however, I have been interested to discover her later work. I see that she turned away from her certainties, at least partially. Before her conversion to Catholicism, she seemed to face into the darkness for a while. For instance her poem "Mass for the Day of St. Thomas Didymus" wrestles with doubt, darkness, and paradox. The style is uncharacteristically blunt and plain, as this passage from the Kyrie section shows:

> We live in terror
> of what we do not know,
> the terror of not knowing,
> of the limitless, through which fearfully

                                          Rae Armantrout

> forever, our dread
> sinks and sinks,
>
> or
>
> a violent closure of all.
>
> Yet our hope lies
> in the unknown.[1]

While I am not truly fond of this writing, which seems a bit dry and abstract to me, I do appreciate the way it engages with "the terror of not knowing." It suggests two theories of the end of the universe, neither of them comforting. In the first the universe expands forever, our world with it, falling or sinking through the "limitless." In the second the universe ends with a violent contraction. The unknown is both a source of fear and, paradoxically, desperately, the only hope.

In her last book, *The Great Unknowing,* she moves back toward celebration, toward a somewhat chastened joy. The poem "Celebration" begins, "Brilliant, this day—a young virtuoso of a day," and ends:

> A day that shines in the cold
> like a first prize brass band swinging along the street
> of a coal-dusty village, wildly at odds
> with the claims of reasonable gloom.[2]

Here she is writing in her top form. I like the surprising personification of the spring day as a young virtuoso and as a first-prize brass band. That latter image has nothing of the grandiose about it. Instead it reminds us of rural high schools and country fairs. It seems to say, we may be a dusty world in a nowhere corner of the universe, but still look at us shine!

I corresponded with Denise briefly after my graduation. I lost her letters somewhere in the great carelessness of my youth. She was a bit uneasy with the direction my writing was taking, and we soon lost touch, but not before she wrote me a recommendation for the creative writing grad program at San Francisco State. It would be easy to say that this gradual breach happened because of my connection with language poetry, but I think it actually occurred before that movement fully coalesced. Still, I imagine (I actually don't recall what she said!) that she found my work a bit too disjunctive. I must have been writing some of the earliest poems in my book *Extremities* then. Now I wish I could have known her in her later years—or maybe, impossibly, that I could know her now. We might have things to talk about—what it's like to be a woman among men, for instance, or what it's like to move away from centers of power and influence.

Throughout her life Denise showed that she was not afraid to change her mind, her tack, her poetic course. She antagonized powerful friends when her work became too polemical for their tastes. I can admire her courage even if I tend to agree with her friends. She must have surprised some of her intimates when she embraced Catholicism too. She was a decisive, brave woman. I saw something of that on the day we first met.

Rae Armantrout

• "NOTHING / LIKE A REAL BRIDGE" •
Rae Armantrout and Denise Levertov

Romana Huk

In the piece that this one serves as companion to, Rae Armantrout recalls being allowed into Denise Levertov's poetry workshop at Berkeley—even before Levertov interviewed the rest of the long line of supplicants awaiting their turn in the hall—on the basis of a poem she showed her that "wasn't great" and whose title she can't recall.[1] I want to speculate about what Levertov might have seen in that poem, even if I don't know precisely what I'm talking about. This isn't easy to write, you'll understand, for this reason as well as others.

Because though Levertov is generously recalled by Armantrout as a teacher and early inspiration in most of her interviews since winning the Pulitzer Prize, she also makes clear in them (as well as in her piece for this volume) that Levertov is not among "main influences" and that she feels rather substantial "reservations about her work."[2] I understand—I feel them too, and for many of the same reasons: her "didacticism," as Armantrout puts it; her vatic knowingness at times; the assumption that she, as "the Poet" (always seemingly capitalized in her usage), was in a position to "prescrib[e] joy." But I've been thinking again about Levertov lately—her philosophical struggles after arriving here from the United Kingdom; her arduous negotiations of "belief" and the road back from Europe's wartime *via negativa;* her formative response to particularly George Oppen's gendered attacks on her in the 1960s (targeting not only her political poetry, like everyone else, but more bewilderingly her "feminine profusion," as I'll explain)—and I wonder whether her prescriptions weren't actually written for her "self," however unusual her evolving conception of that was. Of course that's no excuse for what Rachel Blau DuPlessis reads as her tendency to "moralize."[3] But I find myself interested in what she was battling with and for as well as unsure, increasingly, of such readings of a number of her poems. What so often goes missing in assessments of her writing is the degree to which complicating failure and loss accompany arrivals at joy or epiphany and how such contradictions forced even her developing "metaphysics" in directions that I think Armantrout could respect and possibly extend. But not wanting to claim such large things straightforwardly, I'll think instead about why Levertov may have instantly recognized Armantrout as a fellow traveler in the late 1960s and do so by focusing on one epistemological problem that binds them: time. I don't mean to suggest that they feel the same way about it. But I do see Armantrout's project as furthering what Levertov's began—or, at the risk of sounding overly grand about it, what Martin Heidegger began all those years ago in *Being and Time.* At the very least, both Levertov and Armantrout are poets caught up in similar sorts of ontological/phenomenological investigations and adventures wherein the stakes are rather high (and unlike Heidegger's investigations, often highly topical, political, and overt rather than covert in addressing theological matters). So the first thing I'll say Levertov saw in that student poem was a complex sort of ambition. And she liked it.

I

I'll return to the backdrop I mention above in a moment. But I want to begin by putting the early Armantrout and mature Levertov on the same page, so to speak, by looking at two of their works from the 1970s—beginning with "View," from Armantrout's first book, *Extremities* (1978). As an early poem, it may offer a hint of what Levertov saw in that first sample. More important, it arose in one millennial interview with Tom Beckett as "one of [her] favorite of [her] little poems" and then was featured in Armantrout's "Poetic Statement" and selected by her to include in a twenty-first-century anthology of American poetry, *American Women Poets in the Twenty-First Century: Where Lyric Meets Language.* So it clearly represents something both initiating and enduring in Armantrout's oeuvre.

She leads up to it with recollections of feeling moved, early on, by the poignancy of the imagist project in the hands of poets such as William Carlos Williams, Levertov's greatest American mentor. It was, as she writes, "both an important project and a doomed one." Their desire—not unlike Heidegger's post-Idealist, post-Husserlian one begun just a decade or so before them—was to "make the object speak, to put things in dialogue with mind and somehow make them hold up their end of the conversation."[4] For young Heidegger, the "there" in *Da-sein* must inform post-Platonic "being" of what it is—or "that it is."[5] Armantrout believes the project was, from the start, wittingly impossible: "thing and idea don't really merge, as the poets themselves knew. The world enters the poem only through a kind of ventriloquy."[6] Yet what both that desire and that knowledge have done and still do to traditional conceptions of the poet, poem, and knowing itself have always been at the heart of her critical inquiry. She simply turns it back on itself, as indeed Heidegger did with his philosophical inheritance, analyzing its first figurations and premises and turning clichéd epistemological impulses under, in her case, a new sort of polyfocal phenomenological lens. *Extremities* is well named because, as she puts it, she was "always drawn to poems that seemed as if they were either going to vanish or explode—in other words, to extremes," or Heidegger's

                                                                  Romana Huk

"limits," where being and nothingness reveal something of one another by virtue (or vertigo) of time.[7] But her investigations complicate Heidegger's initially solitary one. Yet I get ahead of myself—here's her "minimalist and neo-Imagist"[8] poem from *Extremities*, "View":

> Not the city lights. We want
> —the moon—
> The Moon
> none of our own doing![9]

The poem "has two dissonant meanings," Armantrout writes:

> On the one hand, "we" (an already suspect first-person plural) want to see the moon as separate from our own activity (a bit of the world caught unawares.) On the other hand, our yearning is framed by deflating clichés. To want the moon is to want the impossible. Our thrust toward the non-human moon can't escape the gravity of language. The purportedly single voice of the nature lover and the words of a somewhat cynical crowd seem to collide. So this is a poetics of collisions and overlaps, of contested spaces. To use dream imagery in a poem, for instance, is to expose something private, but what if a recent film inspired the dream? As I have become increasingly conscious of such contested spaces and the voices that articulate them, my poems have become somewhat longer and more complicated.[10]

Her "Cheshire Poetics," as her poetic statement's title has it, is therefore "one that points two ways then vanishes in the blur of what is seen and what is seeing, what can be known and what it is to know." The moon, above, wanted as "other" to us, "can be known" only as sandwiched between our mute marks—the dashes—and finally as capitalized cliché from 1,001 informing legends and poems (as well as modern send-ups of the same by the likes of James Joyce). The attempt to know or focus one's sights on what exceeds "us"—by repeating it, stopping the flow of associated words in time, building a bridge over that flow to something outside—proves impossible. So too does establishing "present" contact, because first sight slips into all past constructions of "moon," what the poem suggests we're responsible for, "our own doing": our psycholinguistic "worlding," as Heidegger would have it, or as Ludwig Wittgenstein simultaneously theorized it, our vision's relegation to the language that has itself become the limit of our world. Above, it's the manmade "city lights" that impede our seeing the moon we want to see (and the poem's self-reflexivity deepens if we hear in that negated image the City Lights bookshop, repository that it is of even the most "extreme" books of poems). Passionate emphasis just speeds the whole process; the latter capital-ized moon rhymes even more with its literary romanticization, making it dou-bly clearly "our own *doing*" (which takes on a comic scatological component, too). The last two lines become a contradiction, then, or a flimsy denial, most noisily asserted.

"I'm interested in opacity; in the ways the world is opaque. I'm also inter-ested in deception; in how we deceive each other and how we deceive our-selves. I've tried intuitively, almost from the start, to somehow re-enact that in my poems"[11] In other words Armantrout's "doubleness" in such poems can be seen as an update on the imagist project insofar as like them, Bob Perelman suggests, she writes paratactic lyric "under the sign of exactitude"—only what she targets are mistargetings of the real rather than poetic merger or capture.[12] As she herself puts it, "there is more than one model of clarity," and for her a clear exposition of our lack of control over phenomena and each other and "the truth" is anti-imperialist, "inherently political."[13] Whereas the imagist poem offers, by Ezra Pound's definition, liberation as the result of binding disparate intellectual and emotional objects in an instant of time, her doubleness liber-ates instead what will not be brought into relation or control so easily through any "purportedly single" perception achieved in modernist epiphany. Modernist desires to spatialize time, see the world steadily and see it whole[14] again through new art-religious, ecstatic (as in displaced from self) experiences, inform both Heidegger's phenomenological project and poetry through the late modern-ism of Oppen; therefore the latter's "theology," like Heidegger's proposed one, begins with a return to what sounds like an originary experience of being at the vertiginous limits of the self, its "'vertical consciousness of' oneself and god."[15] But consciousness is, for Armantrout, "ambiguous, duplicitous, doubled back on itself," never singular.[16] Such "lack" of singularity is also gendered, as female modernists from Virginia Woolf onward noted, including Armantrout. It pro-duces "slither"—something she recalls Pound praised H.D.'s imagist poems for avoiding, maintaining as he did that she wrote "straight as the Greek."[17] As Perel-man notes, Pound also evokes, with "Greek," "the homoerotic pagan rallying cry" behind its "silence of pristine white marble columns": "when Pound stares toward the poetic body of H.D.'s early work he sees no curves, no threatening liquidity."[18] When she recognized for herself that Pound's rhetoric was "gyno-phobic," Armantrout realized that "I wanted my Imagism and my slither, too. My precision and my doubleness."[19]

Eight years before *Extremities* appeared, in 1970—just after the winter 1969 poetry workshop Armantrout took with her—New Directions published Lever-tov's collection *Relearning the Alphabet,* in which a long section called "Wanting the Moon" appears. In it, two poems, "Wanting the Moon (I)" and "Wanting the Moon (II)," are rethought in devastating ways by the book's penultimate, titular

                                                                    Romana Huk

poem. Armantrout hasn't mentioned any connection between the moon poems in her and Levertov's respective oeuvres, but it seems clear to me that "View" takes Levertov's work in new directions, particularly given the way that the latter's poems begin. Here's a selection from "Wanting the Moon (I)":

> Not the moon. A flower
> on the other side of the water.
>
> The water sweeps past in the flood,
> dragging a whole tree by the hair,
>
> a barn, a bridge. The flower
> sings on the far bank.
>
> Not a flower, a bird calling,
> hidden among the darkest trees, music
> . . . .
> The moon. No, a young man walking
> under the trees. There are lanterns
>
> among the leaves.
> Tender, wise, merry,
>
> his face is awake with its own light,
> I see it across the water as if close up.
>
> A jester. The music rings from his bells,
> gravely, a tune of sorrow,
>
> I dance to it on my riverbank.[20]

The poem's first of several negations shifts the object of what its title signals—"want[ing]the impossible," as Armantrout put it—from the transcendent to the proximate, as Levertov was wont to do by the late 1950s: "not the moon" but rather an ordinary riverbank flower. While many, like Oppen and Robert Creeley, welcomed such moves in her work, reading them as post-imagist/objectivist fidelity to the actual, the "authentic" (as existential phenomenology's jargon had by then prescribed it: the only worthy state and object of attention), they didn't mark her speakers' unwitting failures to connect even with the ordinary in such poems, assuming it to be Levertov speaking "honestly" (as readers have always tended to do, particularly with women's poems).[21] And while fidelity to moment-by-moment perception does indeed guide the movement of this poem, as per Black Mountain dictates, what happens here and in this sequence and finally the book as a whole (which hasn't been taken into account) does more to confirm what Armantrout claims in this volume: that "the world enters the poem only through a kind of ventriloquy" and that the speaker's consciousness will be doubled back on itself. The impossibility of having the wanted in Levertov's erotics of perception is ensured not only by the raging river—a figure for time—that flows between them and her speaker, but also by the river-like, Heraclitean slippage of what "calls" to her: from flower to bird to young man to possibly a lantern mistaken for his "awakened" face (which is not close-up, though she asserts it is "as if" so). And the speaker's insistent personification of natural things that are "none of our doing" transfers the imagined alternative temporality/tempo of the flower, "singing" heedless beside the flood, into the "music" of the bird, which "silences" the destructive flow, and finally into the "bells" of the man out of whom she's fashioned a jester, a "cap and bells" figure straight out of William Butler Yeats's poem "The Cap and Bells," where the jester's cap is a figure for absence that makes the proverbial heart grow fonder, enlivened by desire. Absence plays a fundamental role in conceptualizing presence and therefore "the present" in Levertov's work, as I'll explain later on. Here, her speaker's "danc[ing]" at the end to such imagined music seems a momentary triumph of "transcending" time's flow and the temporal flow of her medium, creating a bridge with her words over it to what she longs for, but it's at best a parallel or invented ecstasy she enjoys. Indeed, we suspect she knows it, having projected her lack of power—erotically and in every other sense—on that tree being dragged by the hair upstream, in time.

This book suggests that all such ecstasies are "doomed," like that "conversation" with the world Armantrout understands the imagists longed for. Here it's undone, crucially, by the "I, J" section of the title poem of *Relearning the Alphabet,* which, at the book's end, returns to this midbook section of poems, critiquing their achievements by "relearning" the language (symbolic as well as alphabetic) through which they were made. In other words the "I" in this section is an instance of Levertov's paradoxically past-inflected, "historied," yet unstable subject—which like a midrashic text continually moves in the flow, rereadable. Here, for example, it finds that, as section "V" has it, "Vision sets out / journeying somewhere, / walking the dreamwaters: / arrives / *not on the far shore* but upriver" (my emphasis). "I" stands for, as the opening line of the section has it, going "*into* the world of continuance, to find / I-who-I-am again, who wanted / to enter a life not mine, / to leap a wide, deep, swift river" (my emphasis). Negating that earlier desire, that possibility of transcendence via connection, the speaker is stuck relating only her encounter with it, as if recollecting a dream for analysis: "At the edge, I stand yet. No, I am moving away, / walking away from the unbridged rush of waters" toward an inward space metaphorically described as her "own clearing." But given that

                                                                                 Romana Huk

"'dreamy, gloomy, / friendly trees' grow one by one there," it sounds like anything but a clearing, and given the internal quotation, nothing like "her own." Moreover the speaker's "not looking where [she] is going," is looking "back, to see / whom [she] called 'jester'"—recognizing that it had been "Picasso's bronze *Head of a Jester*" that "was seen," in "epiphany."[22] In other words her earlier epiphanic moment was born of ecstatic "vision," but through a misreading of her own dreaming-seeing that had recollected another's artwork as a telling cipher, unreadable at the time but increasingly (though never totally)readable in time. The idea of capturing anything in time, purely, when all seeing is a product of it is queried here; and further the idea of capturing the mercurial, even the "inauthentic"—a jester—as sculpture, a spatialized "portrait" of the real, encapsulates a problematic foregrounded in many of her poems. Suddenly reread here too is the second "Wanting the Moon" poem, which begins, "Not the moon. To be a bronze head / inhabited by a god." Desires for stability (and "nobility," as DuPlessis put it)[23] are relinquished as the speaker watches herself "go stumbling / (head turned) / back to [her] origins: // (if that's where [she's] going) / to joy, my Jerusalem," the play with "I, J" letters making "jester" resonate in that last line, too—as "quester" will, by rhyme, in "Q."[24] Immediately afterward the speaker sees herself "weeping, gesturing, / I'm a small figure in mind's eye, / diminishing in the sweep" of those very gestures/jesters, eroding as a speaker even as she speaks. (As do Armantrout's "we" even as they emphasize "their" desire: the moon.)

Bringing desires for transcendence of "our doing," then, back down to earth, back into "the gravity of language," as Armantrout put it, and often by "re-enacting," like Armantrout, "how we deceive each other and how we deceive ourselves," Levertov in her work from this period showcases the difficulty of perceiving instantly or purely that Armantrout later took up as well, however much both wish to see accurately. For Levertov the mistake we make is in not seeing that "all awareness // is an awareness of time"—"the multitudinous interactions in time, space, memory, dream and instinct that at every word tremble into synthesis."[25] Stepping outside it to become aware of things as they are in themselves, onto what Oppen called after Heidegger "the arduous path of appearance," would have seemed like "the impossible" to her. Halting time and what he named her "feminine profusion"—by which he meant not only her political deviations from pure perception and her continual recollection of inherited texts ("German fairytale," as he oddly summarized it)[26] but also her entire way of being in the world, her *mit-sein,* being-toward-others—was what she needed to do in order to participate in his project of knowing via "the isolation of the actual," which begins by isolating the self from external (social) influence and care.[27] He characterized her epistemological tendencies as not only feminine but outmoded and European, a form of consciousness that could not bring itself into the present because it could not face (with the German Heidegger) such pioneering singularity. Yet as Richard

Jackson suggests, Levertov's development of a poetics of "doubleness" had interesting overlaps with ideas Jacques Derrida was investigating at just about the same moment: "In 'The Long Way Round,' the instant and the time preceding it become a unified double structure; self-consciousness occurs 'slowly—for though / it's in a flash we / know we know / yet before the flash there's a long / slow, dull, movement of fire / along the well-hidden / line of the fuse'. . . It is a structure . . . of unachieved totalities—what Derrida calls the play of possibilities initiated by such double-inscriptions of time."[28] And it is not just "polysemy," as Derrida reminds us, but something more radical, more revolutionary: "dissemination."

Unlike polysemy, which lays out entwined meanings in a text in order to control them, dissemination is about the dispersal of meaning given that every word, every concept, every text is connected through all sorts of connotations and appropriations to other words, concepts, and texts that come before it—so that no meaning can be isolated or owned, no object, no poem, no human subject (which is such by virtue of its movement in language). Gendered at the core in his theorization of it, it exposes "the impossible (monocentric, paternal, familial) reappropriation of the concept of the sperm" after the scattering of semen/semiosis.[29] In other words all ideas are not in things or immediate encounter with them but incubated without our knowing long before we know them, well-hidden along an extensive fuse that predates our own being at all. The image, then, conveys her poetry's version of Armantrout's "explosion": it occurs in phenomenological perception of how knowing happens, shattering as it does notions of singularity in any intellectual or poetic breakthrough. Her reading of Heidegger focused not on *Being and Time,* Oppen's favorite work, but on his later interpretations of Friedrich Hölderlin, which begin to rethink being in language differently. She understood these to suggest "that to be human is to *be a conversation*—a strange and striking way of saying that communion is the very basis of human living, of *living humanly.*"[30] She came to critique not only Oppen but also Creeley for their "unsure egoism," for continuing to quest for the impossible: to perceive "discretely," as Oppen put it in one "series" of poems.[31] For her as for Derrida, thoughts, like texts, are inescapably inexhaustible—and even one's own writing is not one's own but rereadable, reinterpretable, something "The Poet in the World" suggests by the way it moves on by, paradoxically, returning to previous poems, though even Jackson's fine reading misses that. We're more likely to recognize it now, given recent interest in Derrida's deconstructive formulations as distinctly related to Jewish hermeneutics and messianic thought. But that's another essay.

Levertov would seem to have found a way, then, through such temporal doubleness to reconcile her European (Anglo-Welsh, Russian) and Jewish understandings of thought as deeply connected to all that comes before with some of the most unsettling of contemporary thoughts about language, time, and being. In other words she began to allow for continual destabilization (or dissemination)

Romana Huk

of her convictions, foregoing earlier notions that "great gaps between perception and perception . . . must be leapt across" and "relinquish[ing] / in grief / the seeing that burns through . . . as acts of magic [she] would perform." These "are no longer / articles of faith. // Or no: it / slowly becomes known to me: articles of faith are indeed / rules of the will—graceless, faithless."[32] Envisioning self as traveler, pilgrim in a continuingly Abrahamic dispersion from "homeland," with no going back, she was able to fold her developing interests in incarnational Christianity back into her Jewish roots to imagine being's embedding in language, the word made flesh, and language's continuance as time itself. This allowed her to, among other things, dislodge from her evolving sensibility the nearly ineradicable influence of midcentury metaphysicians such as T. S. Eliot. One can read this poem as a corrective to the negativity of Eliot's *Four Quartets,* that infamous example of a wartime mystical poem–cum–*via negativa* or self-canceling treatise on being, time, and the present with which Levertov was often in dialogue. She recasts his river imagery from "The Dry Salvages," where the "strong brown god" of the Mississippi (which rhymes with "the brown folds" of her river's "cloak") stands for "Time the destroyer," which is also "time the preserver," one of Eliot's many crossed-out images. All has already been enacted in his extraordinary vision of foregone conclusions; all there is to be longed for are time-stopping visions of "mid-winter spring" or the impossible future when "the fire and the rose are one" and we escape from the temporal altogether. Therefore the poem exhorts its readers cheerlessly: "Fare forward, travelers! not escaping from the past / Into different lives, or into any future // . . . time is no healer: the patient is no longer here."[33] But in Levertov's poem, where the past is also always already with us, it's "not farewell, but faring // forth into the grace of transformed / continuance"—the last line break foiling the appearance of some transformed "presence" with a new form of "grace" in what we normally fear: difference and deferral (the basic conditions for language). At the sequence's end, the "fire" in her imagery doesn't indicate any Yeatsian or Eliotic mysterious afterward: "the blaze addresses / a different darkness: / absence has not become / the transformed presence the will / looked for, / but other: the present." As she puts it in an earlier poem in the volume, an absence—another condition of language, which substitutes for presence—is itself "an absolute / presence / calling forth / the person"; she begins, in other words, to go into the generative gap rather than imagine the "leap across."[34] "All utterance" has led her speaker here, though it takes arrival at "a distant region" and the "stranger" of her epigraph (from Heinrich Zimmer) to call up being, too, by its sudden absence, its struggle into articulacy before otherness. Her conception of "being as conversation" can be seen to connect with the more famous one of Emmanuel Levinas, for whom its emergence depends on being called forth by another, whose wholly/holy irreducible difference shatters any self-coherent epistemology or worldview and demands response.

Perhaps the "beloved stranger" at the start of this poem was met upon her arrival in the United States, that "distant" land. Donna Hollenberg points out that the title of "Overland to the Islands"—the poem by Levertov that Armantrout most admires, as she makes clear in "Denise and Me"—signals an impossibility; "in reality, one must cross water to arrive at an island."[35] Hollenberg's reading of it as Levertov's repression of the ocean that separates her from home (the British Isles) is quite interesting, though I want to read it here more simply as signaling just what it signals: an impossibility, as impossible as it was for her speaker "to leap a wide, deep, swift river." There is no arrival if "every step" is one, as Levertov's final quote from Rilke has it—which I think opens up the poem rather than shuts it down, as Armantrout suggests. With it she relocates, pointedly, what she admired most in the American sensibility: its desire for arrival anew, in a new world, as Oppen described it in "The Mind's Own Place"; she seems to see it as an "impossible but important" dream (like the imagist project that Armantrout described) moving, nevertheless, in time. And time ensures that her metaphorical dog-as-perceiver in this poem "keeps moving"; "Let's go," the poem begins, rewriting Eliot's paralyzed Prufrock—because the arrival, for her, is within continuance itself. There is no "real" bridge over it to the (isolated) islands we long for; as her poem puts it, "a barn, a bridge" all "go" in that flood.

II

As Armantrout might say, such metaphors must, of course, go too—those figurative bridges, with their displacing heuristics—at least as constructive of "the present," "what is," or "articles of faith."[36] As Armantrout puts it in "My Problem": "When the dog is used / to represent the inner / man, I need to ask / 'What kind of dog is it?' ("man" here jokily slipping into an exclamation rather than a noun: "man!"). "It is my responsibility / to squeeze / the present from the past / by demanding particulars"—by returning what we say to experience and next analyzing *experience* as a term even while analyzing how we moved from touchable vehicle to invented tenor.[37] But she admits metaphors are unavoidable in the process of knowing in language, wherein "a familiar predicate," as Derrida writes, must be transported toward "a less familiar, more remote, *unheimlich* (uncanny) subject," which is then named "by the indirect detour of what is nearest."[38] The willed bridge results in illumination of aspects of each member connected but it clearly isn't real—though language forgets its provisionality. And although "always sensory and material" at the outset—even "not exactly metaphor" in its original figuration, Derrida claims—it becomes so "when philosophical discourse puts it into circulation." It becomes, in other words, "the sensory figure which is sheltered and used (up), to the point of appearing imperceptible, in every metaphysical concept."[39] Always interested in displaced operations of meaning and perception and

    Romana Huk

the dark operations of the disavowed, Armantrout in "Ongoing" writes that "when I'm metaphorical / I'm happy"—because not yet doubled back upon the figure in critical perusal of its activities, one of her poetry's most frequent moves.[40] And perhaps happy because, as one interview exchange with Lyn Hejinian suggests, this traditional project for poetry connects it to the "joys" of religion, in that both circumvent the realities of being in time by "manufacturing" (an important word for Armantrout) "pleasurable confusion" and "timelessness":

> *LH* • . . . The concept of "lyric time"—arrested moments in which accumulated time resides . . . doesn't seem relevant to your work. . . . I could imagine an argument that would put time at the heart of religion, naming "time" as that which reconnects. This argument would base itself on the etymological source for the word "religion," which is from the Latin verb, *relegere*—"to gather up again," "to collect again," but also "to travel through again," "to sail along again," which suggests that religion as interrelatedness is a (temporal?) process.

> *RA* • Is that what religion means? Then it's a lot like metaphor—"to carry across." I think that in the moment when a connection is made, when a and b are linked, there can be a paradoxically brief sensation of timelessness. (A pleasurable confusion, perhaps.) And that's one thing the work of art can do, perhaps especially the "lyric poem." I suppose I like the sensation, but I also, perversely, like to foreground its possibilities and impossibilities—the conjunction of brevity and timelessness, for instance. Maybe this recapitulates, in more abstract form, my fascination with and resistance to religion.[41]

Such "perversion" is typical in Armantrout's work and constitutes (in my view) the power of her verse—or "per-verse," as I think of it: writing that, unlike the lyric it looks and often sounds like, unpicks "likenesses," "rhymes," "resemblances," and the satisfying sense of stayed time that results from the bridging of disparate *a*'s and *b*'s (therefore her most recognizable, part-by-part form, "that is not one"). "How much present tense / can any resemblance make?" she asks in "Manufacturing," playing on the copula most often used as the connective in metaphor. Just as her recollection of metaphor's etymology (*metaphérein*) incarnates it again, as a physical "crossing over," here she jokily plays with its efficacy in sums and measures, the bottom line in all industry. Thinking through the shift from the one-off making of things into the manufacturing of her title, and the debasement of difference and relation into the sameness that characterizes not only consumer capitalism but also the language it lives in—where "So. Cal. / must connect with / so-called // to manufacture the present" (even though the "so-called" is not the new but pejoratively past tense, a repetition)—she ends the poem with a bathetic image of "the new thinking" itself: "the new in-joke / is a pun / pretending to be a bridge."[42] She'll produce one herself, as the title of her Pulitzer Prize–winning book, *Versed*—a word that, aside from its several better-known meanings of well-schooled or "knowing" (i.e., versed in a subject) offers a pun on poetry's character and on one of the word's literal meanings: the rise of the arch of a bridge. It's always been not only poetry's but philosophy's job to hoist metaphorical bridges toward knowing—though Armantrout does so deconstructively, too, as in the fifth poem in the volume, "Vehicles" (a term, of course, in metaphor's construction), which playfully begins: "Pairing matched fragments, / then pausing— / archly?—."[43] The question being: Is the pause stopped time, a finished bridge between fragments? or a sudden meta-metaphorical reflection on the construction, the progress of her own matchmaking? In this as in her earlier volumes, Armantrout continually pauses, questions, turns, doubles on her constructed bridges; indeed *versed* also has its root in the Latin *vertĕre:* to turn.

And turning happens in time, even though it doubles back on time, as in Levertov's work. I've tried to suggest that it may be their abandonment of poetic "vision" in the old style, "seeing in an instant of time," that connects Levertov and Armantrout in their various doublenesses. As well as their awareness of "the gravity of language," their contemplations of the accumulated textuality of nonsingular self-hood and the collaborative nature of memory, their sense of the poignancy of selves writing into time (or as Armantrout's poem "Writing" has it, "I, myself, was always a forwarding address")—and even their interest in the telling, internal otherness of dreams.[44] What goes without saying are the enormous differences between them, of course, which one would expect, given the powerful rise of Language poetics at the time of, and in part through, Armantrout's first writings. Most obvious is the discrepancy between their dispositions toward language itself—and, in related terms, toward linguistic inheritance. Levertov's particular "care for language" registers somewhere between her earlier neo-Romantic regard for it as given to poets in "sacred trust," her Jewish half's reverence for it as both a highly material and simultaneously spiritual gift, "a *form of life* and a common resource to be cherished and served"—something which explains, for me, her peculiarly material method of processing abstractions)—and Heidegger's poetic phenomenology from the 1950s onward, which fears the eroding stewardship of "natural" or "traditional" language (*überlieferte Sprache*) as opposed to "technological" language, especially on the part of poets.[45] Armantrout might well be sympathetic to his fears about technological language—given her "anxiety about 'use,'" as Stephen Burt reads it in her work. But for her, *no* bit of language escapes the influence of the same; there can be no pre-served divisions between what Heidegger romanticized as our "essential" language,

                                                                 Romana Huk

"original" writing, and the technological—or "effective"—language in the capitalist world that Armantrout constantly probes in her work.

And even more importantly, whereas Levertov assumed a positive flow of time in language as her "authentic" experience in the world, even though notions of time's "moving forward" are at core metaphorical, Armantrout turns on such assumptions about the space-time continuum as extracted from "experience." "Something (is it history?) has contracted so much that familiar images (Elvis) are now symbols of representation," she mused in interview. "Symbol as meta-symbol, like money or postage."[46] Are time and language—"the present," our "currency"— impacted by repetition and circulation? Or as she asks in her investigation "Ongoing," are we "corporate-funded / homunculi // in an infinite regress"?[47] Even "are we really moving?" at all, as "Autobiography: Urn Burial" wonders:

> I could say
> "authenticity"
>
> will have been about trying
> to overtake the past,
>
> inhabit it
> long enough to look around
>
> say "Oh,"
>
> but the past is tricky,
>
> holds off.
>
> So are we really moving?
>
> or is this something
> like the way
>
> form appears
> to chase function?[48]

Her understanding of existential phenomenology's authenticity is signaled immediately by putting it in scare quotes: it's manufactured, just as autobiography is (like her own, *True,* whose title she chose to call up its opposite); it attempts the impossible, "overtak[ing] the past," building bridges backward as well as across time to that terrain that sounds (once again) like "the moon," where we must linger just long enough in our space suits "to look around" and achieve a sudden (present) illumination: her wonderfully deflated "Oh." Unlike Levertov's emergence into "the present" at last, through doublings back upon herself, Armantrout characteristically just doubles back again, and, like Derrida, asks another question.[49] Here the questioned are, in part, spatial metaphors for time's movement "on"; if the past "holds off," how do we know we're "past it" (an interestingly failed expression) or that it isn't "the future"? Therefore her final questions, too (enacted via a metaphor): if forms chase function rather than produce new ones, insofar as the desired function informs the form, what does autobiography as a form do? "You want something; that's the pretext. . . . You can see it, since you asked," she writes at the start of "Birthmark: The Pretext"; her playful second-person address suggests that both the speaker and we in general must submit even asking itself to a Pascalian-cum-Derridean question: would we know what we're seeking if we didn't already have (perhaps at some linguistic, shared level) what we want?[50] Does autobiography after all access the past (in a different sense) if writing a form of ourselves through asking about it allows us to see our "pre-text"? Levertov's more innocent notion of organic form as a "doing" that reveals or discovers the present—"Relearn the alphabet, / . . . the world understood anew only in doing"— is less aware of the force of that want, which for Armantrout always also means lack.[51] Not only in the female sexual sense, as read by Sigmund Freud, both also as what in Jacques Lacan drives all selving in that, as she understands it, "the subject experiences self as lacking and projects possession on some other"; "only later he / she suspects the other may be lacking too." One might say that human relations, like time, are shaped by the forces of space or nothing; Armantrout is "fascinated by the way scientists, too, conceive of space as active"—and lacking, which we also can't see, curves interactive experience in time.[52]

Levertov's formation of a poetic project, born in her time of emergency, as she saw it, would subordinate her own questioning of human lack and its projections to faith in the development of "living humanly" (as she put it through her reading of Heidegger) by recognizing self as a "conversation," already composed of the other who calls it into being—her metaphysical translation of psychoanalytic suggestions that we need the other in order to come into language to begin with, even to exist at all.[53] Armantrout may agree to some extent, but objects to her avoidance of the full picture; as she writes in "Denise and Me," "[Levertov] often underestimates the perversity of human nature" and its manifestation in the language we speak, our forms, which emerge from pretexts of desire gone subterranean in our processes of knowing and controlling. As the middle stanza of her titular poem in *Versed* has it: "Metaphor forms / a crust / beneath which / the crevasse / of each experience"—suggesting that our Heideggerian world with its outer crust made of such forgotten operations avoids the holes or fissures between experience and figuration, which therefore may rule invisibly, undetected, like the dark matter of the

                                                     Romana Huk

title to the second part of *Versed*.[54] Therefore her response to both Levertov and our own time of exigency might involve quoting her most important American mentor, Emily Dickinson:

> Faith is a fine invention
> When Gentlemen can see—
> But Microscopes are prudent
> In an emergency.
> (#185)[55]

But this is not to say that Armantrout has no interest in what Levertov would call "mystery" and I, lacking an adequate modern-day language for the matter, might call metaphysics. In fact I think it's in contemplation of such that something sympathetic most closely joins these two writers: their willingness to take their intellectually rigorous investigations to "extremities," as Armantrout puts it, where safe bridges explode, identities (selves, metaphors) implode, and the apprehension of what Heidegger in "What Is Metaphysics?" called nothingness, with reverence (as it makes being appear), leaves work gaping, potentially bereft, like the end of a Samuel Beckett play, but perhaps instead facing absence as a presence. For Levertov, as we've seen, that arrival into absence is renamed experience of the absolute, the present that, like "the stranger," generates her self and writing; therefore the end of *Relearning the Alphabet*—which returns to "the ah! of knowing in unthinking" that began the sequence—revisits but rewrites Gerard Manley Hopkins's conclusion to his poem in the praise tradition, "God's Grandeur": "And though the last lights off the black West went / Oh, morning, at the brown brink eastward, springs— / Because the Holy Ghost over the bent / World broods with warm breast and with ah! bright wings."[56] Levertov's update of Hopkins foregoes his traditional imagery for timeless generative energies and relocates them as paradoxically incarnate in experienced absence, in time: that is, in operations of "sacred language." Armantrout's response to the same poem in "Day" should render moot any attempt to link Levertov's "ah!" with the later poet's response to absence or silence as phenomena; her day "flashes / but doesn't gather // It rhymes and does not / confirm."[57] Missing the leap into faith and faithful seeing that animates Hopkins, Armantrout can see nothing but the same occurring again—not progress, not affirmation—in these natural events; hers is not Levertov's tendency toward praise as Susan Stewart has described it: "affirmative—it reveals, augments, and at the same time creates surpluses in excess of what it discloses."[58] But it is poetry that, as Henry David Thoreau put it, "trembles on the brink of science,"[59] and does all those same things Stewart lists by noting how what it can note in the world depends on what it can't, "is the inverse / shape of what's / missing," as she puts it in "Dark Matter" (which refers to those invisible forces that constitute most of the universe and are responsible for its unexpected, continuing expansion). Thinking about how "Missing Persons"—"God and her mother" in the poem by this name—continue to shape her; wondering always at the limits of knowledge and about what we think we know by virtue of naming or numbering (as if anything in the world is yet provably singular or finally knowable)—in "Integer" she asks, "One what? / One grasp? / No hands. / No collection / of stars. Something dark / pervades it." She dispenses with the "no hands" ease of knowing by letting our machines roll, like bikes, accumulating knowledge as we have always done: by assuming everything from one thing, seeing the universe in grains of sand. "But the part is sick of representing the whole," as she puts it in one poem. Each integer/ instance is different—as even her line from "Day" suggests about each new day, too, with its line end: "It rhymes and does not." "Time flows / because no set / of proofs // can be complete. / Bring me the friendship / between solving / and dissolving," as she writes in "Relations."[60] Like Levertov, Armantrout works in whatever sort of unstoppable flux it is we call time, and at a dangerous epistemological edge—still at extremities—trying to understand how it might be that it's precisely what we don't see that controls what we do see and even sense. "There's a need," as she puts it, tentatively, "to indicate the space of the ineffable, perhaps, in the world. There's a need to point to it. Like there's a need to point to things."[61]

We can't build bridges to such spaces and forces with language, no more than the imagists and objectivists could be in conversation with the things that drew them. Nor does Armantrout (any more than Levertov) "want to talk about absolute silence in an ontological way" (as she says in one roundtable discussion, continuing on from Michael Palmer's observation that silence too is a metaphor, since as John Cage pointed out, "strictly speaking, it ain't there").[62] Instead she's interested in the impact of (relative) silence on both experience and perception: how nothing can make something happen—as in "Language of Love," where "expectant solemnity / . . . seems to invite a kiss."[63] And the poem that follows it in *Veil*, "Getting Warm"—as in the sense of "getting close to the jackpot," as well as getting sexually excited—suggests that perhaps there are asymptotic points of contact between even our "manufacturing," our physical feeling, and the invisible, "ineffable" forces such as silence that could well power both, be they what they may (she won't assume them to be good—she won't, like most post-Heideggerian theologians, ontologize them). But in this poem nothing is involved in fabrication to make something real appear, like magic: that one brief experience of ecstasy or joy that we may arguably know—orgasm:

> Tingle:
> a shaft must be imagined to
> connect the motes
> though there is no light.

Romana Huk

The notes.
If she's quiet
she's concentrating on the spaces
between cries, turning
times into spaces.

Is it memory or physics
that makes the bridge appear?
It looks nothing
like a real bridge.
She has to finish it
so it can explode.

She is in the dark,
sewing, stringing holes together
with invisible thread.
That's a feminine accomplishment:
a feat of memory, a managed
repletion or resplendence.[64]

The speaker's own "shaft" (or penis) "must be imagined," given female lack; hers sounds like an industrial mechanism—a mining shaft, perhaps. And so she becomes industrious, turning her own vaginal tunnel into something that holds nothing—which in Shakespeare's time (and plays) was a pun: "nothing" (for "no-thing"). She's composing, like a poet or musician, but by connecting "the notes" that rhyme with the silent "motes" of imagined light in that shaft. In other words this is partly the work of metaphor, which we know is capable too of "turning / times into spaces"—except here her linking fabrication is a matter of "sewing" not matched things together but "holes"—real silences "between cries" to get where she's going (rather than Levertov's string of "all utterance"), stitching together by memory their accumulatively real, "explosive" physical effect. Here "nothing" is "like a real bridge" and nothing like one—which raises a problem, a contradiction, from which all genuine new thought might be said to arise. The question asked is, I think, honestly posed, like so many of Armantrout's questions: "Is it memory or physics / that makes the bridge appear?" Does one inform the other? In my view such questions lie at the heart of her "metaphysics"—a word we might reconsider to mean "after physics" again, as involved with physics, or perhaps even residing within. "There are limits to knowledge and imagination," as she put it in an interview; "maybe, when I leave spatial and logical gaps in poems, I'm trying to envision it": that space for the invisible and silent that both scientists and her speaker in "Getting Warm" know is active.[65] She invites something other in, as did Levertov; but her speaker "manages" it just that crucial bit more self-reflexively as both a connection, a bridge built, and a construction that must be exploded to achieve pleasure. Now I choose to connect Armantrout's orgasmic "repletion" on a fare of nothing with Levertov's "ah!" upon reaching absence, her presence; both are, as my title neatly has it (quoting as I do), "nothing / like a bridge." And I'll use that connection for my purposes in conclusion—drawing these two willfully into relation, perhaps their original relation. I do hope something mutually illuminating has occurred in the course of this comparison.

But it is, of course, time to explode.

• INTERVIEW WITH BRUCE WEIGL •

Donna K. Hollenberg

DH • Hi, Bruce. How and when did you meet Denise Levertov?[1]

BW • The first time I met Denise was in college. I was an undergraduate at Oberlin College. It must have been 1971 or '72 and it was a great place to be for student writers in those days because they had enough money to bring writers who would spend time with the students. Denise taught a workshop, and then in this small creative writing office we sat on the floor at her feet and she sat on a chair and took questions for a couple of hours. The first thing that happened to me was that I fell deeply and madly in love with her. I thought she was the most beautiful woman I had ever seen in my entire life.

DH • That's very interesting, because she had very little self-confidence in herself as a woman.

BW • Yes, I know. I don't know whether it was the gap in the teeth or what . . . but she had this glow about her, and she was so sweet and so generous with us.

DH • Did you tell her you had been in Vietnam?

BW • I don't think so at that time. The war was still going on, and we had learned very quickly that it wasn't a good idea to advertise that. There were still a lot of funny feelings about veterans, even at Oberlin, which really surprised me. So I might not have.

DH • But you were writing poems . . .

BW • I was, yes.

DH • But not about the war.

BW • Barely. Well, I had sent a few around, and the response wasn't very good. I remember even being told that . . . I think the language was something like, "This has already been done."

DH • Could you explain that?

BW • Well, this is in the period when many well-known writers embraced the subject—in the 1960s for a while. After the war was over, when the soldiers came home, then *they* were writing about it.

DH · I see.

BW · It was really thanks to people like Tim O'Brien that doors started opening. But it wasn't something that, when I was a young writer, I felt was a subject upon which general approbation would be bestowed.

DH · Yes, I read and taught his novel, *Going After Cacciato*. When you were sitting in this group at Oberlin, how many people were there?

BW · There were probably about six or eight of us sitting there.

DH · And she had read your poems?

BW · Yes, she had read some of our poems, and she talked very directly about them. I was sitting very close to her, just as close as I could without sitting on her lap!

DH · I wonder if she saw in your writing something that you were keeping in.

BW · I'll tell you something, Donna: there was a lot going on that day about which I was unaware. Yes, I think she saw something, but I wasn't smart enough to think of that. We weren't talking about it. There was no narrative yet.

DH · Did you talk with her again?

BW · Not on that trip. We had been introduced to her work as part of her visit, a lot of her poems, randomly, but I think *Footprints* had just come out, and I fell in love with that book, and I started carrying it around with me.

DH · That's right after *To Stay Alive*. I'm really glad to hear that, because she took a lot of flak from critics about those poems.

BW · She did. But if you read it today, it really holds up. It's amazing how strong it is today.

DH · I was appalled when I looked back at the reviews. In those days, you were not supposed to write political poetry in the U.S., I guess.

BW · Yes, and this one is not as political as *Relearning the Alphabet* and *To Stay Alive*. The thing about *Footprints* was that I felt real close to it. So then the only connection was me following her work and reading her work, and every once in a while we would correspond, but just very formally. And then one year I was in New York with Reginald Gibbons, who was being given some award by the Academy of American Poets, and so I went to the ceremony. Denise was also there and was being given an award, and I wanted to meet her, but she had this entourage around her, so I thought, oh well. At one point, because it was hot in there, I went outside and was having a cigarette with someone, and Reg Gibbons was standing there and a couple of other writers, and I saw Denise come out with some people, and it looked like she was leaving, and we kind of made eye contact, and she came over to where I was standing, and she said some really kind things about my work. I started to tell her about when we first met, and she cut me off and said that of course, she remembered. That was probably in the 1990s.

DH • Wow, she remembered.

BW • Yes, she remembered, and she gave the sense that she'd been paying attention to my work. So then we did start corresponding and talking on the phone as well. I made her a book. I had a terrible nine-year insomnia—due to PTSD—and she would give me all these different cures.

DH • The '90s. By that time she herself had some illnesses. She died in 1997.

BW • But she didn't really talk about that, to anyone, I don't think.

DH • That's correct.

BW • The last thing she would have wanted was someone like me, or anyone, worrying over her illness. That's certainly the kind of woman she was. The sad thing that's occurred to me, thinking about talking about her and looking at some of her work again, is what a distinguished body of work it is and how widely it's ignored in this country.

DH • Well, that happens after someone dies. But New Directions published a *Collected Poems* in 2013, and I hope my biography will help. I think she'll be revived.

BW • We tend to do that a lot, often for the wrong reasons, but in this case, the work is so strong. It really holds up, and I don't know why no one really said that. Even at the time, I don't think they said it enough. If you read the kind of poetry that's published today and then you read something like her "Feet," it's like reading someone from junior high school and then reading a master.

DH • Yes, but that was drafted in 1996 and published posthumously in *This Great Unknowing*. Well, you told me it was also published in the *Seattle Review*.

BW • But feet imagery shows up quite a bit throughout her canon.

DH • I looked at it again after you asked me to read it, and that made it so much more meaningful to me. It was as if I had missed it before, because when I was reading from the perspective of a biographer, I was thinking about her mother, because she is in it, but when I read it this time, I wondered what Bruce loves about it. What do you love about it?

BW • I think one of things that I love about her work in general is that she manages to walk on this thin line between narrative and lyrical. She is able to retain elements of narrative, of storytelling, that she likes and that readers like. At the same time, the stories are not told in a traditional narrative way. Once upon a time this happened or that happened and we lived happily ever after. They're told through a juxtaposition of imagery, which makes it a little more abstract, a little more difficult, a little more physical, too. I think in that poem she does that perfectly without a glitch.

DH • And she brings in so many aspects of her life. Of life in general.

BW • It's full of allusions and analogies. Yes, it's a deeply autobiographical poem. I'm sure you know more about that aspect of it than I do, but I love the beginning, and I love the retelling of the mermaid story.

DH • Yes! That's the part I noticed again.

BW • I want to read to it to people coming out of the *Beautiful Mermaid* movie![2]

DH • The part about the mermaid turning her tail into legs and feet and the pain involved in taking each step and that she does this "for love, and the dream / of human joys and a deathless soul."[3] I wondered, Bruce, thinking about you and why you love this poem. Is that what writing poetry takes? Is that about writing poetry, that section?

BW • In what way? What do you mean?

DH • Well, to be able to write about the painful?

BW • You know, once Bill Matthews showed me an essay he was working on. It was called "Teaching the Afflicted." And I don't know whether he ever published it, but you know, when you're teaching a literature class and there's always this kid who sits in the back with the jacket and sunglasses and doesn't ever look up and doesn't talk to anybody and yet, when it comes time to talk about the story or the poem, seems to get right at the heart of it, and that's the kid to whom something bad happened. So there seems to be a connection between having a deeper understanding of your own mortality and having those kinds of insights. Then, Donna, on the other hand, there's *The Red Badge of Courage,* written by a man who never saw a day of combat. One of the great antiwar novels of all time. But I have neurologist friends who work on this who say, yes, there's definitely a connection between the two.

DH • This time that part of the poem really hit me in a way it didn't before.

BW • I'm really glad to hear it was written so late. So here she is, strong as ever.

DH • I think her late work is her strongest work. It takes all that time to be that good. You have to earn it.

BW • You're right, she changes.

DH • One of the questions I asked you, since we're talking about her later life, she turned back to Christianity, and then at the very end she became interested in Buddhism. Am I correct that you were raised Roman Catholic?

BW • That's right.

DH • What happened: did you reject it, or did you add Buddhist meditation?

BW • No. I stopped being a Catholic. I don't know if I ever formally rejected it. I loved the church when I was a kid. My Yugoslav grandmother was sort of the church matriarch, so she's the one who took me through Communion and confirmation and all that. It was an Eastern European church, and I loved the priest and the whole thing. Only until I went to the war. I was at a place called L.Z. [Landing Zone] Stud that was set up in preparation for an assault on Khe Sanh in an operation called Operation Pegasus, and I was coming over this hill, and I saw a priest and he had a surplice on and his whole outfit on. I could just see him from the waist up, because

                                                    Donna K. Hollenberg

of the hill, but I could see that he was doing a blessing, so I thought that maybe he was having some kind of Mass up there or something, so I kept walking up the hill. And then when I got up high enough to see, I saw that there were a few other people there, but what he was actually doing was blessing this cache of ammunition and armaments. And, you know, I was just eighteen or nineteen years old, and watching him doing this, I thought, I don't get it. This goes against everything my priest taught me, so I decided at that moment, I'm not going to be a Catholic any more. Kind of adolescent frenzy, I guess. Then many years later, I spent time around some people, and I approached it from a scholarly point of view for a long time and read a lot and studied. Then one day a Buddhist friend of mine said, "Why don't you stop studying and be a Buddhist?" So I started trying to be a Buddhist, and it's been about fifteen years—twenty years now.

DH • I see that there a number of poems that refer to that aspect of your life—sutras and reference to Buddhism.

BW • I have a book that's just coming out in which I try to keep it out, because I don't like the ring of that pseudo-Buddhist poem, but after a while it just becomes part of your life.

DH • Right now, I have your book *The Unraveling Strangeness* open, and the first poem in that book, I just love. It's called, "Oh, Atonement," and I think the part that resonates for me personally is the second page, where you connect with the "giant thunderhead" on the flat prairie plain, and that's where you'll pray.[4] To me that's such a subtle way of conveying what Mircea Eliade means by "an open existence," one with a transhuman structure, because it's to the thunderhead, not the rainbow, not the blue sky, and yet it is atonement.[5]

BW • Maybe it's like Ahab's atonement. It occurred to me that what I was doing as a writer and what I and others want to do is a kind of neo-romanticism. We have so much in common with that movement. Although we must account for some horrible things that happened between now and then. But we still struggle to find our place in the natural world, even though we go on violating it to do that sometimes. You know, we drive our recreational vehicles deep into the forest and then drive the motorcycles we've tied to the bumpers even deeper, and the high-pitched engines keep the deer from procreating, and that's our idea of communing with nature, but we're still trying to do it, and I think in a poem like that it is the only salvation.

DH • Yes. Denise was certainly a neo-romantic.

BW • That lyric/narrative tendency I described earlier is part of that neo-romanticism. Wordsworth wanted it that way. He wanted the best of both of those worlds. And so did Keats. Keats got trapped in this traditional apprenticeship, but then he's writing little poems like "This moving hand on the border" while he's working on a longer homage to Milton.

DH • In your poem "The Hand That Takes"—another one I really loved because it was so unflinchingly honest—where you say, "I have loved war . . . And after that dangerous love / no woman could save me / from the meaning of things."[6] And in other poems, too, you talk about the love of war. What do you mean?

BW • I think it has to do with before you come to the understanding of what you're doing and how it is based on, in fact, lives, and you have to remember the average age of soldiers, eighteen and a half, so there weren't a lot of bright lights walking around there. We believed what we were told and did what we were told. There was a kind of beauty in the way that things worked. We were pretty well trained, and because we did what we were told, when things worked the order, the idea that all of this is contributing to this larger sense of glory, that you're actually preserving the democratic principles for people, whether they want them or not! The unambiguous nature of it is another thing. There's "them" and "us"; there's "die" or "kill." When you talk about romanticism, that's the romantic ideal. I wrote a poem about a man who remembers having been forced to perform fellatio on an older man when he was a child. The last part of the poem is "See it clearly, you make it beautiful, no matter what."[7] And the punishment's been taken to task for many different reasons, but one thing the people who wrote about it didn't get was that in my mind, that was always a challenge to romanticism, that line. That's my criticism of romanticism. It is possible to say anything in such a way as to make it beautiful. Perhaps that's a flaw of language, that we can do that.

DH • It reminds me of Jorie Graham's "The End of Beauty." I think you have a poem about beauty, too, that is critical of the beautiful in those terms. But "no woman could save me." In other places you do say that the love of your wife and family did save you.

BW • Yes, when how I think I was able to survive, in every case . . .

DH • You were just saying that it was the love of your grandmother and your mother that saved you.

BW • Yes, my grandmother, my mother, my sister. There were a lot of strong women in my life. You know my grandmother had seen people go off to war, and so had my mother. My relatives were from Yugoslavia, and so they knew something about suffering and about how to welcome me home. That was something the country didn't provide for us in any way back then.

DH • Well, I'm very glad you pointed that out. Something else: I was moved by *The Circle of Hanh*. The fact that you and your wife went back and adopted

Donna K. Hollenberg

a Vietnamese child, a daughter. That's such a beautiful thing. Obviously, she's a grown-up now, right?

BW • Yes, she's twenty-four.

DH • At the time it must have been hard. You talked about how hard it was—just getting to do it.

BW • Yes, the embargo wasn't lifted yet, so it was really difficult.

DH • You must have learned some Vietnamese, because you've translated.

BW • Yes, I did, a little bit, but, you know, there were enough people who were speaking English, and I had made enough friends in Vietnam by then so that if I needed an interpreter, it was really easy for me to get one. But it was quite a journey. When I look back, it was very interesting and very difficult, and there times when I didn't think it was going to work and it was pretty crazy, but I had a lot of help.

DH • Does your daughter still speak Vietnamese? She was eight, so she must.

BW • I did a little research before she came, and I learned that, basically, without Vietnamese school lessons, she could lose her language within a year, so I basically committed myself to that and found her a teacher. I was teaching at Penn State at the time, and I found a Vietnamese couple from Hanoi who were graduate students. And we all became friends. They became godmother and -father to her. Her Vietnamese has stayed great. In fact, last year she published a translation of my memoir, *The Circle of Hanh,* in Vietnamese. She's published several articles in Vietnam, which she wrote in Vietnamese. They love her writing there and they love her story, especially that she was able to stay deft at her speaking and reading and writing skills in Vietnamese.

DH • The act of translation must be exciting for you.

BW • Yes, it was. I love doing the work. I'm going back in March for a week or ten days.

DH • So you go regularly?

BW • I try to, yes. I think eventually maybe I'll start spending part of the winter there. Hanoi is like San Francisco in the winter. Only cheaper than SF.

DH • In *The Circle of Hanh,* you write that "the story circles back on itself if you let it have its way."[8] And I know you have the collection *The Archeology of the Circle,* so obviously the image of the circle is important. I was reminded of Levertov's late poem "Evening Train," in which she writes "everyone has an unchanging age (or sometimes two) / carried within them, beyond expression."[9] I wonder what your core ages are and why?

BW • I thought about that question, and I'm sure not quite what you're asking me.

DH • Well, in the poem she's sitting across from this man, and one of her 'core' ages, that she still feels in her heart, is fourteen. Sometimes I do, too. I can still feel my teenage self. So I wonder what are yours?

BW • I guess eighteen would have to be one.

DH • When you went to war.

BW • The funny thing is before. Because I remember the difference. The before and the after, which is a very distinct thing, distinct in the sense that I thought, "Oh, my God, one day I was like that." And I was like that all my life up to that point. And then the next day I was different. That moment.

DH • That reminds me of Levertov's mermaid sequence. Sometimes when I think of my own core age, I like to think of the pleasurable things. I don't want to think about the painful things. But yours were so overwhelming. You couldn't just throw that person aside, or you'd be a mess.

BW • Yes. For the first time, my health care—everything—is being taken care of by the VA, and it has been a good experience—mental health as well as physical stuff. It's nice dealing with people who consider that aspect of your experience, where other doctors typically don't. And you really should.

DH • Do you find that writing helps with that?

BW • Not really. Drinking helps with that!

DH • I thought maybe writing did, because some of your poems have a lot of pain in them.

BW • You know I don't like the idea of writing as therapy, because writing is too hard. Therapy is a lot easier.

DH • Did Denise share her experience in the protest movement with you, when she got involved in some pretty violent stuff?

BW • I asked her about Mitch. She told me some stories about meeting Mitch and about some things that they had organized and done together but nothing really graphic.

DH • She had to make a decision about whether she would get involved in protest groups that threw bombs—like the Weathermen.

BW • I knew about that, but she never talked to me about it.

DH • Well, I think she regretted some of what she did, later, and that's probably why she didn't. She got in over her head, and then she realized it later when she was in other protest movements, like the environmentalist movement, where people weren't saying things like "Off the pigs" and behaving really over the top. At the beginning it was in response to the police beating them up, but then it got out of control.

BW • Although there's nothing to apologize for, is there?

DH • No, there isn't, when you remember what was going on. Your poem "Snowy Egret" (from *Monkey Wars*) deftly conveys the ways in which the culture of war infects even a young boy's relation to nature. He seemed to shoot the bird in spite of himself. I was also moved by your response to his actions. The fact that you hugged the boy. What is the genesis of that poem?

   Donna K. Hollenberg

BW • I'll tell you the whole thing. I dreamed that my neighbor, who is nonexistent, shot an egret in my backyard. I woke up, and it was such a vivid image that I told my wife, and then it stayed in my head that day, and I wrote it down. I just took the phrase "I dreamed" off and said that my neighbor did this. And then I started asking myself questions: why did he do it? It went from there and just took off. I liked the poem and where it was going, and I sent it and some others to Reg Gibbons at *Tri-Quarterly*. (He was editing *TQ* at that time.) He called me on the phone a couple of weeks later and said he especially liked "that Vietnam poem." And I said, "I didn't send you any Vietnam poems." He said, "Yes, you did," and I said, "No, I didn't, I haven't written any Vietnam poems for a long time." And he said, "Yes, the one about the egret." Then I went back and read it, and sure enough, it was a Vietnam poem.

DH • In your poem "My Good-Bye" you allude to (and reject?) T. S. Eliot's famous mermaids.[10] Your sense of reality is much more down-to-earth than his. Levertov read Eliot, too, of course, but preferred W. C. Williams. Both, like you, "live among dogs." (I'm thinking of the black bitch in *Paterson* and Levertov's poems with dogs in them, for example, "The Dog of Art" from *Collected Early Poems* and "As It Happens," from *Poems 1960–1967*. In your case I think of the "dogs of war." Could you say more about your relation to Eliot and WCW, as well as Levertov, and what it means to live among dogs?

BW • You know, there are at least two distinct versions of Eliot, and I feel very close as a writer to the *Four Quartets* version of him. That's the Eliot that makes a lot of sense to me as a poet, although I love the other stuff, too, for how it turned our heads and made us look at the world differently. The *Four Quartets:* it's the personalization of the vision instead of the intellectualization of the vision, as *The Waste Land* is, but I also love *Paterson. Paterson* is what we needed in terms of showing us a direction formally, because we began to break down form, but then there was so much bad free verse, because people thought that because we weren't counting anything or measuring anything, it didn't matter where you broke the line. *Paterson* has such a wonderful, jazzy form. It shows that you don't have to count, but it still has a musical element, the line. It may not be music in a metrical sense, but it's still rhythmic somehow. The great thing that Denise taught that day, long ago—I teach every student of mine this—we were talking about the line break. And it's so important when you're talking about her poems to pay attention to the line breaks, because if not, the whole meaning of the poem can change, so it's a line like "I'm dying / for a bowl of ice cream." And she says that the line break is half a comma. I love that. It has been so helpful to me as a writer. It's such a small thing, but it's a little jewel.

DH • Denise was a wonderful reader of poetry. I once remember crying in her class, and she wasn't even reading her own poetry. . . . Is there anything more that you'd like to say?

BW • I may have spent my ringtone . . .

DH • Well, Bruce, thank you so much.

Donna K. Hollenberg

• GENERATIONS OF POETS •
Denise Levertov and Bruce Weigl

Reginald Gibbons

In the 1960s many American poets born between about 1915 and about 1935 (whatever their individual aesthetic paths had been) participated in a poetic change that, after decades of accumulating pressure, decisively shifted poetry in American culture, in terms of its engagement with social realities and its craft. This was only the latest turn in the continuing unfolding of poetry through history, but it seems to have had a longer-lasting effect than any other such turn in the poetry of the English language. For Denise Levertov (born 1923) two kinds of earlier artistic invitation were most important. And the poetic innovations in her work were part of the permission received a generation later by Bruce Weigl (and other poets) to develop an intensity of response to the waste and cruelty of warfare and of the politics of warfare and to write for a broader audience by using small narratives and the materials of everyday life.

As the twentieth century advanced in technology, decade after decade, and thus in medicine, warfare, and communication, while simultaneously grinding its way through its social, political, and military traumas, and advanced too in the general acceptance of broader ideas of human rights, most American poets came to feel—especially during the 1960s and 1970s, those years of renewed ideals and a growing poetic culture of poets and readers, in the midst of, and perhaps because of, artistic and social turmoil—that the freeing of the poetic line brought with it a freeing of thought. In Levertov's poem "September 1961" she names three of those she called "the old ones," whose poetic innovations and permissions had opened poetry in craft and range of materials—Ezra Pound, William Carlos Williams, and H.D., all of them by 1961 rendered speechless by afflictions of old age:

> They are not dying,
> they are withdrawn
> into a painful privacy

learning to live without words.
E. P. "It looks like dying"—Williams: "I can't
describe to you what has been

happening to me"—
H. D. "unable to speak."

One of the two artistic legacies on which Levertov (born in England and educated by her extraordinarily literary family) drew was the fully American craft of Williams's short line, with unpatterned and vigorous rhythms created by speech stresses and enjambment. Levertov often combined these with a rhetoric of delicate, precise perception (as in Williams's exemplary "Young Sycamore"), which she conveyed with lively simplicity. The other legacy of which she made greatest use was the uniting of intensely felt perception with half-deconsecrated spirituality—not something that Williams pursued at all. She united the presentation of perception itself with other things, too: a self-conscious thinking about feeling, even in the midst of the poet's elaborating of the poem's stages of feeling; a mystical conviction about what might be holy in everyday life, especially in bodily experience; the idea that one of the functions of poetry was to create (again) a counterdiscourse opposed to the dominant political and social discourse; a conviction that poetry could be potent—where rights of free speech are allowed, just as where the right of free speech was absent, in samizdat cultures—in voicing strong dissent. These values she fused with poetic craft derived in part from the "old ones," and she combined them in addressing not only inner life but also the life of human communities—those of residence and those of values.

Levertov mingled perception and apperception in the same moment, we might say, mixing imagery with abstract and sometimes didactic discursiveness. She often asked her readers to see in her vivid literal images the symbols of her urgent attention to being, to the body, to the sense of the spaciousness of inner life, and to suffering and to the causes of suffering—wrong action, hateful public and political discourse, and the horrific waste of life in war and in social suffering. In the poem that is quoted below, she inverts William Wordsworth's poetic ideal of withdrawal from the messy compulsory pursuits of everyday life—not because she rejects nature, which for Wordsworth was his antidote to spiritually poisonous "getting and spending," but because for her a risky openness of spirit to both nature and society was a moral imperative if poetry was to say anything to the world—whatever it might say about the world. Here is the beginning of a poem, once perhaps her most famous, that she titled by its third line: "The world is / not with us enough / *O taste and see* / the subway Bible poster said." She also wrote this (from "Life at War"):

　　　　　　　　　　　　　　　　　　　　　　　　Reginald Gibbons

> . . . burned human flesh
> is smelling in Vietnam as I write.
>
> Yes, this is the knowledge that jostles for space
> in our bodies along with all we
> go on knowing of joy, of love;
>
> our nerve filaments twitch with its presence
> day and night.[1]

We need to harken to that twitching, not deny it: Levertov valued a poetic engagement with our lives as social beings who lived where much of what was done in our name should be decried. And the ruination of the twentieth century, with its particularly intense suffering, folly, hatred, and destructiveness, its presidents' wars and dictators' oppression, its malevolent great-powers scything of life here and there around the planet, effectively compelled two poetic responses at once: a prizing, amid all that, of a sanctuary of inner life, dignity, compassion, and humane imagination and at the same time a poetic engagement—preferably straight on—with the horror, so as to name the good and to call evils evil and to refuse to be silent about either.

When a poet accepts—intuitively, temperamentally, or with conscious deliberateness—an offered poetic invitation, then the obligation imposed by art itself is to use it for new purposes and thus to extend it to others. Levertov's work and her life as a poet seem to have offered a particularly important invitation and permission to Weigl (born 1949), who had heard the bombers flying overhead and had fought in the war on the ground. (In those days, when war news on television was much less censored than it is now, we often saw death and wounding at 6 P.M. on our little glowing screens and felt the shock of it. And the shock of American newspaper photos of Vietnamese scenes of killing were more honest about brutality than such photos have ever been again. (In those days offending a sensibility of niceness was a gesture of truth-telling; now it is regarded by too many as an offense against patriotism or a trigger of inner traumas.) The social and media context of poetry, as for public discourse and for nearly everything, was very different from what it had been during the Korean War and World War II, the wars of the biological and poetic mothers and fathers of the poets of Weigl's generation.

One of the many poets of the generation born beginning around 1943–1953, Weigl began to publish in the 1970s, and like others he could take for granted the craft and the uses of poetry that his recent predecessors had received from the modernists and also the ones that they themselves (Levertov among them) had created and were now offering to their successors. Every aesthetic or stylistic turn is also a turn—to different degrees in different poets—in what people believe poetry does and in what they want it to do. Levertov wrote poems that named the American war in Vietnam and opposed it; Weigl has written poems that describe that war and enact the aspects of inner aftermath that never leave the soldier who fought it.

At the age of twenty-one, Weigl had already returned from active duty in Vietnam, where like other infantrymen he had carried a heavy weapon and a heavy pack, had worn a heavy uniform and boots, and had been assaulted by heavy danger and the stark contradictions of combat and boredom, the necessarily rigid chains of command and the distorted social world off base. Like his contemporaries, Weigl has been able to choose more freely than could Levertov what to make poems of and how to let them say what they say.

His poems have as much urgency as Levertov's but without her particular rhetoric of anger. They present an intimate speaking voice that is frank, quiet, meditative, faithful to the real suffering and folly of war, and pressing—not always calm, but even when calm, nevertheless pressing. His lyrics rise from recollections of childhood and later battle, from contemplation and recuperation, from love and anger; they tell of physical or psychic suffering, the restoration or inaccessibility of inner peace, America and Vietnam, then and now.

Levertov, like almost all noncombatants, could not imagine the reality of soldiering and combat. Nor could she, as Weigl can, grasp the complex inner lives of veterans. Weigl imagines all this well—not because he has lived it but because he can imagine what he has lived—with the powers of language to evoke the physical reality of the body, including the effect on it of fear and of violent impulses, the tastes—so to speak—of being, whether pleasing or bitter: "all that lives / to the imagination's tongue," as Levertov put it.[2] Through the poetic self that Weigl creates on the page—supremely articulate but often in oblique ways—he conveys a sense of life that is frank about suffering (both as victim and as combatant) and about elemental existential doubts, and at the same time he is solicitous of our little spirits, which sometimes can accept what must be accepted and yet also seek and find renewal in the clear consciousness of nonsuffering, which Weigl inflects by attending to Buddhist thought and practice.

Weigl brings the scale of shared powerlessness (in politics, in battle, and in existence itself) back to the individual and to the continuing process, ever after, of articulating the changes in inner weather that follow the experience of the outward storm—the storm that has been survived. In fact the storm that lasted, for Weigl and many others who survived active duty in Vietnam, turns consciousness in such a way that even all that was not storm may also be seen as the contradiction of suffering and survival. Weigl moves close to the everyday violence that is nearby, that is not simply a potential in each of us but is already an active reality in and around us. We can confront and name it: the old man who amuses himself by teasing his shocked small grandson with the bloody head of the chicken he has just killed; the two yelping dogs unable to free themselves from their copulating; the boy who, as if he thought it could be a secret, shoots and kills a wild bird, an egret, near his own back-yard, helpless against the compulsion to do so; the tired man home from work whose dandling of his small sons scares them; the sexual predator who seizes a small boy.

Weigl alludes in Donna Hollenberg's interview with him to the beauty of Levertov's graceful lines and syntax and also to her passion for speaking to what most disrupted her times: state violence as war. But Weigl offers us few traces of any protests like hers. Here is a craft of image and language, brought as an instrument of vision and language to articulate a different world, a different kind of paradox from those of Levertov's generation. The poem's last line serves as its title, "When Saigon Was French":

> I remember Françoise crossing
> the room in a naked blur
> in the hotel on Trung Hung Do—
> dark except for flares
> falling in the cemetery
> catching on the window
> as if the caches of weapons would be visible.
> She was looking for something, a cigarette
> or some more clothes, it was her idiosyncrasy
> to move around afterwards
> as it was mine to lie still
> with the understanding that this was a war
> in which no one was called to duty,
> a war with no fronts.
> I was a day away from leaving
> and didn't want to go—a boy
> come six thousand miles from Ohio
> to fall in love with a French girl,
> to lord over my block of the black market
> and spend my money on cocaine,
> all that beautiful dying
> when Saigon was French.[3]

Wordsworth's legacy, which every poet has inherited, was to have made everyday life and ordinary people worthy subjects of poetry and a literary version of every-day speech a worthy poetic mode; but perhaps we should say that he made poetry worthy of such subjects and such language.

Levertov saw in everyday life what she regarded as holy—including the simple realities of bodily, sensuous existence that restore the spirit after it has been soiled, bedraggled, by what we do. The ending of "A Romance," the title poem of Weigl's first book (1979), already articulates the irresolvable contradiction of our "holiness" and our unholy impulses:

> I don't sleep anyway so I go to bars
> and tell my giant lies to women
> who have heard them from me,
> from the thousands of me
> out on the town with our impossible strategies
> for no good reason but our selves,
> who are holy.[4]

And for Weigl—as only rarely for his predecessors—atonement, too, on a scale both social and intimately individual, is a compelling subject or focus. What he often presents is the inner conflict between—on the one hand, or as if held physically *in* that hand—knowing too much of the wrong thing and having done too much of it, and on or in the other hand, self-knowledge that must reckon with such knowing and doing. For this reason I have elsewhere called Weigl's stance toward life a pondering of "dilemmas of awareness."[5] In his poem "One Lie" from his book *The Abundance of Nothing* (2012), we read:

> You can say that one thing is connected
> to the other, and so on, and so forth, on past our wildest
> imaginings, so that you may believe that the world is
> held together somehow, and that the shapes of things,
>
> and the million dialogues, and the billion monologues
> all add up to something discernible, sometimes something even holy.
> Anyhow, it's a beautiful lie. It's a lie you can strap on
> and live with for a long time, and imagine is your life.

Levertov wrote of wanting to feel for herself stinging, smothering tear gas to atone for not having been among the bombed ("At the Justice Department November 15, 1969"); she cherished the fragile human body yet felt almost a rage that made her, too, want to be damaged and want to damage in return. Weigl offers us very little detail of his experience of warfare, hardship, suffering, fear, and grief. He is discreet about the episodes; for decades he has been deeply meditative over the images and symbols.

We can't forbid or decry the contradictions that every person lives. The contradictions live in us, live us, especially those of conscience and restraint, of being hurt and being hurtful. What we live is often beyond articulating or sometimes is not quite beyond it—just by a millimeter, just by the slight difference

Reginald Gibbons

between this pistol and that one, just by the difference of the width of a surgical thread, just by the weight of a heron's feather or the measurable electrical energy in a facial expression of loving kindness, just by the difference between this word and that.

Poems may simultaneously say one thing and its opposite. This is the poetic legacy not of particular poets but of nearly all: the human mind, especially in language as poetry uses language, can thrive in thoughts and feelings that push and pull against each other. We find ways forward (or inward or outward) from the opposed pressures of wind on the sail of each of us and water on the keel. Through book after book, Weigl has written fearlessly right along the fast course of greatest pressure, where one's individual little boat of being may capsize. War and aftermath have not been his only subjects, but they have given his work its strength by opening up his other subjects and setting the course of his work at the dangerous angle for the craft. If our own poetic age has created identifiable legacies—rather than a universal craft set that has now explored every possible way of putting meaningful (and meaningless) words on the poetic page—then we can hope that the most courageous poets, writing for the sake of the greatest human stakes, will in the future be welcomed by other poets who accept their permissions and their invitations to the voyage.

Weigl's *The Abundance of Nothing* is a mental traveler's journey to and through things that cannot be accepted and must be accepted. It is both a somber train of thought and a triumph of acceptance. The craft of the shaping of these poems and the sequencing of them is like a spiritual practice, cool, clear air in the lungs as one reads, the breath itself a mode of thought, as it is line by line in the first poem of this book, "Quiet Fountain":

> I love the guest house on Nguyen Du. I slept
>> inside the linen net, my windows open wide
>> to let the spirits in who come to visit
> from the lake. I've seen them in a chorus,
>> their white shapes in the garden where the lotus blossom
>> has to be content to swirl in
>
> just one place, the fishpond crowded, the quiet fountain
>> only barely there. I share my room
>> with geckos on the wall who chirp their discontent—
> lack of bugs, my modern pesticides—
>> with a rat who visits when I shower;
>> he cleans himself beside me on the floor,
>> and soon, I wish like him, beyond the gaze
>> that knows there's room for both of us to live.[6]

• POET'S EAR, POET'S VOICE •

Susan Eisenberg

In spring 2011 I read poems about Israel and Palestine at the Women's Studies Research Center at Brandeis University, where I'm a resident artist/scholar. "Can people with Jewish last names write poems about Gaza?" opened the first discussion ever held there on that issue. I designed the event as a closed session, for scholars only, hoping that the general goodwill and respect within the community would carry us through our deep differences. In the weeks preceding, I received strong encouragement from some while from others, a series of challenges suggesting reasons—academic and personal—I might be wise to cancel. The Middle East wasn't my area of expertise, the topic raised painful history, the community would become divided. Even the premise in my poem "Seder Plate," that homes in Gaza had been destroyed, was questioned.

The publication of that poem in *Blind Spot* had caught the agitated attention of a man who believed that no one should criticize Israel, especially people with Jewish last names. A threat from him in fall 2010 was menacing enough that I was advised to report the incident to police. A community disorders detective now follows the case. But something about standing in a police station with a big, burly Boston Irish cop leaning across the front desk saying, "Let me get this straight. You wrote a poem about Gaza, about the West Bank. He doesn't like the poem," made me more aware of my own self-censoring, as well as the cues at the center to avoid political discussion of the Middle East. The day after I filed a threat report, I scheduled the talk, deciding to read the new poems I'd been writing in what I call the Forbidden Series.

I began the reading by talking about being a poet trained by Denise Levertov to hear silences, and how silence can become painfully loud, with poems a means to ease that pressure. Everyone who spoke in the discussion that followed seemed to be drawing from their own deep well of unspokens. The authenticity of each voice allowed sharp disagreements to surface without explosion. I'd like to think that Denise, whose many encouragements nurtured me through the long plateaus and backslides of my early years as a poet, would have appreciated the moment and that her point that engaged poetry refers not only to content but community had been heard. "Your poems made me feel happy because you have grown so much. Your writing has matured. Your persistence has borne fruit. And your *range* has extended."[1] I remember sobbing as I read that letter from Seattle—relieved by the affirmation of progress from someone who was always a blunt critic but, even more, overwhelmed by the constancy over time of her belief in me as an artist. It was November 1994, almost nineteen years since I'd first sent Denise three poems as my application to audit her Creative Writing: Poetry class at Tufts University. The Seattle note went on to critique one poem she thought didn't work but might if pared and to quibble with my use of noun as verb in another poem (a point of disagreement). She then gave a frank reflection on the long breakdown of her marriage—indicating acceptance of my response to her last letter, which had taken me to task for my divorce, challenging whether I had considered seriously enough the consequences for the children. Her letter went on to suggest that my daughter, immersed in ballet, might be interested in her poem "Dance Memories" and concluded with comments about the "unspeakable election [the Newt Gingrich / Contract on America victory] & the naked espousal of totally inhumane policies, discarding even the old hypocrisies." Poetry, love, family, politics.

Having experienced other teachers in the arts whose insecurities led them to belittle their students and, as a parent, having witnessed the cruelties of ballet training structured like a sieve with students continually cast out and replaced when their lack of talent was revealed, I am amazed by my good luck to have been introduced to the craft of poetry by Denise Levertov. There were times over the years when she looked at my newest poems and found them much weaker than previous work. Or she found my life choices wrongheaded, like when the theater company I directed opened a play the weekend of a major antinuclear demonstration. "Sorry yr play opens just as people shd. be heading for the U.N. if they possibly can," she wrote, having already scolded me over the phone for that poor judgment. "But I hope to see a later performance."[2]

Although her disapproval could be caustic, her commitment and high expectations remained stalwart. Even uncomfortable conversations were energizing, sending the mind off in a new direction. In her company I always felt challenged not only to be a better writer but also to be a better human being. At the memorial in Boston at Arlington Street Church celebrating her life, I was struck that person after person stood up and said the same. Because she didn't discard after she criticized, she was able to convey, even when her comments were harsh, that you and what you did mattered—not only to her personally, but to a larger effort in which you were joined.

Whenever I teach a poetry class, I find myself telling the story of my March 1975 interview with Denise to audit her Tufts course. She liked to add the perspectives of older students with life experience to the classroom conversation; I was twenty-four. We sat in her living room at 4 Glover Circle in Somerville, and she asked me questions about the three poems I had dropped off at her house a few weeks earlier. Within two months the *Boston Globe* headlines declared the end of the long war in Vietnam, but Denise's focus was on my poems, as though they were a matter of great importance. Why had I broken the line here, not there? Why had I used a period rather than a semicolon? Why had I chosen the verb *to hump*, which connoted a particular image system, rather than other, more fitting choices?

With a growing sense of panic, my answer to each question was the same: blank, a shrug. It wasn't that I hadn't revised the poems but that the choices were all from instinct and my training in logical prose. I was certain I had failed the interview. Fortunately, as it turned out, Denise's questions were not for entry but were more the course description or first lesson. Now her questions became practical ones. I could audit only if I committed to being at every class, Tuesdays and Thursdays, 3:30–6 P.M., for the year and to doing all the work. I agreed.

It would be hard to overstate Denise's impact on my life as a writer and artist, a reflection—especially in retrospect—not only of her legendary generosity as mentor and friend but also of the model she offered in turbulent times of a considered and meaningfully engaged life that placed high value on human relationships and other pleasures. (She introduced me to Russian vodka.) She both challenged you to be self-aware and to act from your principles and knowledge and made you laugh. I remember once, in her kitchen, Denise recounted a story in which a dog appeared. When she got to the dog's part, suddenly she was on all fours, barking. Like many of her stories, the telling ended with infectious laughter.

For me she was a life raft: not only the person who first taught me the craft issues of organic poetry—the tools for creating my own life rafts—but also an adult who at a crucial time offered an alternative path through the Scylla and Charybdis of apolitical cynicism and destructive stridency. She stood out as someone who acted from a sense of the political moment's urgency while conveying a long-term and expansive view of what it took to become a political artist.

Raised in a liberal Democratic household in Cleveland, where my sister and I sang patriotic songs on our front porch when we hung the flag on holidays, I left for the University of Michigan's Residential College in Ann Arbor in 1968. The uncritical framework I'd been taught in junior high school civics—already cracked by the mid-'60s racial violence in Cleveland and Detroit that split apart my dad's family and saw my hometown occupied by the National Guard—collapsed under the war's daily news and a college environment that questioned authority and challenged assumed truths. The beating of protestors at the Democratic convention, the murder of 158 students in Mexico City and dozens of Black Panthers across this country, the use of napalm in Vietnam, and the complicity of my own university's research in some of the atrocities of the day shocked me. I went to Woodstock. I went to teach-ins. I became an activist, self-righteous as I was earnest. Before I left Ann Arbor for Boston, the new framework also shattered from its own

Susan Eisenberg

contradictions, and my trust in words faltered. Relocating began a long process of rebuilding. Still an activist, still looking for the systemic roots of social problems but also addressing my own blind spots, I tried to approach issues—and people with whom I disagreed—with more humility than I had in college.

In Boston I joined the Somerville Women's Health Project collective as it opened a free clinic in what was then a working-class community, and I began to train in theater, drawn first to mime and then to physical acting based on the work of Jerzy Grotowski's Polish Lab Theater. I heard Denise read poetry at antiwar events, but I owe meeting her personally to a friend who had taken her poetry class at MIT in 1969 and later been invited to house-sit at Denise's home near Tufts. She brought Denise to a 1974 performance of Firesticks, a woman's theater ensemble in which, common to that period, each woman told a personal story. Wearing a Pulcinella costume, I performed a piece about the impact on me of my father's cancer. Afterward Denise told me that I had *duende* as a performer. I didn't understand the comment, but I was captivated. Knowing I wrote poetry, my friend urged me to ask Denise if I could become her student.

The class met September 1975 through May 1976. I had left the Somerville Women's Health Project and moved to Boston's Jamaica Plain neighborhood to live with my boyfriend—later husband and father of my two children. I earned money teaching theater workshops in the Boston public schools through funding related to desegregation while continuing to perform with, and then direct, the Firesticks company. But I made my way back across the Charles River religiously every Tuesday and Thursday, sometimes hanging out after class with Denise back at Glover Circle. I was dedicated to the class, and what I began to learn that year transformed my writing and came to anchor me to poetry as an artist, although I would always juggle between genres or mix them, and for the next decade it was really theater that had the strongest hold.

Classes were a combination of lectures on poetics and workshopping of our poems. It was my introduction to William Carlos Williams, Muriel Rukeyser, Rainer Maria Rilke, Pablo Neruda, and Tom McGrath. Because I had a vague understanding that Denise was famous and because the class was my first encounter with poetics of open form—the poems I'd been reading in underground newspapers of the day and copying into my journals—I was clueless as to how bold and groundbreaking the concepts being conveyed in class were. I took Denise's lessons about indented lines, line breaks, stanza breaks, and the like as accepted concepts, not ones being newly articulated and forged. I still have a Xerox copy of "On the Function of the Line," written on a manual typewriter, with handwritten proof corrections that Denise must have given as a class handout. I was eager for the tools that would get me beyond the shrugs of my living room interview.

Looking back now, my poems written before that year had imagery and descriptive detail that were sometimes well-chosen, with an urgency behind them, but lacked any rhythmic awareness or drive or sense of how to develop the effective kernel into a full poem. Much of what I learned technically that year, like listening to stresses, I would have been taught in any good course. What probably was particular to studying with Denise was the exhaustive reading aloud and listening to silences, in class and at home, learning to distinguish the subtle and not subtle shifts of meaning created by even the smallest shift of white space, including the visceral reaction of the reader to what the eye saw in the arrangement on the page.

Denise was relentless about scoring what was on the page so that it could be read by the reader exactly as the poet intended. We read each other's poems aloud, so that the writer could hear any wrong scoring. Our reading aloud of our own poems was critiqued against what was on the page, with any mismatch brought to attention. Like practicing scales when I studied flute, Denise had us read line breaks, indentations, and stanza breaks so that choices would be made with a deliberation that appreciated their significance. Beginning that year, poems in my journals would be revised as I wrote them, line breaks and indentations appeared and were crossed out or moved as part of my thought process.

Not surprisingly my first experiments showed an overly exuberant use of line breaks and indentations. To demonstrate Denise would show how, without any change in words, the lines of my poem could be reshaped more effectively. As someone who can be a control freak, I am amazed that I didn't find this upsetting. I think because I felt that Denise was interested in helping me to write my own poems, not hers, and because she enabled me see opportunities I was looking for but not yet able to see, I accepted what otherwise might have felt intrusive or even shaming. I started the course well trained in complex sentence construction and, from theater training, attuned to stream-of-conscious thought that followed emotional nerve lines. The tools I added from Denise's instruction freed me to take larger risks, find new structural supports for what I wanted to express, and seek musicality in the interplay between line and syntax to carry my poems forward. A launching.

Technical issues were only a small part of what Denise taught. What happened inside and outside class blended. I'm sure that her own untraditional education contributed to her overriding of the boundaries of class hour and course term, as though that were normal and not, as she sometimes acknowledged, at a cost to her own solitude and time for writing. For myself, I welcomed what I absorbed in the more casual time.

Denise was adamant against attempting political poetry too soon, that political poetry was the hardest to write and needed to wait until one had developed adequate skills. I found this a release. Attending readings was part of one's training. Again it was not only the poetry but also the person. One day class was canceled so we could hear Grace Paley in Cambridge. One of my strongest memories of that

   Susan Eisenberg

year was going to an evening reading Denise gave with the Iranian poet Reza Baraheni on February 28, 1976. It was my first encounter with someone who had been
imprisoned and tortured. I was struck by his quiet demeanor. A leaflet recounted
the various torture methods used under the Shah, including against prisoners'
children. It mentioned that, while in solitary, Baraheni had heard another prisoner
reciting his poem. That image has, ever since, stood for me as the best description
of the communal sustenance that a well-wrought political poem can provide.

That July my partner, Danny, and I vacationed in North Carolina and back-
packed into the old-growth hardwood virgin forests at the western edge of that
state. I brought *Relearning the Alphabet* with me and read for the first time "A Tree
Telling of Orpheus" in that landscape. I was ecstatic. It was the perfect meeting of
place and poem and somewhat of an unexpected graduation exercise or recognition of a new fluency: because I could read the line breaks, I could read the poem.

Two years later, in 1978, when I gave my first poetry reading, for friends, in
Danny's and my apartment, it seemed natural to invite Denise and natural that
she came. Danny picked her up in Somerville since she didn't drive, but otherwise she was one of the group, not a special guest. Afterward she told me that
everything I'd read was a poem, which I appreciated. Neither self-absorbed nor
coy, she seemed to have sensitive instincts about her position, able to be democratic while acknowledging difference of status and development. That same year
I founded Word of Mouth Productions (WOMP), a theater ensemble that focused
on issues of working women and lasted a decade, launched with my one-woman
show about Calamity Jane. Denise came to performances of almost all our productions, including one held in a firetrap building with milk-crate seating, and gave us
permission to perform her "El Salvador: Requiem and Invocation."

Also in 1978, the year Affirmative Action guidelines opened the construction
industry to women, I began a four-year apprenticeship with the Boston local of
the International Brotherhood of Electrical Workers (IBEW), working for the
next fifteen years in heavy construction. Before the tradeswomen pioneers of that
era, the only women working on construction sites were selling food from coffee
trucks or were prostitutes. Depending on who was making the judgment, female
apprentices in the craft trades were seen as invading aliens or serious and able
students. Not only one's training, but one's safety, was in the hands of the super-
vising journeyman. Some jobs were exhilarating, others so terrifying I cried on
my way to work. To survive apprenticeship I crafted my impressions into poems
that helped me acknowledge and understand what I was experiencing. I sent them
on to Tom McGrath, whom I'd met in 1981 at a cultural conference in Minnesota,
whose organizers Denise encouraged to invite WOMP to perform *Why Don't You
Find a Rich Guy and Marry Him?* McGrath gave me the important advice to be
unafraid to use jargon from the worksite. Denise published four of these poems
when she guest-edited the journals *Hanging Loose* and *Harbor Review*.[3]

With her expansive view of the content and perspectives that belonged in poetry and the community of poets required to create that literature, Denise showed particular interest and support for the poems I began to develop from my work in construction. I organized the poems into a dramatic order and read them as a performance piece, the stage empty except for a four-foot ladder, with me sitting on the top wearing a "diamond hardhat," an image from "Hanging In, Solo" that appears now in my touring mixed media art installation *On Equal Terms*. Whetstone Press asked to publish the poems as a letterpress book and asked Denise to write a foreword for *It's a Good Thing I'm Not Macho* (1984). I am sure her foreword helped the book catch the attention of Canadian poet Tom Wayman, editor of seminal anthologies of poetry written from inside the experience of daily work. Tom invited me to participate in the 1986 Split Shift Colloquium on New Work Writing in Vancouver, British Columbia, where I met American and Canadian poets who wrote about an array of jobs, from logging to secretarial, and joined a still-ongoing conversation and community.

The work poems also connected me to a national community of tradeswomen. I began to hear from women plumbers, carpenters, and line workers from across the country who read the poems and identified, helping us all to begin to understand and examine the commonality of our perspectives. I've been reframing these experiences now for three decades, sometimes as poet, other times as activist, researcher, performer, or installation artist, and been involved in policy work locally, nationally, and internationally. The grassroots tradeswomen community I first connected to through the early poems has remained my touchstone throughout this long dialogue—and in some respects another training for me as a writer—with a community of readers who grew along with me. It's a dynamic relationship with a readership that I've carried into other content arenas.

Coming from a family that was not always safe, with the predictable abandonment issues that accompany, I might have clung to my relationship with Denise forever had she let me. A few years before she left for Seattle, she booted me from the nest when we met for drinks at 33 Dunster Street in Harvard Square. She responded to a question with "You can't ask me that anymore," telling me that there was no answer, I had the tools; the decisions were mine. It was a complicated and painful separation, because it was combined with affirmations of love and respect and encouragement to stay in touch and because of the history I brought to it. I tried to respect the distance she—and I—needed, though I wasn't always clear what that meant.

As I work across genres, I find myself applying the lessons about organic form—with intention dictating the poem's shape—to choice of medium, sometimes expressing the same material in nonfiction and poetry, art installation and personal essay, or public policy argument and performance. In the 1990s I began to understand poetry's place at the core of my artistic work, whatever the genre.

Susan Eisenberg

I've come to consider my art installations to be three-dimensional poems and my best photographs to be ones that begin from the same open inquiry that launches a poem. This became particularly clear as I began to conduct interviews with pioneer tradeswomen across the country for the nonfiction book *We'll Call You If We Need You: Experiences of Women Working Construction*.

I knew that the book would be a response, through the stories and voices of tradeswomen, to the official interpretation of Affirmative Action's failure (policies should have led to women's being 25 percent of the workforce, yet they remained less than 3 percent) that faulted the women themselves. It was the kind of question that might drive a poem, and I counted on the women I spoke with to lead me not only to content but also to the book's structure. I wasn't interested in writing a personal memoir, which one agent suggested, but a record of the collective experience. This required being able to hear people whose backgrounds, experiences, and opinions were different from mine, in some cases radically, and to find the cross threads and interwoven story. As I listened I realized that I had been trained not as a sociologist or reporter might be, to take down words or incidents, but as a poet is trained: to hear the pauses and silences, the shifts in tone and volume, the particularities of diction, the meaning beneath the meaning.

Knowing that the material in *We'll Call You* would be controversial, and that the women construction workers I was interviewing were taking an enormous risk, I felt I had to write the best book I possibly could. I'd also had a death threat for my activism and for other reasons was ready to leave working in construction. Getting a graduate degree seemed to address both problems. I considered various PhD options, obviously a more sensible route, but decided on an MFA in poetry at Warren Wilson College, with Denise as a reference on my application. I've never regretted that choice and believe the critical success of *We'll Call You* is owed to poetry. Not only for the nonfiction, but for the poems I wanted to write as well, I found myself once more needing to refresh and expand my toolbox. When I met Eleanor Wilner at the opening reception of my first residency, I immediately recognized a kindred spirit in politics and humor and knew I'd again found wise and trustworthy hands for my writing. A few months after Denise's death, my poetry collection *Pioneering* was published by Cornell simultaneously with *We'll Call You*.

In an earlier letter from Stanford in January 1989, Denise had written that my recent poems had shown "a great leap forward to another level of work. I don't mean this as a put-down of earlier work, but as artists we must keep developing, mustn't we—and that's what you've been doing. Your experiential concerns, which were the main quality one perceived earlier, now provide the necessary steel frame for the building itself, which is 'the *poetry* of the poem.'"[4]

Of all her gifts, perhaps that was her greatest. By maintaining a connection, by acknowledging both advances and stalls, she conveyed something of the persistence and reinvention required by the artistic process.

• THE EXPANSIVE VIEW •

The Poetry of Susan Eisenberg and Denise Levertov

Martha Collins

In her essay about Denise Levertov, Susan Eisenberg refers to the rigor the famous poet brought to the teaching of craft—a rigor that often surprised students, who suspected that (political) content would be enough to satisfy their (very political) poet-teacher. Equally surprising to students was what Eisenberg cites Levertov as saying: that political poetry is the most difficult to write and that one can't really do it until one has the necessary craft.

Eisenberg took the rigor to heart. And while her collected poems, at least, have almost always had "political" content, she has moved ever more deeply into the emotional and intellectual complexities of pressing political and social issues, focusing on the places where the personal and the political intersect. In addition to lessons in craft, Eisenberg mentions Levertov's "expansive view of the content and perspectives that belonged in poetry, and the community of poets required to create that literature." I'd like to focus on that expansiveness as a way of moving through the trajectory of Eisenberg's work and briefly consider community as well.

Although most of the poems in Eisenberg's first book, *It's a Good Thing I'm Not Macho* (1984), are reproduced in her second, *Pioneering: Poems from the Construction Site* (1988), with slight revisions, it's both useful and delightful to read the early book on its own (though I will quote the revised versions here). Eisenberg's experience as an apprentice electrician (she was one of the first women to enter the trade) gives the book both substance and structure: it's organized dialectically, in three parts, the titles of which suggest the tension between their terms: "As a Woman," "As a Mechanic," "As a Woman Mechanic." The dialectical structure also shapes the book's first long poem, "Hanging In, Solo," which answers the question "So what's it like to be the only female on the job?" in three sections, moving from sunny days to "mudcold-gray-no- / sun-in-a-week days" when "at each mistake, a shrill siren / alerts all tradesmen on the job / to come laugh at me," and finally to "most days, those / partly sunny days that bridge" the others. Here is the first section:

On the sunshine rainbow days
womanhood
clothes me in a fuchsia velour jumpsuit
and crowns me with a diamond hardhat.
I flare my peacock feathers
and fly through the day's work.

Trombones sizzle
as my drill glides through cement walls
through steel beams.
Bundles of pipe rise through the air
at the tilt
of my thumb.
Everything I do
is perfect.

The "scoring" of this section captures the experience of doing the work well: the pause and indentation between "tilt" and "of my thumb" make the action seem almost magical as both thumb and poem make "bundles of pipe rise" (note the assonance). And because, again, of line break and indentation, Eisenberg is able to convey the feeling rather than the fact of what follows: "Everything I do / is perfect."

The difficult days—made especially so by the words and actions of male workers—surface in a number of poems, including "First Day on a New Jobsite," where the speaker has to think of women in other cities also "passing / through construction site gates for the / first time" in order to "keep going." But even that poem has an upbeat conclusion: "the workers all strangers all men / myself the only 'female' / and yet / we find, almost easily, the language / that is common."

That language is one of the joys of these poems, used either metaphorically or in celebration of the electrician's work. Here is part of "Through the Ceiling, Maiden Voyage," its sense of wonder enhanced by the fusion of work and worker through metaphor and invented words like "buildinglife":

Sliding
under an airduct, then
scrabbling crab-like along pipes and crossbars—
. . . .
I ask the stillness,
has another woman passed
before me?

>to witness this
>pulsation of buildinglife:
>arteries of plumbing pipes branch across
>electric nerve lines sinews of metal
>secure airducts
>pumping coldbreath/warmbreath
>to the skeletal framework of iron beams.

The excitement of Eisenberg's trailblazing apprenticeship is the dominant emotion in this first book and is reflected in the trailblazing nature of the poems: who had ever written about such an experience—new in history as well as poetry—before? The last poem in the book, addressed to the poet's left arm, ends: "Only as a balanced whole / can the body / redress history. / You have taught me: / all hands are needed."[1]

As Eisenberg notes, this book led to a conference on "work writing," which in turn inspired her to edit the anthology (and produce as a theater piece) *Coffee Break Secrets* (1988), a "cycle of poems about work" by twenty poets. Eisenberg's mingling of her own poems with those of others seems like a precursor of her groundbreaking nonfiction book, *We'll Call You If We Need You: Experiences of Women Working Construction* (1998), which carefully and poetically collages selections of interviews with other women and her own voice, the latter only occasionally recounting personal experiences.

Published simultaneously with this important prose book, *Pioneering: Poems from the Construction Site* also honors the collective voice of tradeswomen, in this case by using the third person *she* in all but a handful of the new poems that occupy the first and largest section. The contrast between these poems and the mostly first-person ones reprinted from Eisenberg's first book is striking in other ways, too. In most of the new poems, Eisenberg has moved beyond apprentice to journey level—and in the process has had to acknowledge, as she says in the introduction, that in the earlier poems she had "understated" the "difficulties and hostilities" she and other women had faced. The title poem follows a woman from her difficult beginnings in the trade ("The loud ones argued / to throw her out immediately"), to her relative success ("She became a regular— / always on the fringe / expected to help out / just a little more"), to the end, which confounds even her critics:

>After all those years hurling back cannonballs
>womanizing the barricades firing
>only if she saw the whites of their eyes
>it was the lonesomeness
> of pioneering
>that broke her resistance.

Martha Collins

The military metaphors are telling, as is the metaphor that precedes an implicit death threat in "Partner #3," one of a sequence of nine poems that focus on different partnerings between an unnamed woman and man: "She smelled dynamite on his shirt."

Some of the poems in the "Partner" sequence are more positive, as when the woman is paired with an old-timer, a black man, or just someone with whom, after some months, a process of "seeding a friendship that defied harsh soil" occurs. There are occasional moments of exuberance comparable to earlier poems too: "Did She Tell You about Running Pipe?" celebrates both work and women workers by fusing the language of the two, the pipes "slicing the vault air / spinning leaping kicking / their powerfully rounded thighs in perfect / unison."

But while the woman in the title poem had "wedged in the doorway / for other women" a "welcome mat," the last of the new poems is a sequence titled "UnWelcome Mats at the Construction Site." The new poems are also conscious of the physical dangers of working in the trades: a male pipefitter apprentice falls, and in "Tell Me" the speaker asks, in hauntingly short lines: "What / shall I / do / with the / woman's / hand / left / on the table / of the radial / arm / saw / she was not instructed / how to use." Here syntax turns physical disaster into complaint with the surprising turn at the end, as well as the period that follows in place of the expected question mark.

Economic difficulties are more apparent in these poems too: in addition to threatened layoffs, the poet notes class distinctions, as in "Following the Blueprints," the poem that opens the book:

> To the open possibility
> of steel against sky
> we weld, bolt and strap
>
> wide staircases of marble, arched
> skylights, commanding views
>
> serviced by windowless corridors
> where ceilings hang low, as though
> the ones who will push carts and carry trays
> are unusually small or
> prefer to scurry, like mice
> in closed dark spaces
>
> or as though
> extra headroom might give them
> ideas.[2]

I love the way the language of the poem, focused through line and stanza breaks, seems to "open possibility" in the first two stanzas, the first of which seems like another praise song for work, only to shut it down in the last two. Here and in "For Money, at the Hotel," Eisenberg uses the construction site to move beyond the tradespeople themselves to those for whom they are working, and thus to explore a class system that includes both the more fortunate rich and the less fortunate scurrying workers to come.

That expansiveness becomes even more apparent in Eisenberg's third book, *Blind Spot* (2006), in which the poet notes, among other things, her interest in "the intersection of family and historical moment." The territory here seems somewhat new: family had made only cameo appearances in Eisenberg's earlier books, and history was experienced in the work poems primarily as history in the making.

The intersection is most obvious and controlled in the first of the book's three sections. Focused on the poet's grandmother, it opens with "Heirlooms," a poem that in seven lines manages to juxtapose not only the grandmother's past and present but also Rumpelstiltskin and the grandmother's own mythmaking:

> She unstitched all remnants
> of the girl from the shtetl
> and spun our gold into skeins of straw
> washed, dyed, and sewn by hand into
> her proudest dress, woven
> in perfect English: *I was born*
> *in New York City.*

Five poems whose titles begin "My Grandmother Hated" follow, the first showing the grandmother's contempt for her orthodox neighbors, the second her "missing" of Jack Ruby's killing of Lee Harvey Oswald on television. The grandmother also hates the sexual freedom of her daughter and others, but her narrowness is never simply derided. Countering the "hate" poems, Eisenberg creates three delightful poems titled "Imagine," in one of which the grandmother proposes to send cookies to the imprisoned activist Lori Berenson. The poet both contextualizes and laments immigrant history in "Capitalism Takes": "we never caught on that / our elders / traded our circle for a place in line," she writes, and then: "My grandmother never showed me / the dance she danced on a tabletop / while her father clapped a clapping / that echoed through shtetl rooftops."

In the last poem of this section, "Seder Plate," Eisenberg writes from the intersection of her own Jewish heritage and contemporary events:

> This year even the charoses tastes bitter,
> salt water over everything. Enough

                                                                   Martha Collins

rejoicing at plagues—as though God
uproots olive groves and smites
first-born sons. Let the shank bone signify
orphaned arms and legs.
Let the roasted egg signify
eyes blinded by rubber bullets.
Let the matzo signify peace
without justice: fragile and tasteless.

Keep the door open all night for Elijah.
He has been wandering
since seven tanks swallowed his house in Gaza.

The juxtaposition of Seder foods with the history being made in Palestine, held together by the apparently calm and repetitive language of ritual ("Let the _____ signify") as well as the similarly shocking but quiet last stanza, makes this one of Eisenberg's most powerful poems.

The poem also prepares for the second section of the book, which moves more broadly and distantly into both history and oblique political commentary, opening with poems based on nineteenth-century Massachusetts mill girls and a woman who owned her half-sister slave. The poet then places herself in more recent historical moments, sometimes in juxtaposition to the past, as when, discovering the shocking and perhaps murderous deaths of tradeswomen, she references the 1911 Triangle Shirtwaist Factory fire or when, in a collage of memories of the 1960s, she notes:

Blindfolded, gunbarrel to the temple, *boom*
slump forward *boom* slump forward *boom*
that one VC shot a thousand times on news
brought to us by Saran Wrap and GE

souring forever off-key on my tongue
the patriotic medley sung from the flag-
flying porch of childhood.

The section gradually moves closer to the present, with poems about Andrea Yates, post-9/11 airport surveillance, and the Iraq War, always with emotional complexity: Eisenberg sees beyond the obvious and acknowledges her own complicity, her "own mute throat."

Finally, reversing the pattern of many books (and also of many poetic careers), Eisenberg moves in the last section of *Blind Spot* to more personal poems, all focused on family: a sequence about a sister shot during a robbery, several poems about her children (preceded by "Miscarriage"), a very funny poem about divorce, and a sequence about her aging father. The poems are not simply personal: the awareness that much is wrong in our world makes its way into one of the poems about children, "Public School at Open House":

> Parents tour the carcass
> of classrooms picked clean
> by the pennysavers.
> The science teacher
> needs paper cups.
> The kindergartens:
> paint. No red
> in September,
> by October:
> no yellow.
> Trees grow bare.
> Bulletin boards
> sprout pictures
> with no sun.

But the last of the father poems ends with a memory of the father giving driving directions that resonate throughout the book: "Go straight. The lights will change for you."[3]

That advice seems increasingly difficult to maintain in Eisenberg's most recent poetry, which explores both personal and political struggles that offer no easy solutions. The most personal work, her book *Perpetual Care,* recounts in its first two sections Eisenberg's journey into illness, beginning with the poem "Pre-Diagnosis," and is reminiscent of her brave account of moving into the trades in her first two books. The language similarly uses metaphors of struggle, as in "Lupus Outwits Me, Declares Martial Law":

> Who would dream to awaken from fevered sleep
> stun-gunned into paralysis by their own
> ruthless doppelganger:
> power stations overtaken in a pre-dawn coup;
> from every organ of the body
> a triumphant, unfamiliar flag!
>
> Who wouldn't be humbled
> by their double's brazen brilliance? Or,

Martha Collins

begin at once to plot in whispers
the first frantic steps of resistance?

The emotional vicissitudes of learning to live with illness give these poems a varied texture, as do shifts in form: among the longer poems are a number of short ones, including haiku. Here are two, "Lupus Flare," and "The Technician Who Just Ran Your Tests Pops Back in the Room / Asks a Tip-Off Question / Disappears, Reappears Haiku" respectively:

> I'm simply a serf.
> Fatigue raises its scepter;
> my eyes bow in sleep.
>
> She'll sound nonchalant,
> *The doc wants to speak with you.*
> Steel yourself: bad news.

These two haiku suggest some of the tonal range in the collection, the first relying, like many of the poems, on metaphors of power relationships, the second on compellingly effective assonance (*nonchalant/doc/want, speak/steel, you/news*). There is also, as in much of Eisenberg's work, humor—as in the title of the second haiku and in an even shorter poem, a one-liner called "Auto-Immune": "How dumb-is that?"

As in the work poems, *Perpetual Care* is also given broader significance by shifts from "I" to "she" and by the inclusion, in the last two sections, of poems about the illnesses of family members and others. But the most important way that Eisenberg moves beyond her own situation is by placing it in a larger political context. As in the work poems, the struggle is not just immediate; a greedy economic structure is part of it, as in the beginning of "Chronically Ill":

> Corporate giants battle in cell-to-cell combat
> across organs, joints, blood. Knocked
> to my knees by the Agri-Industrials,
> I'm now acolyte to Big Pharma,
> those *liberators*
>
> who overstay
> and bring their own trouble.
> Religiously, on Sunday mornings,
> I assign
> into seven plastic boxes (like a row
> of miniature coffins) an arsenal of pills.[4]

The multiplicity of pills is matched by a multiplicity of bills in another poem, and the patient's struggle is interrupted throughout by satirically witty pieces spoken in institutional voices—that of a hospital social worker who explains why a patients' art gallery has been discontinued, that of a corporate voice lamenting the death of someone who had been part of an "I'm-a-Survivor campaign" that represented a "major capital investment."

Whatever poetic techniques a political poet may discover and develop, there's always a question: however effective the poems, how many people will read them? Quite a lot, Eisenberg found, when her first published poems led her to a community of tradeswomen. But it's also worth noting that Eisenberg has been creating art installations that incorporate her own and others' voices since the 1990s, when she created an early version of *On Equal Terms,* the mixed-media installation that has been touring the United States since its opening in 2008. A stunning compilation of two- and three-dimensional artwork, written texts by Eisenberg and others, and audio recordings of interviewees, the installation both embraces the larger community of workers and extends into and beyond it. Eisenberg has similarly created an installation called *Perpetual Care,* first displayed in a cemetery (from which the resonant title of the poetry collection is derived) and later displayed in photographic form along with the poems. These expansions of poetry, off the page and into the gallery and world, are further examples of Eisenberg's far-ranging and change-seeking art.

Where will she go from here? The beginning of her essay on Levertov mentions what she calls her "Forbidden Series," poems-in-progress that focus on Israel and Palestine. One of the most powerful of these is "Poems about Gaza by Jews," which references a man who threatened her after reading "Seder Plate." Each of the poem's ten couplets begins with the same line, "He found me browsing the poetry section of a bookstore"; most end with something the man says about her poems, including "One of those poems should *not* have been written," "Someone with my last name should not have signed that poem," "That poem should never be read aloud"—and then, the only time the statement crosses the stanza break, "He granted one caveat. The poem could be read aloud— // . . . in a closet. To myself."[5]

In a closet to herself is exactly where Susan Eisenberg's poems should not and have not been read. They reach out to those of us troubled by the political and economic concerns that seem increasingly to define our times, as well as to those who may not have thought much about the issues she explores. For all of us who read Eisenberg's poems, the complex connections between her ever-expanding subjects—women and work, family and history, illness and the economy, Palestine and Israel—will never look quite the same, or feel quite as separable, again.

• THE INTEGRITY OF WORDS •

Kathleen Norris

Denise Levertov once gave me a powerful lesson in the integrity of words. She also taught me how to give a poetry reading. I was in my early twenties, attending an event in New York City in which Denise had been paired with a much younger poet, who read first. Fresh from a prestigious MFA program, she weighed her poems down with the trappings of academia, prefacing each one with a lengthy explication. Seemingly intent on impressing the audience with her acuity and brilliance, she succeeded only in making each poem a disappointment, not nearly as interesting as the remarks that had preceded it. The performance was flashy, occasionally witty, and so discouraging that I would have left except that I wanted to hear Denise.

And then Denise took the stage, and with a bare minimum of preparatory remarks, she began to read a poem. Immediately I felt as if I was inhaling fresh air again; I was like a thirsty person gratefully drinking a glass of cool water. Her words did not provide easy comfort, as they challenged me to pay close attention, but they were a restorative and a balm. The frothy and self-aggrandizing verbiage I'd been subjected to for the previous twenty minutes faded away, and I knew that I was hearing genuine poetry. My boss at the Academy of American Poets, Betty Kray, a longtime friend of Denise's, believed that people came to poetry readings for the relief of hearing language. Now I understood what that could mean.

In spare, oracular speech that was never portentous or pretentious, Denise gave the audience room to listen. There was none of the "see what a clever girl am I" of the previous reading. Denise herself seemed to disappear behind the words, hospitably inviting the audience to a shared experience of language at its most meaningful and intense. Listening to Denise, I learned that to a great extent a true poem can stand on its own, its very cadences and sounds resonating with wisdom, beauty, and even hope.

Yet the words of Denise's poems were mostly ordinary, everyday words, and that greatly appealed to me. A few years before, as a college student, I had discovered James Wright's *The Branch Will Not Break* and marveled at his ability to convey strong emotion in plain, stripped-down language. Listening to Denise, I was reminded that even the simplest, well-chosen words can be trusted to hold great significance, carrying considerable emotional and moral weight in a way that seems effortless. I believe that it was this reverence for language that allowed Denise to tackle so deftly and consistently the charged themes of politics and religion without losing either the beauty of words or their poetic intensity.

At the time of this reading, in the early 1970s, Denise was presenting new work, but I was grateful that she included some earlier poems that were familiar to me. She had been one of the few contemporary poets I enjoyed reading on my own in high school. I especially delighted in her play with the Bible in *O Taste and See,* the title itself being from Psalm 34. In high school I was still attending church with my parents, but religious faith seemed abstract to me. And poetry was largely a matter of looking for the hidden meanings so I could get the right answer on a test. What I found in Denise's work was a poetry that was delightfully transparent: plainspoken, accessible, yet suffused with mystery. In a way Denise was writing psalms for the contemporary age. She did not shy from wonder and praise or stint in her harsh criticism of human folly. But one sensed that there was a deeper source behind her words, an inexhaustible fountain that left both poet and reader thirsting for more.

When I was in my twenties, I thought I had left religion behind. New York City is full of churches—there's one on nearly every street—but I did not deign to enter them. Poetry was substituting for religion in my life, and attending readings was how I grounded my spiritual life. Although I did not realize it at the time, Denise's reading was a milestone in my coming full circle, reclaiming my religious heritage even as I deepened my love for literature. After that night I could no longer see the two as mutually exclusive.

In doing research for *The Virgin of Bennington,* a memoir of my postcollege days in New York, I found a letter that Betty Kray had written to Denise in the summer of 1966. As head of the YMHA Poetry Center, Betty had invited Denise to give her first major reading in New York. And she had sent Denise on the nationwide college poetry reading circuits she established in the early 1960s. Now Denise wanted to dedicate a book to Betty, as an "ardent and steadfast friend of poetry." Betty replied: "I am trying to figure out how to explain to you who grew up in an atmosphere charged with language how it was to have grown up in a relatively mute world [in which] language was regarded either as a practical instrument for everyday dealings or as a didactic instrument, and as such blunt and heavy. A killer!" She explained that her "grandfather wrote didactic articles and as a consequence spoke pompously, but he would lapse into biblical idiom—and that saved him."[1]

This statement reveals to me one reason why Betty had long been attracted to Denise's poetry. Having one's language grounded in a biblical idiom means that

　　　　　　　　　　　　　　　　　　　　　　　Kathleen Norris

one is well-grounded in the English literary tradition as well. Using a biblical image of her own, Betty described poetry as "a River Jordan, sluicing the barren West."

But a true poet, at play with words, is never a slave to tradition. I believe that Betty sensed in Denise, both as poet and friend, someone who understood language as a primary drive toward something keenly sensed but hidden from view, glimpsed in passing, and all the more valuable for its transitory nature. In the letter Betty offered a definition of poetry that I believe serves as a good description of Denise's work. As serious-minded as that work can be, it is also "like an otter's toboggan slide, for fun, merry-making, a quick plunge, of infinite use."

• FROM DENISE LEVERTOV •
TO KATHLEEN NORRIS

Peggy Rosenthal

> Menstruation is primitive,
> no getting around that fact, as
> I wipe my blood from the floor
> at 3 A.M. in the monastery guest room,
> alone in this community
> of sleeping men.

So begins Kathleen Norris's poem "Land of the Living," written in the mid-1980s. The poem could not be Denise Levertov's. Getting down on hands and knees to scrub her menstrual blood off the floor is just not what Levertov did in her poems.

Nor can I picture Levertov evoking, as Norris does later in this poem, the "young monk, laughing," who "splashed my face / with holy water" at the end of bedtime prayer at this monastery where Norris was on retreat. Laughter bubbles up in Norris's poetry much more than in Levertov's, as does the sort of wild imaging that follows the holy water splash:

> he flew down a banister, and
> for one millisecond
> was an angel—robed,
> without feet—
> all irrepressible joy
> and good news.[1]

And yet "Land of the Living" illustrates much of what Norris says that she learned from Levertov. First there is the making of poetry from "ordinary, everyday words." Listening to Levertov at a poetry reading in the early 1970s, Norris "was reminded that even the simplest, well-chosen words can be trusted to hold great significance, carrying considerable emotional and moral weight in a way that seems effortless."

All of Levertov's poetry exemplifies this complex meaningfulness that she was able to draw out of "the simplest, well-chosen words." Take, for instance, "City Psalm," a poem published in *The Sorrow Dance* (1971) and therefore one that Norris might have heard at that reading. The poem evokes the corrupt atmosphere in the United States during the Vietnam War, with the air "bear[ing] the dust of decayed hopes." The poem's speaker is

> breathing those fumes, walking the thronged
> pavements among crippled lives, jackhammers
> raging, a parking lot painfully agleam
> in the May sun.[2]

Every word here is measured; every word does its work of precisely describing while at the same time "holding great significance." Just those "jackhammers / raging" express the emotional and moral weight that impressed Norris.

As Norris came to absorb this lesson into her own poetry, she found a different voice—her own voice, as is natural for any fine poet—with which to entrust ordinary words with significance. Her poetic voice is more colloquial, with a midwestern no-nonsense solidity. Here, from the mid-1980s, is the beginning of "Housecleaning," which again finds the speaker on her knees:

> Kneeling in the dust, I recall
> the church in Enna, Sicily,
> where Ceres and Proserpine reigned
> until a Pope kick them out
> in the mid-nineteenth century.
>
> This is my Hades, where I find
> what the house has eaten.[3]

Or Norris's images of her sister giving birth in "Ascension":

> It wasn't just wind chasing
> thin, gunmetal clouds
> across a loud sky;
> it wasn't the feeling that one might ascend
> on that excited air,
> rising like a trumpet note,
>
> and it wasn't just my sister's water breaking,
> her crying out,

the downward draw of blood and bone . . .
It was all of that,
mud and new grass
pushing up through melting snow,
the lilac in bud by my front door
bent low
by last week's ice storm.

Now the new mother, that leaky vessel,
begins to nurse her child,
beginning the long good-bye.[4]

There could hardly be more simple, accessible words than these. Yet through them Norris creates a powerful poem about the cosmic significance of new life. As her sister's blood draws downward, nature pushes its new grass upward "through melting snow." And the sister's nursing of her newborn child is the beginning of both a new relationship and "the long good-bye"—because the child now out of her womb has begun its own journey.

While Norris's "Ascension" exemplifies what Levertov had modeled for her about simple, well-chosen words carrying great significance, the poem illustrates as well the other lesson she says she learned from Levertov. Even reading Denise in high school, Norris found "a poetry that was delightfully transparent: plainspoken, accessible, yet suffused with mystery." *Suffused with mystery*: Levertov's poetry did always have this quality. "One sensed," Norris adds, "that there was a deeper source behind her words, an inexhaustible fountain that left both poet and reader thirsting for more."

Born in 1947, Norris would have been in high school in the early 1960s. Levertov published her collections *The Jacob's Ladder* in 1961 and *O Taste and See* in 1964. Both volumes have explicitly biblical titles, and both contain poems that find transcendence in everyday experience. Although Levertov considered herself an agnostic at the time, she later wrote of this period that "as an artist I was already in the service of the transcendent."[5]

Indeed, in a 1968 lecture, Levertov said: "The poet—when he is writing—is a priest; the poem is a temple; epiphanies and communion take place within it. The communion is triple: between the maker and the needer within the poem; between the maker and the needers outside him . . . ; and between the human and the divine in both poet and reader. By divine I mean something beyond both the making and the needing elements, vast, irreducible, a spirit summoned by the exercise of needing and making. . . . Writing the poem is the poet's means of summoning the divine; the reader's may be through reading the poem, or through what the experience of the poem leads him to."[6]

In another lecture, in 1970, Levertov speaks about poetry conveying readers "to the heaven of that deepest reality." She continues by calling the poet to "an ecstasy of attention, a passion for the thing known, that shall be more, not less, sensuous, and which by its intensity shall lead the writer into a deeper, more vibrant language: and so translate the reader too into the heavens and hells that lie about us in all seemingly ordinary objects and experiences: a supernatural poetry."[7]

So when Norris attended that poetry reading of Levertov's in the early 1970s, these were the convictions behind the poems that she heard. Hearing them, she says, was transformative for her. Although raised in a practicing Presbyterian household, by this time in her twenties and living in New York City, she thought she had "left religion behind," as she put it in her essay in this volume. Poetry was "substituting for religion" in her life, and she grounded her spiritual life in attending poetry readings. Although she didn't realize it at the time, Denise's reading was a milestone in reclaiming her religious heritage even as she deepened her love for literature. After that night the two were no longer "mutually exclusive."

Within a decade Norris was writing poems with explicitly Christian themes. She had moved with her husband from New York City to the small town of Lemmon in rural South Dakota, returned to the Presbyterian Church of her childhood, and befriended the clergy couple there. This couple introduced her to Benedictine monastic spirituality, which increasingly informed her poetry. So fully did Norris come to identify herself as a Christian poet that in 1986 she wrote an essay for the *Christian Century* called "Finding a Place for Poets in the Church." There she names among her favorite contemporary poets self-identified Christians Kate Daniels and Patricia Hampl. In their work, Norris says, "the holy is found quite readily in the profane, and sometimes it startles."[8] As it does, I'd add, in Norris's "Ascension," composed in the mid-1980s.

Norris's association with the Benedictines became more formalized when she accepted an invitation to become an oblate (a layperson who promises to follow the rule of life of a religious order). Out of her deeper absorption in monastic liturgy and the rhythms of monastic life grew her prose work *Dakota: A Spiritual Geography* (1993), which made the best-seller list and brought Norris national fame. In the interviews that followed on this acclaim, she speaks comfortably about her calling as a Christian writer. "The Benedictines, the farmers [of the South Dakota plains], the fact that I'm a writer, all of this comes together so easily in my life . . . . Poets love to draw disparate stuff together and play with it," she told the *Critic*.[9] And in a subsequent interview with *U.S. Catholic,* Norris names some of the poets other than herself "who are writing and identifying themselves as Christian poets": Scott Cairns, Andrew Hudgins, Anne Porter, and Levertov.[10]

By that time Levertov had been baptized into the Catholic Church and wrote comfortably as a Christian. Her own journey to becoming a Christian poet was quite different from Norris's. Levertov's father had been raised a Hasidic Jew in

Russia but while a university student in Germany had converted to Christianity. He married Beatrice Spooner-Jones, from Wales, and by the time Denise was born, they had settled in England and he had taken orders as an Anglican priest. So in Denise's background there was not only Christianity but also the special Hasidic sense of divine presence hidden in every particle of creation.

Yet during her early adulthood and the first decades of her development as an acclaimed poet, Levertov considered herself an agnostic—an agnostic, however, with a finely tuned sense of the transcendent present in everyday things and occurrences. Gradually she became "more and more occupied with questions of belief," as she put it in a 1990 essay, "Work That Enfaiths." Then something extraordinary happened during the writing of a poetic sequence called "Mass for the Day of St. Thomas Didymus" in 1979–80. As Levertov describes it in "Work That Enfaiths":

> The poem began as an experiment in structure. I had attended a choral recital from which the choir director had put together parts of Masses from many periods. . . . And I thought to myself that it might be possible to adapt this framework . . . to the creation of a poem. . . . I still considered myself an agnostic. I thought of the poem as "an agnostic Mass" (using the word Mass merely as a formal description) . . . , basing each part on what seemed its primal character: the Kyrie a cry for mercy, the Gloria a praise-song, the Credo an individual assertion, and so on: each a personal, secular meditation. But a few months later, when I had arrived at the Agnus Dei, I discovered myself to be in a different relationship to the material and to the liturgical form from that in which I had begun. The experience of writing the poem—that long swim through waters of unknown depth—had been also a conversion process.[11]

After this unexpected experience, Levertov delved deeper into Christian liturgy and tradition in her poetry. She adopted the fourteenth-century Christian mystic Julian of Norwich as mentor and wrote several poems meditating on her writings. In the mid-1980s, she began attending Emmanuel Episcopal Church in Boston but then was drawn toward the Roman Catholic Church, into which she was baptized in the early 1990s.

Levertov continued writing poetry that issued forth from her previous passions: the natural world, precious human relationships, political activism. But to these were now added poems exploring the Christian narrative and her practice of contemplative prayer. How to imagine the full mystery of the Incarnation continued to motivate her poetry, and she wrote several poems trying to get inside of Jesus's experience on earth: "Salvator Mundi: Via Crucis," "On Belief in the Physical Resurrection of Jesus," "Ikon: The Harrowing of Hell," and "Ascension" are among them.

Peggy Rosenthal

It's instructive to compare Levertov's "Ascension" with Norris's. Both begin by evoking the natural world's engagement in the miracle of an ascension, and both envision a simultaneous downward and upward push. Remember Norris's lines: "it wasn't just my sister's water breaking, / her crying out, / the downward draw of blood and bone . . ."; here is Levertov's first stanza:

> Stretching Himself as if again,
> through downpress of dust
> upward, soil giving way
> to the thread of white, that reaches
> for daylight, to open as green
> leaf that it is.

But while Norris connects her poem with the biblical account of Jesus's Ascension only by quoting as epigraph the angels' words in the book of Acts, addressed to the disciples who had just witnessed the event ("Why do you stand looking up toward heaven?"), Levertov's entire poem focuses on the experience of Jesus himself. She ponders how "arduous" it must have been for him to "relinquish . . . human cells, / molecules, five / senses" in order to return to eternity. And she likens Jesus's leaving the earth to his entering it at the Incarnation:

> He again
> Fathering Himself.
> Seed-case
> splitting,
> He again
> Mothering His birth:
> torture and bliss.[12]

Childbirth, intriguingly, plays a role in both poets' "Ascension." For Norris it is the core of the poem, the miracle of childbirth likened through title and epigraph to Jesus's Ascension; for Levertov it is almost the opposite, with childbirth as final image for the experience of Jesus.

The contrast holds true for much of the explicitly religious poetry of both poets. Levertov uses her poetic imagination to enter Gospel scenes or to explore her own religious experiences. Norris uses hers to evoke scenes of daily life—her own, her family's, the Benedictine monks'.

A fascinating meeting of their poetic minds is where both these poets come to see metaphor itself as "incarnational." Norris spoke about this in the interviews she gave in the mid-1990s. She told the *Critic* that "the Incarnation itself, it seems to me, is a metaphor in the sense that it yokes the human and the divine. That's what metaphor does; it's yoking two disparate elements."[13] She elaborated for *U.S. Catholic*: "I get in trouble when I refer to the Incarnation as the ultimate metaphor daring to yoke the human and the divine. To a literalist, I have just said that the Incarnation isn't real. As a poet, I think I have said that it *is* reality. It's alive; it is the new creation. So metaphor to me actually has a holy purpose. God made our minds to think metaphorically so that we would be able to live holy lives, to really accept the Incarnation of Jesus Christ. Most sensible people are afraid of metaphor. You can't control it; it is powerful, so it is scary."[14]

Levertov would have agreed, I think. Yet I'm not aware of her speaking about the topic in prose. Rather, in "The Showings: Lady Julian of Norwich, 1342–1416," she muses on Julian of Norwich's motive for desiring Christ's wounds in her own flesh:

> it's the desire to enact metaphor, for flesh to make known
> to intellect (as uttered song
> makes known to voice,
> as image to eye)
> make known in bone and breath
> (and not die) God's agony.[15]

Commenting on this passage in an issue of *Renascence* devoted to Levertov, critic Paul Lacey noted that for Levertov "the Incarnation, the supreme act of relinquishment, because it *enacts* God's promise, is also the supreme act of artistic creation. *Enacting* carries a great deal of power for her."[16]

This is why, I think, Levertov's friend Judith Dunbar, writing in tribute to Denise after her death, called the spirituality of her poetry "at once contemplative and prophetic."[17] Both contemplation and prophetic vision are forms of enacting. There is nothing passive about contemplative prayer, as Levertov knew. She never tired of composing poems that tried to find apt metaphors for her natural struggles in prayer. "Flickering Mind" plays with the metaphor of currents of water to dramatize her mind's restlessness when she tries to pray; "Sands of the Well" evokes the process of meditation in terms of grains of sand stirred up and then settling in a well; "'In Whom We Live and Move and Have Our Being'" imagines God as the air we "inhale, exhale, inhale" as we cower like fledging birds "in cliff-crevice or edge out gingerly / on branches close to the nest."[18]

Prophetic vision, too, is an enactment of the imaginative powers. Like the Hebrew prophets, who decried the injustices of their day in the light of God's call to righteousness, Levertov cried out in her poetry against the political outrages of her time. She was doing this long before her conversion to Christianity. After her conversion what was added to her prophetic vision was her repeated attempt to grasp with her imagination the Incarnation's meaning for our suffering world. "On a Theme from Julian's Chapter XX" (in *Breathing the Water*) explicitly probes this

Peggy Rosenthal

question. "Salvator Mundi: Via Crucis" (in *Evening Train*) then personalizes it, as the poem speculates on what "the burden of humanness" must have been for Christ:

> that He taste also the humiliation of dread,
> cold sweat of wanting to let the whole thing go,
> like any moral hero out of his depth,
> like anyone who has taken a step too far
> and wants herself back.

"Wants herself back": Levertov had experienced this dread many times in her political activism. And so, as the poem continues, she can imagine that "Incarnation's heaviest weight" must have been

> this sickened desire to renege,
> to step back from what He, Who was God,
> had promised Himself, and had entered
> time and flesh to enact.[19]

Contemplation and prophecy merge for Levertov in a poem such as "To Live in the Mercy of God" (in *Sands of the Well*), which reaches for metaphors that enact what a life fully trusting in God's mercy could be like. "Primary Wonder," in the same collection, continues this meditation, as do the "Psalm Fragments"—the last volume that Levertov published before her death.

Norris had sensed as early as that 1970s poetry reading that "in a way Denise was writing psalms for the contemporary age." And it's true that well before her conversion, Levertov occasionally drew on the Hebrew Psalter for inspiration (as in "City Psalm"). But after her conversion, many more of Levertov's poems have a psalmlike feel: that combination of praise, petition, unsettled questioning, and awe.

Norris has drawn on the Psalter as well. "Land of the Living" takes its title from Psalm 27. "What Song, Then?" plays with Psalm 137's image of singing God's praise on "alien soil," though Norris transposes the alien soil to her inner being. Like Levertov, and like the Psalter itself, Norris moves deep into her personal experience to speak of a hoped-for intimacy with the divine in the midst of life's trials.

It's interesting to note these similarities in the textures and inspiration of some of Levertov's and Norris's poetry. But what's most important, in my view, about the religious work of both is that it helped open the U.S. poetry establishment to religious experience as an acceptable subject. Through most of the twentieth century, the intellectual world was suspicious of religion, considering it outmoded and superstitious. Secularism was the reigning ideology. Talk of ultimate meanings was scoffed at, and major poets moved into ambiguity (Robert Frost) or solipsism (Wallace Stevens). Irony was the measure of a poem's value.

Many forces converged in the mid-1980s to change the intellectual establishment's attitude toward religious experience. Deconstruction, which was the reigning methodology, claimed that all systems of meaning were equally unreliable, hence putting religion on the same slippery footing as other belief systems. More positively a hunger in American culture for the spiritual was increasingly expressed by poets themselves. Each poet came to this through unique personal experience, as we've seen in the cases of Levertov and Norris. Yet as more and more major U.S. poets composed poems out of a religious sensibility free of ironic detachment, a critical mass was reached. By the early 1990s, the quarterly journal *Image* was launched, with its subtitle *A Journal of the Arts and Religion*. Levertov joined the *Image* editorial advisory board in 1994, as Norris did a few years later.

I'm not suggesting that Levertov and Norris were alone in bringing religious poetry back into favor. But they were among the major writers who led the way. Remember Norris saying of Levertov's poetry reading that she attended in the early 1970s: "Although I did not realize it at the time, Denise's reading was a milestone in my coming full circle, reclaiming my religious heritage even as I deepened my love for literature. After that night I could no longer see the two as mutually exclusive." Levertov opened for Norris a possibility of the convergence of poetry and religion, a possibility that both then opened to readers and other poets in the decade that followed.

At the end of "Work That Enfaiths," Levertov articulates the value that this convergence can have for the larger culture: "A poet speaking from within the Christian tradition and using traditional terms (though not necessarily upholding every orthodoxy) may have more resonance for our intellectual life than is supposed. The Incarnation, the Passion, the Resurrection—these words have some emotive power even for the most secular minds. Perhaps a contemporary poetry that incorporates old terms and old stories can help readers to re-appropriate significant parts of their own linguistic, emotional, cultural heritage, whether or not they share doctrinal adherences."[20]

Surely this is true of Norris's poetry. Take her "Body and Blood," the closing poem of her 2001 collection, *Journey*. The poem's speaker, "worn, spent, / torn with sorrow," is out walking in the early dawn light. "Stupid with worry," she pauses before a neighbor's "weedy hollyhock." And there:

> I hear the bumblebee
> before I spot him
> entering a blossom,
> his body quivering
> like an infant's mouth at the breast,
> drinking the milk of the world.[21]

Peggy Rosenthal

In the depths of her exhausted misery, she is able to see new life, fragile yet real. As in Norris's "Ascension," fragile new life is imaged as an infant nursing, and the Christian mystery of death and resurrection draws the poem to itself—subtly, only through the poem's title. Yet the title moves us to see incarnational wonder in the smallest events of daily life: a bumblebee entering a blossom. Here is a poet, as Levertov says, who is "speaking from within the Christian tradition" in words that open the tradition's "emotive power" for all readers, believers or not.

• DEAR, DEAR DENISE •

Fragments of a Mentor

Ben Sáenz

I

On September 26, 1989, Denise Levertov wrote me a letter—in longhand. She never typed her letters. She had just moved from her home in Massachusetts to a house she had bought in Seattle.

Dear, dear Ben,

What a pleasure to get your letter & Ms.! I had a few other commitments (plus a million irritating household things) to take care of before giving the poems my attention, but have done so. It's a fine book I think and have a couple of suggestions for publishers which I'll add at the end of this. I've also had a fine letter from Ann [another Stegner Fellow who was a mutual friend], and she told me about your almost getting killed [she is referring to a car accident]—for God's sake do take care, 2 scrapes are a warning—I think life does give one warnings, saying slow down or words to that effect, now and again. You have too much to do, to live and to give to be careless with yourself.

I crossed the states (with 2 drivers, people I know) in a 24-Ryder truck. It was a good adventure especially the Grand Tetons and Idaho. But my oldest close friend (I have one even older but not so close) died while I was in transit, so 3 days after I got here I flew to London to her funeral and spent a week with her brother who is an equally dear and close friend of mine.

So really I've only been here since the 8th when I returned, & I'm preoccupied with such things as a damp basement that needs fixing, windows I can't open and close, spiders (of which I'm mortally afraid—I have a pest control person coming day after tomorrow), need for more bookshelves, chimney sweep to see if my fireplace is safe, etc. etc. etc. However, the place is gorgeous. I've seen the eagles (1 of a pair) in the park a block away, I can see the lake (a bit) from my windows, and Mount Rainier comes and goes like the most beautiful of mirages, not quite visible from my house but superbly present from very close by. And people are really nice, both of my neighbors are black, & one is coming to tea tomorrow, Miss Juanita Alexander, isn't that a nice name. This week-end I go to Durango, Colorado to read and October 25th I leave for a month at Bellagio on Lago di Como where I have a fellowship—bad timing, just when I should be settling in, but one can't (or shouldn't) "look a gift horse in the mouth"! My local church is really racially diverse and I think I'll get properly connected to it. The lector turns out to be the brother of a SF writer who used to be a part of the scene when Jack Spicer had a coterie there—not a group I felt warmly towards, really, but the priest himself seems very nice. I'm thinking about formalizing my relation to the Catholic Church, what do you think? There are a whole lot of issues I (obviously) don't accept the official line on—but then nor do a lot of people within the church. It's a question of whether in the process of "ritualization" I would have to foreswear/perjure myself. . . .

There's a very nice publisher here, only a year old, called Broken Moon, which so far has mainly done Sam Hamill. It's 2 people doing it for love & with enthusiasm, supporting it by working at computer stuff— John Ellison and Lesley Link, Broken Moon Press PO Box 24585 WA 98124–0585.

I told them I'd be suggesting 2 or 3 people to them and they said they'd be glad to give their attention to anybody I suggested.

I'm having a hard time getting back to creative work—all these months of mundane preoccupations. Maybe Bellagio will help. . . .

The realizations about global warming, what it implies, are filling me with dread, & pain for Earth. Hard to think through, or about, & not despair. I don't feel one should pray for direct intervention, it is not playing fair—so one can only pray to be guided. . . . But I am not in despair, only anxious.

Much love,

Denise

She attached a business card from John Ellison and Lesley Link of Broken Moon Press and wrote on the card: "Ben—I read them a poem of yours when they were here. They would like to see your MSS. Send as soon as you can—it doesn't have to be in final shape."

Shortly after, I received the manuscript I had sent to her, and she had taken a great deal of care in going over my poems. She made remarks and offered critiques, and I remember reading her comments and thinking that the manuscript needed a great deal of work. To begin with I hated the working title: "Autobiographies of the Desert"—it was beyond awful. I was grateful for her generosity and decided not to send the manuscript to John and Lesley right away. I also asked Simone Di Piero to read it, and she, too, made some very helpful comments. Eventually I rewrote the manuscript, threw out the poems that Denise rightly felt were not working, added some new poems I had been writing over the summer, and came up with a new title: *Calendar of Dust.*

I can't remember if I sent the final manuscript to Denise before I sent it to Broken Moon Press. I do remember getting a phone call from John Ellison telling me they were publishing my book. Denise was thrilled for me, and she offered, of course, to write a blurb for the book. And her endorsement was very generous. I don't remember if it was Denise that first sent me a copy of it or if it was John. I do remember being very happy and grateful for her generosity.

I remember the spring day I got the book in the mail. I was living in Menlo Park in an apartment complex. The weather was awful—it was windy and rainy. I tore the package open, and there it was, my first book. I remember holding it, almost as if I couldn't believe it. I admit to being a sentimental man. I cry easily—a gift I inherited from my mother *and* from my father. There's nothing to be done about it. I remember reading Denise's blurb again and again on the back cover: "I salute the publication of a new poet whose work moves me and expands my life as poetry should."

The publication of *Calendar of Dust* in 1991 changed everything for me. That book was awarded an American Book Award by the Before Columbus Foundation and got the attention of the Lannan Foundation. In 1992 the Lannan Foundation contacted me and invited me to read from my book in their poetry garden in Los Angeles. The members of the board had gathered for their annual meeting—a fact I did not know anything about at the time. A few months later, I got a phone call, and I was informed that I had been awarded a Lannan Poetry Fellowship. On the list of fellows that year was a familiar name: Denise Levertov. Looking back, I'm almost ashamed of having been in her company.

II

Calendar of Dust was reviewed in the *Minneapolis Star Tribune* by a young man who had a great love for poetry. That young man's name was Michael Weigers, my current editor at Copper Canyon Press. Life is full of coincidences—if you believe in them. What else is there to believe in if you don't believe in fate or destiny or some kind of preordained plan? What I know is this: it was through Denise's intervention that I have a career as a writer and as poet. She quite literally helped to change the course of my life.

As I said, I'm a sentimental man—especially when it comes to matters regarding my mentors. I think about Denise and realize how much I loved her, how much I miss her, how much I still think about her. She was one of most complicated human beings I've ever encountered. I still have her in my head sometimes when I'm working on a poem. Even after all these years. I'm fairly certain that Denise would not have liked the work I have produced of late. I tell myself that she might have liked *Dreaming the End of War*. She would have liked the expression of my politics, and she would more than likely have appreciated the aesthetic expression. Maybe. Probably. But she would have hated much of *The Book of What Remains*. The aesthetic would have been all wrong to her. She believed in distilling, in paring down, in arriving at rhythm through the use of line breaks and the arrangement on the page. She was always looking for a kind of precision that was to be found in a minimalism that I have almost completely discarded. My aesthetic in *The Book of What Remains* would have sounded—to her ear—as nothing more than prose. I also think that she would have viewed me as having turned into some kind of emotional exhibitionist, a charge I certainly may be guilty of. Suffering over what she might have thought or said about my work is an interesting pastime for me. I am pained by that prospect—though I don't know why it should matter. *Why shouldn't it matter?* But the difficult fact remains that the respect of those who taught us always matters. And perhaps it should always matter. What are we without those who brought us into being? Isn't that what mentors do—bring us into being? They intervene, they share their knowledge, and, if we're lucky, they share their lives with us. Not to be in dialogue with them—even long after they're gone—seems a supreme act of ingratitude.

In fact Denise didn't like my second book of poems, *Dark and Perfect Angels*, nearly as much as she liked my first. My work was beginning to shift toward a different aesthetic. I was experimenting with longer lines and fragmented narratives in my longer poems. I remember when I was visiting her once I asked her point-blank if she thought my second book was as good as my first. I think she would have refrained from commenting had I not asked her. But once asked, she didn't hesitate. Denise didn't have it in her to lie about such things. She was honest to a fault—even when she wanted to spare your feelings. "No," she said simply. She did point to one poem, "El rio no sabe que se llama rio," and said, "This one." I think she was saying that if my work had to shift, I should let it shift in the direction of this poem. That particular poem had long lines, but it had music and rhythm in it—and had a politics she embraced and a humanity she understood. I think she very much liked the sensibility of the poem.

Still it disturbed me that she felt my work was weaker in my second book. We always like to think that we're progressing, that we're getting better, that each book will transcend the weaknesses of the previous one. That isn't always the case. But aren't we all the worst critics of our own work? But are our mentors the best critics?

All in all her critique of *Dark and Perfect Angels* was gentle enough. She thought I was less disciplined with my language. I got the feeling she would have liked it very much if I had let her see it first. Perhaps she would have liked for me to continue showing her my work before it was published. I don't know. I can't know. I do know that I was ready to write my own work without having anybody's input. I had to learn to be a poet and stop being a student.

But she wasn't harsh in her criticism. Mostly she shied away from discussing that book with me. I had so wanted to please her, to enter into her world as a kind of equal, but I don't know that it's possible to be an equal when it comes to our mentors. Our mentors always remain our mentors. And when they love and respect us, they don't want to hurt us. So we did a dance around my second book. That was the way it had to be between us. She wasn't going to offer me false praise, and she wasn't going to disapprove of me, either. And I couldn't apologize for poems I believed in. So we moved on to other topics much more important than my work.

It says a great deal about her influence over me that even after she's been dead for all these years, I still care what she would have thought about my work.

She's dead, and I still care.

No, no, she's not dead. Her voice is not extinct in my head—and it never will be.

III

I keep a picture of Denise in my office. I often stare at it. In the picture she and I and another poet, Ann Neelon, are marching at a protest in San Francisco. We are protesting against the first Gulf War. I am carrying a sign: "Poets for Peace." Denise is holding up a crucifix. The crucifix was mine—something I had hanging on my wall in my apartment. I'm not entirely sure why I thought it was appropriate for me to take a crucifix to a protest march. Probably the vestiges of my reading liberation theology while I was in the seminary. I like the fact that she was the one who carried the crucifix. In the end it was she who was the true believer and not me, the ex-priest.

In those days Denise seemed tireless to me. She was as vital a woman as I'd ever met. I was in awe of her energy and her optimism—though she had her moments when she felt that perhaps humankind wasn't ever going to evolve, as her letter to me attests. She was disciplined and stubborn, which made her a great poet and an interesting human being. She was probably one of the best-read intellectuals I've ever encountered. In her house in Seattle, her books stretched from one end of the

　　　　　　　　　　　　　　　　　　　　　　　Ben Sáenz

house to the other—all alphabetized. I admired her politics as much as I admired her work, or should I say, I admired the way she managed her politics and her writing. There is a real art to the negotiation between one's politics and one's poetry.

By example she helped me find my own way. By example I knew that everyone must, at one time or another, be fierce and unafraid, be true enough to oneself to risk alienating even the people you love. She was so tough, and she was also so, so soft. As I write this, this thought passes through my mind: *she was my mother's age.* But I never thought of her like that. I always thought of her as being young. *Because she was young.* I still have a memory of her in a pair of jeans, bounding up the steps to her house in Seattle. She wore the smile of a girl, and I tried her to imagine her as she had been.

IV

I first met Denise when she came to read in El Paso back in the spring of 1985. I remember her sitting with a group of graduate students at a restaurant that was situated literally on the border. She was gracious, attentive, articulate. She was, on that occasion, almost shy. She certainly didn't hold court—not on that particular day. She asked us questions. She wanted to know what our program was like. She asked us about our literary influences. There was something very girlish about her, and I'm not using the word in any pejorative sense. I suppose I mean that she somehow managed to keep her childhood curiosity. I thought she was charming.

When I first heard her speak, I was surprised by how English her diction was—though perhaps I shouldn't have been. I knew she was born in England, but having known her only through her work, I had always thought of her as being thoroughly American. To my ear she really did write in an American idiom. I don't know what I was expecting, but I wasn't expecting the Denise Levertov sitting across from me at the restaurant. I think all of us sitting at that table were a little starstruck. The occasion was a typical one that is reproduced all over the country each time a famous writer visits a university. Graduate students gather around the writer to absorb a piece of unearned wisdom. That was exactly what it was like that afternoon as we gathered around Denise as she spoke about poetry and asked questions. And yet there was something about her that was humble and generous. She wasn't superior or arrogant, refused the role that she could so easily have played.

I remember her asking me about the name of a particular desert bush. I could see her making a mental note. She thought it was important to know and be able to name the particulars of your physical environment. She insisted on being precise. She was always searching her brain for the right word. You could almost see her mind working.

She gave a memorable reading. Not all poets are good readers, but certainly she was. She read her "score" beautifully. Always. A few years later, in a workshop, she accused one of the students of committing "poem murder." She said something like this: "It's a perfectly fine poem, but you must learn how to read your own work." And then she read the poem aloud. And it was, as she said, a perfectly fine poem. She knew how to write a poem. And she knew how to read one.

I didn't know, at the time, that she would become one of my most important mentors and that we would become friends. I don't think the thought occurred to me. I was never one to insinuate myself to famous writers. I found that sort of thing embarrassing. The following year I went to the University of Iowa on a fellowship to study American literature. I hated Iowa. It was too cold and was too much the university town. I don't like places where everything centers on the university. The late Arturo Islas, another mentor of mine, urged me to apply for a Wallace Stegner Fellowship. I almost didn't. I didn't think that it was actually a possibility for me. Arturo badgered me into applying. God bless him. I sent in my application on December 31. I didn't think about it after that. No one was more surprised than me when I got a phone call one cold Iowa spring day, telling me that I had been selected as a Stegner Fellow in poetry.

I have no doubt that Denise had a big role in selecting me. She saw something in my very raw work. And it was very raw. I was a much better reader and critic than I was a writer at that point in my career. In fact, what career? What I had was something that Denise had. A hunger.

Denise was learning to play the piano when I met her, which may seem to be an insignificant detail in a life as full as she led. How many accomplished people have the patience to begin learning how to play a piano in their sixties? Through a group of friends that were politically involved at Stanford, I became a friend of Denise's piano teacher, Sarah Doniach. Sarah was a gifted pianist, and she only took on children as students. I think Sarah took Denise on in part because she admired Denise's work. But she also mentioned to me once that Denise possessed the wonder of a child—and because she possessed that quality, Sarah decided to make an exception for her. I don't know how good Denise got at playing the piano. I knew her to be stubborn at times, and one of her colleagues referred to her as being a "difficult woman." Denise could be difficult and stubborn—but those qualities are what helped her to survive. There are some people in this world who find it nearly impossible to compromise when they feel strongly about what is true. Denise was one of those people. That meant she could be absolute about certain things—things she felt very strongly about, her politics, her sense of aesthetics in a line break, her morality about what one should or should not write about.

She told me a story once about Robert Bly. At some conference Bly, in the most aggressive and public manner possible, told her, "Denise, stop terrorizing your students." I asked her, "And how did you respond, Denise?" She said, "Well, I cried." I don't know why I've always remembered that small anecdote. Perhaps because to many people, Denise appeared to be impervious to what anybody thought about her, but that was not my experience of her. She was personally always kind to me, always generous with her time and her resources.

IV

The Jacob's Ladder

> The stairway is not
> a thing of gleaming strands
> a radiant evanescence
> for angel's feet that only glance in their tread, and need not
> touch the stone.
>
> It is of stone.
> . . . .
>
> A stairway of sharp
> angles, solidly built.
> One sees that the angels must spring
> down from one step to the next, giving a little
> lift of the wings:
>
> and a man climbing
> must scrape his knees, and bring
> the grip of his hands into play. The cut stone
> consoles his groping feet. Wings brush past him.
> The poem ascends.[1]

Denise wrote "The Jacob's Ladder" in 1961. It is a poem I often go back to. I like to read it aloud. For me her poems insist on being read aloud. I can almost hear her reading them. I certainly picture her reading this precise and beautiful poem.

I never gave much thought to what drew me to "The Jacob's Ladder." But right now I'm thinking that this poem has everything to do with religious faith. Denise struggled with faith almost all of her life—but her struggle (even during her periods of agnosticism) was as a believer. In the end, as her letter to me predicted, she did formalize her relationship to the Catholic Church. I found her conversion completely consistent with the Denise Levertov I studied with at Stanford in the late 1980s. I always felt that one of the biggest reasons she and I became friends was the fact that I was a former Catholic priest. I think she found that to be an interesting and important part of who I was. I think she saw in my writing a religious sensibility, and she could see that my work was colored with my Catholic imagination.

But my journey has been opposite to Denise's journey. I suppose some people would say that I have lost my faith. From a certain perspective, I suppose that's true. But it isn't so much that I don't believe in God; it's that I've grown tired of religions and their claims to speak for God. Certainly I have lost my faith in Catholicism. It has taken me a lifetime to come to terms with my sexuality. Frankly it's difficult to belong to a church that hates you. And one other thing: the institutional church has turned its back on the poor and adopted a right-wing political stance. The church I grew up in was a "big tent" church that was big enough for the Left and the Right. The church has taken a large step toward the right—and I will have no part of it. I can have no part in it.

Not that I don't understand and respect why Denise became a Catholic. I can see in this poem her obsessions and the pure and distilled articulation of her faith, not only faith in the human journey toward God but also complete faith in poetry. In Denise's poem the graceful movements of the angels are contrasted with the human struggle to climb toward heaven—which is a difficult and physical labor. The entire movement of the poem hinges on the last line: "The poem ascends." The poem that ascends is the labor of the speaker. I admire the faith Denise had in the power of poetry. Her words may have been written with a doubtful sky in the background, but there is no irony here—nor is there any hint of doubt in the simple and elegant last line.

Last year I was looking through some of Denise's work and stumbled on her poem again. Maybe it wasn't an accident. I read the poem, and it made me smile, thinking of her. I wish I had heard her read that particular poem, but I never did. For some reason I was moved to write my own poem in response to hers. I wrote it as a tribute to her—though I wonder what she would think of it. I wonder how she would mark it up with comments if I presented it to her for a critique.

Jacob's Ladder

In memory of Denise Levertov

There are no angels on this ladder. Jacob,
always on a journey, addicted to his pilgrimage. Eyes
searching for God, always traveling through
the desert. If a holy man cannot find his God, he prefers
the solitude and cruelty of the burning sands. A holy man
is not interested in comfort. A holy man is not
interested in the talk of idle men. Offer him a piece
of bread but do not offer him coins. Offer him
water but do not offer him wine. Do not
offer him words.

Ben Sáenz

Jacob. He used a stone for a pillow
and dreamed. I have given up on holiness but I have *not yet*
given up on ladders. Sometimes, I picture a young man
sitting on a ladder, reading a book, the earth below him.
Maybe he is reading the Bible. But I doubt it. This is
my brain drawing the picture. I think it more certain
he is reading a book of poems or a strange story
by J. G. Ballard. I never know whether that young man
on that ladder is me. I try not to spend my time
on questions of identity. Those questions can never
be solved. And anyway I am no longer young—though
a young man still exists somewhere in the stubborn
corners of my body. The young man inside me
is an inoperable tumor and likes to laugh. He likes
to cry too. And read. He likes to climb on ladders.
He likes to ascend and then descend, traveling in between
the heavens and the earth. Maybe the young man
I picture sitting on the ladder is an angel. So the young
man can*not* possibly be me.

He must be Jacob as a young man.

I am staring at
one of Manuel Alvaro Bravo's photographs. Diego
Rivera is standing on a ladder. He is painting
a mural. For Rivera, a ladder is a tool. I do not believe
Rivera gave ladders much thought. He was not
the kind of man that appreciated the things
he stepped on. In another photograph, an old man
named Francisco is sitting on a ladder. Francisco
is a peasant. For him, a ladder is a place of rest.
In another, a ladder is leaning against the wall.
According to the title, the ladder is there *para
subir el cielo.* Richie Valens is singing that phrase
over and over in my head. The only thing we need
to reach the sky is a ladder. A good ladder
is made of wood. It is a resurrected tree. I like
to imagine that leaves can sprout from every step
of that good ladder. I see leaves everywhere.
Sometimes the sky is full of them. Leaves falling
to earth, floating, becoming birds, becoming
pages full of words, descending—but never

ascending. The Rabbi claims that the angels' descent
and ascent are dependent on his actions. If
he forgives, the angels will ascend. If he sins,
the angels will descend and live in exile on
the bitter ground. The Rabbi is arrogant. What
depends on what *I* do? I want words to ascend.
But do they? Can I will myself to climb the ladder?
Can I ask the young man living inside me to
help me climb? Can I order him *Climb! Climb! Climb!*

V

I just turned fifty-eight. I shouldn't need a mentor anymore. Isn't it my turn to be
a mentor? Isn't it my turn to teach others what has been taught to me? Isn't it my
turn to pass on my own legacy to an apprentice? Somehow I feel like I have so
much more to learn. Somehow I feel too inadequate to be a mentor.

There are days when I would like to talk to Denise again. I would like to show
her a poem. I would like to talk to her about faith and about poetry and the work
that it does in the world. I would like to talk to her about the state of the world and
its cruel politics.

Let me go back to the letter that Denise wrote to me. If you read the letter
with care, it contains all of her obsessions and preoccupations and opinions about
the world she lived in. She mentions concern for me after two car accidents in a
row. And she gently tells me to be careful. This was Denise—she cared about her
friends. She mentions her intentions to become a Catholic. In passing she mentions her lack of affinity for Jack Spicer and his "coterie." She always had something
to say about literary movements and writers she had encounters with. Denise had
her share of disagreements with other literary figures. She was a writer with definite opinions. She could be argumentative. But she was fully engaged, and she
could never disengage. She cared too much. I think her greatness lay in her caring.
She didn't know how not to care. Yes, she fought with people. There's a long list of
literary figures with whom Denise had strong disagreements. But she didn't disengage. Not ever.

I think she showed her care for the world through her work, through her
poetry, through her commitment to articulating her craft to others. I no longer
share Denise's aesthetics. I don't have her faith in Catholicism, and I certainly don't
share her belief that "the poem ascends." For me poetry is work. *Climb! Climb!
Climb!* I have to tell myself to keep going, to keep writing—even if I don't believe
anything I write will ever have any influence in the material world I live in. I wonder sometimes what keeps me writing. It saddens me that I don't have Denise's
profound faith in the power of poetry. I think it would sadden her, too. Just as my

Ben Sáenz

lack of faith in Catholicism would sadden my mother, who died in February 2012. My mother was born in 1929, not long after Denise.

I thought of Denise at my mother's funeral. I remember thinking that she would have liked my mother. And certainly my mother would have liked her. It's a painful thing to lose the people who loved and nurtured you. We receive nurture and support in many different and distinct forums. My mother nurtured me in all the ways we think a mother should nurture a son. Denise nurtured me in the ways that a mentor should. She once accused herself of being a bad mother. I thought she was being too hard on herself. To my mind she had all the attributes of being a good mother. She cared enough to tell you the truth. She was fierce in her loyalty, and she was affectionate. She was disciplined, and, more than this, she expected her students to be disciplined as well. She understood all too well that undisciplined people were unhappy people. Denise confessed to me once that she was disappointed in matters of love. She might have been, at times, disappointed. But she never lived her life in despair. On the contrary she lived her life in with a rare and genuine optimism.

I hope I share that optimism—despite myself.

When Denise died, Rose Catacalos, a former Stegner Fellow and also a friend of hers, called me on the phone and told me: "She's gone. Denise. She's gone." I remember going to my office and grabbing one of her books and holding it in my arms. I wept like a boy. In my third book of poems, I included a poem I wrote for her:

"Denise Levertov, poet and political activist, dies at 74"

> That was the headline
> in the obits in
> *The New York Times.* December.
> A good month to die.
> '97 was a warm winter
> on the border. Was it cold
> in Seattle?
>
> It was night
> when Rose called.
> I couldn't talk.
> I picked up your last
> book. I held it
> in my hands. I stared
> at your poems. That night
> they were just words.

Poetry can praise, can dispense
wisdom, can console. Denise,
there are times that
words are shallow—
to utter them is to
insult the dead. And
to insult the living too.

I couldn't talk.
*
I had a dream.
        I heard a voice:

When you are hungry
        that is when you know food.
When you are thirsty
        that is when you know water.
When you are dead
        that is when you know death.

I woke and asked
        When do you know God?
*
Did poetry matter in the end?
*
What was the last question you asked?
*
You were as old as my mother. I never
thought of you that way.
*
I see you riding a bike.
I see you looking into my
face, explaining something
urgent. You are trying to make
me understand. You think
I am being stubborn. I think
you are being stubborn. I see
you climbing the steps to
your house. You are surrounded
by flowers. You know the name
of each of them, know which

Ben Sáenz

seasons they will bloom. You turn
and point at a heron on the lake.
I am walking next to you
at a march. I turn and read
the sign you hold. The words
become a poem and you are
reading it. I see your hands
moving across the keys
of a piano. Never
enough music, books, rain.
*

I don't remember if I thanked you
in the end. For what you gave.
*

Denise, you believed
in politics and art
and poetry and God,
you who became Catholic
in the end, tell me
that death is not
a bitter thing. There
has been enough loneliness
and rage in the living.
Tell me we are done with that.

Tell me the poor were saved.
Tell me the poor were saved.[2]

I don't remember writing that poem. I look at it now, and I grieve again for what
I have lost, for what she meant to me. I would not be the poet I am today were it
not for her. I may be many things, but I'm no ingrate. I am happy to tell anyone
who will listen that Denise Levertov changed my life, and that change was all to the
good. She will never be dead to me. She still makes me want to be a better poet. She
still makes me want to be a better man. *The poem ascends. Climb! Climb! Climb!*

• DEAR BEN, DEAR DENISE . . . •

A Lament and a Praise

Alison Hawthorne Deming

I

In 1965, one year out of high school, I was living in Cambridge, Massachusetts. Denise Levertov then was living nearby in Somerville. She was a fixture in the Cambridge antiwar and antinuclear movements. Her poems were everywhere. And so was she at protests and demonstrations. I was beginning, through her example, to feel poetry as an expansive force for social good. I had known it before this time as the music of intense and private emotion. T. S. Eliot. Sylvia Plath. Anne Sexton. Robert Lowell. Poems wrung from mindful anguish and emotional privation. As a teenage mother and college dropout—not the script written for me by my blueblood New England family—I was starving for affirmation, not only for myself but also for a culture that seemed to be plotting itself toward doom. Starving to know how to stay alive and inhabit the choices I'd made for myself and my infant daughter. To find a community of belonging and safety. Dumbfounded. The 1960s. Things were breaking right and left. Patriotism meant war. Political speak. Sexual decodification. Stanzas (those rooms that poems inhabit) and living arrangements teetering. I was reading Adrienne Rich and Denise Levertov. I loved them both for taking their activism from the street to the page and from the page to the street.

I was hanging out in coffeehouses with my notebook. I wanted artists and intellectuals to see me as one of their own. Where did I get the idea that this was a place I belonged? Perhaps from a Jules Feiffer comic: bohemians in Greenwich Village making a joke and a culture of their artistic appetite. In truth I'd grown up in a family that treasured the arts and in which women were as deeply engaged in producing art as were men. My mother was a playwright, my great-aunt an impressionist painter, my grandmother a haute couture dressmaker, and I was a student of classical piano, modern dance, Latin poetry, and acting. Still, as a young adult, I was looking for evidence to tell me what it might mean to be a woman and an intellectual, to live in and for books, and for such a life to matter within the anguish of history and politics. Would I have thought of myself as a poet?

Certainly not. Though I had a hunger to dignify the inner life and knew by intuition and family history that art was its banquet table. I studied modern dance at the New England Conservatory, I worked at the Fogg Art Museum, I went to concerts and plays at Harvard and Brandeis, took Harvard Extension courses: Art and Literature of the Renaissance, The Art and Religion of Japan, Dante's *Divine Comedy*. I skirted the edges of the political upheaval and sought the avant-garde in art. I did not believe in violent revolution. I hated war and the self-righteous rhetoric of a leftist friend who was learning to make bombs in order to dismantle the war machine. I hated injustice and traditions that kept unfairness embedded in the American way. I wanted art to lift me out of the mire of the times.

Levertov wrote in one of her "Entr'acte" poems that the real singing would begin when the rhythms of revolution and poetry meshed. I don't know what she meant by that. She had a romantic relationship with revolution. I feared it. She writes:

> And I
> know such violent
>
> revolution has ached
> my marrow bones, my
>
> cracked heart tolling
> such songs of
>
> unknown morning-star
> ecstatic anguish, the clamor
>
> of unquenched desire's
> radiant decibels shattering
>
> the patient wineglasses
> set out by private history's ignorant
>
> quiet hands,—.[1]

Still I saw her, through her poems, as having a political courage that I lacked, a great heart for the world that was braver than mine. Her poems claimed that politics and art were one, when I had felt that art was a refuge from the political, an alternative way. Her sensibility came to apply not only to her treatment of the war and nuclear threat, but also to her intimate relationships, as defined in poems such as "The Ache of Marriage" and "The Woman Alone." The poem was a means to the end of being mindful of the terms of one's existence and historical time. "O taste and see," she invoked, countering William Wordsworth's exhortation with her own: "The world is not with us enough." Yes, poetry should help us to taste and see, should take on political material with aesthetic intent, should be "a record of the night," that spiritual unknowing that makes us hunger, and poetry should guide us to

> Praise
> god or the gods, the unknown,
> that which imagined us, which stays
> our hand,
> our murderous hand,
> and gives us
> still,
> in the shadow of death
> our daily life,
> and the dream still
> of goodwill, of peace on earth.[2]

Perhaps my adulation of Levertov's work through my twenties and thirties was a set-up for a reality check. William Butler Yeats wrote that a poet "is never the bundle of accidents and incoherence that sits down to breakfast."[3] I think as young poets seeking role models we yearn for poets to embody the emotions and values contained in their poems. Is it fair or even sensible to ask that the poet be the poem? Or is the poem by its nature a transcendence of the limitations of character? Are the limitations of character what drive us to become poets? Levertov's poetry changed my life by bringing aesthetic aspiration into alignment with the longing for peace and social justice. My personal associations with her, however, were vexed with chilly tensions, the great heart for the world that she demonstrated on the page and as a public artist and intellectual a matter of literary persona more than of personality.

After Cambridge I moved to northern Vermont, where I lived from 1969 to 1979 as an urban refugee following the hope for cultural renewal in a rural place. If the culture was poisoned by its appetite for violence, maybe, I thought, the antidote lay in nature. It seems now an ill-conceived aspiration—trying to leave one's culture behind—though perhaps not unlike what the Chinese poets of the mountains-and-rivers tradition practiced for centuries, leaving the corruptions of politics and commercialism for a simpler way. Vermont seemed a healthy place to raise my daughter, where our poverty was received in a neighborly context and sustenance came from the land. I kept reading and writing. I was all about aspiration, some hunger that drove me beyond the need to make a living, attend to

Alison Hawthorne Deming

family responsibility, and seek romantic love—though I did all of these things. Yet the sense of artistic purpose, a calling that had to do with repair of both self and culture, was strong. That sense of purpose drove me deeper into language as a means to explore the experiences of my life (to paraphrase Levertov). I became involved with the small-press group Poets Mimeo Cooperative in Burlington and studied the Black Mountain poets and the San Francisco Renaissance. Levertov was the most prominent woman of accomplishment informing those movements. Her poems and essays were the touchstone for my growth as a poet through her articulation of principles of organic form and her enactment of them on the page. In Levertov the poem scored movements of mind freely with a line that took white space seriously and form as a "revelation of content."[4]

In 1980 I returned to school to work on a low-residency MFA at Vermont College. I was writing strange and derivative poems—open-field poems, surrealism, cut-ups, lyric gestural drawings. I distrusted narrative and received form. I hadn't thought much about meditative poetry as a mode, though that's where I was headed, on the heels of Levertov, a meditative poetry grounded in personal and cultural history. Carl Rosenstock, a poet with a deep historical imagination, was a close friend in grad school. He was writing dense poems informed by literary and historical research. He'd made a stab at a piece titled "Letter to Nathaniel Hawthorne," but it never got off the ground. Carl knew of my familial relationship to the author (he was my great-great-grandfather on my father's side) and gave me his research notes and false starts. "Maybe you can do something with this," he said. I'd always felt the anxiety of influence about my literary aspirations, wondering if they were really mine or simply the echo of claims I'd heard since early childhood about the importance of this lineage. It seemed presumptuous to try for literary expression when the bar had been set so high by my own ancestor. Carl's gift catalyzed my interest in digging into this history and interrogating how family history had informed my ancestor and how it might inform me. I sent the poem off to *Nimrod*'s Pablo Neruda Prize, heartened that Levertov was the judge that year. I must have felt that my near-twenty-year apprenticeship to her work would shepherd the poem into her fold.

The poem won the Neruda Prize—and I think it was the sense of history that Levertov admired in the piece, so much lyric poetry eschewing the longer view for the sake of expanding the present moment. I was invited to fly to Tulsa for an award ceremony and writers' conference. I'd hardly flown in a plane. I was phobic about flying. The few times I'd flown were panic trips with death sitting on my shoulder chiding me for taking such a risk with my precious life. I required magical thinking to get on a plane. Surround yourself with white light, I'd tell myself, only to fantasize the white light becoming an explosion. I made my flight reservations and called Fran Ringold, then editor at *Nimrod*. "Oh, great," she said. "You're on the same flight with Denise. Maybe you can get acquainted on the plane!" I was flying.

When I arrived at the gate, I scanned the seats, thinking I could at least shake Levertov's hand and thank her before boarding the plane. She was not there. I waited and waited. The last minute to board arrived. I asked the gate agent if Denise Levertov had checked in. "Yes," she said; "are you traveling with her?" "Yes," I said. "Would you like to sit with her?" This was 1984, clearly a more casual time in the airline business than today. Why not? Yes, I said, magically thinking I would fly under her protection.

It turned out to have been the wrong answer, but how could I have known? I felt connected to the poet through her work. And now through the Nimrod contest, my work had spoken to her. Surely she would want to meet and talk and share the excitement of artistic kinship. I boarded the plane, saw the empty seat and Levertov reading. I sat down and introduced myself. She looked up. "Oh," an icy surprise. "Well, I had other plans," and buried her face in a book. She made an enduring nimbus around herself for the flight, and when we landed for our layover rushed to the exit. As I boarded the connecting flight, I spotted her in her seat spotting me heading her way. She gathered her things and fled to an unassigned seat. How had I managed to so offend her?

At the award ceremony she praised the poem and the importance of its engagement with history. We sat together on a panel. She dismissed or refuted anything I had the temerity to say.

My brain spun as it had in childhood when treated dismissively. I blamed myself for having been brash on the flight, but given some decades of perspective, I know her lack of civility had more to do with Levertov's inner weather, or perhaps personal circumstances of that time in her life of which I was unaware, than my undue enthusiasm.

Five years later I won a Stegner Fellowship to Stanford and sat in her workshop in the winter quarter. I hoped this would be a time when I could bridge the distance and learn from her. She had a knack for curt and dismissive criticism. And with certain of the fellows—especially Dean Young—a genuine antipathy. I got along. I had decided to be tough enough to learn what I could from her. Some of the younger workshop participants—the most doelike of women— would be reduced some days to tears. Levertov did not understand either the hostility or the woundedness among her students. There was no mending of ways afterward. Her pronouncements were just that and not facilitation of craft discussion. I lingered after a particularly bumpy workshop session. She asked me why so-and-so had been upset. I said I didn't think she understood how vulnerable a person can feel putting her poems up for criticism before a roomful strangers. Some might say that a writer had to be tough and get past that vulnerability. I remember the words of John L'Heureux, then director of the Stanford program: "Art is difficult and rare and ought to be surrounded by a wall of fire." Understood, though that has not become my pedagogical style. Levertov said she'd never taken a workshop. Had studied nursing and ballet while growing up in England. Understood.

I remember putting up a poem called "The History of Marriage," in which I'd tried to tell the story of my maternal grandmother's two marriages: first an arranged one when she was nineteen years old, marrying a Cubano and moving to Mexico City, and the second, after her first husband died of tuberculosis and she returned to New York City to run her mother's dressmaking salon, to a civil servant who abandoned her shortly after their daughter was born. The importance of history. The poem was written in a roughly stanzaic form. Unrhymed and unmetered. Overburdened with information. Denise said, "I don't believe in poems like this." End of discussion. We all moved on. It was a fundamentalist dismissal. What precisely did she not believe in? The stanzaic form? The clutter of detail? The attempt at psychologizing the grandmother? Was the language too flat? A linearity of mind? Any and all of that may have had to do with the poem's weakness. Its lines surely were wooden, its music stunted by intention. But what might have been a pedagogical moment became nothing but a rebuff. I still can't stop wondering what she saw or did not see. The poem never came back to life for me.

I say this for the record, because poets' lives matter and because the mystery of person versus persona in the poet is a grand one. I say this with no intention to disrespect a poet whose accomplishment matters to twentieth-century poetry and poetics. I remain grateful for her support of my work and the generosities she showed in selecting it for the Nimrod and the Stegner, generosities that made a real difference to me as a poet coming up.

I admit I envy the warm relationship Benjamin Sáenz describes having with Levertov, and I did see the kittenish side that Ben describes. She had a childish sweetness, an innocent quality—that gap-toothed openness—that seemed strange in contrast to her more autocratic teaching style. At the end of the quarter, she made herself available for a full manuscript critique. I thought I'd be a fool not to take her up on it, though I dreaded it like a visit to the dentist. She invited me to her apartment—a little place on campus for visiting faculty. She had an upright piano there that she'd rented, as she was taking classical piano lessons. Otherwise the place was quite stark and lacking in domesticity—temporary quarters for the academic quarter. She made us dinner—a little precooked supermarket chicken, potatoes baked in the toaster oven, and I suppose there may have been some supermarket salad. Plenty of wine. She seemed a bit embarrassed, a bit cute and coy about the meal. We ate and drank and went page by page through the manuscript. Somewhere I have the notes from that session. What did she say? Few comments of a specific craft nature, more suggesting the poems she thought strongest. Little stays in my mind from that evening, other than her warmth, the awkward sweetness with which she welcomed me into the privacy of her evening as I sat by her side and savored the moments during which she treated me like a real poet.

"Stop terrorizing your students," Bly told her. But I want to believe she didn't see it, and so she could not stop. In "Looking for the Devil Poems," with its epigraph "Tell Denise to write about the devil," she wrote:

> Tell Sam
> it is (perhaps) the devil
> made me so goddamned strong
>
> that I have made myself
> (almost)
> numb,
> almost unable
> to feel in me
> (for now)
> the beautiful outreaching of desire.
>
> And tell him
> it is perhaps the devil
> inserted these parenthetical
> qualifications.[5]

I knew that numbness in her, and I understand now that the poet is not the poem. That what one sees in a poem (in one's own poem) may be impossible to see in one's daily actions and interactions. That a poem may embody a great heart for the world, but the poet may be aloof from that world. And poets must be forgiven for this. We write not only out of aspiration but out of limitation. And through the poems, perhaps, we rise into the world better than ourselves.

In the early 1990s, when I was working as director of the University of Arizona Poetry Center, I invited Denise to come to campus for a reading. *Evening Train* had just come out, a book of the quiet poems of spiritual direction that she wrote in her last years while living in Seattle. We had a wonderful time reminiscing and bitching about Stanford and people in our workshop. She wanted to see the desert, so we took a long drive out past the cotton fields in Eloy. The crop had been harvested, and great bales of cotton the size of semitrailers were perched beside the road. She was amazed that this was cotton and wanted to see the plant. We stopped and picked up a few pods, the cotton puff erupting out of the stiffened, dry petals. She carried one of these in her hands all the way back to Tucson, fiddling with the raw cotton puff as it expanded in leaving the pod. We shared a moment of wonder over something so complicated as cotton, its history intimately chained to that of slavery in the United States, reduced to the simplicity of natural object, an invitation to poetic image.

Alison Hawthorne Deming

After that visit I had a phone call with Ben, who'd been in touch with Denise. We were friends from Stegner days. "How was your visit in Tucson?" he'd asked Denise. "Oh, wonderful. I had a great time with Alison. I don't know why we never became friends when she was at Stanford." Ben and I had a good laugh. Despite his friendship with her, he was not blind to the rougher edges of her character.

I keep that cotton boll still on its stem, in an old ink bottle beside my desk, and have for twenty years. So there it is, forty years of adulation, apprenticeship, wounding, love, and gratitude to a master whose memory I hope to honor with these words.

A poet is best honored by the sustainability of her work. Does it continue? Does it feed work that comes after? Levertov is among a cadre of the most influential poets of the age, fusing open-field poetics with political urgency and spiritual quest. Ben Sáenz is of a new generation of poets, a citizen of the borderland shaped by the violence, anguish, and aspiration of the region. His politics have grown not out of ideology but out of his experience of the "bullets and deserts and borders" of his homeland, as he writes in "The Fifth Dream" of his book *Dreaming the End of War.* While tuned to the anguish of terrorism, domestic and global, his great reckoning is with the invisible war against immigrants in the Southwest. He lives with a sense of brokenness—his Mexican father laboring on and losing a farm, Ben's "rows and rows of books" owned now as a man juxtaposed with the "rows of crops" he knew as a kid, his sense of being lost in a homeland where his thirteen-year-old niece was "shot in the back of the head, executed / in some barbaric ritual." What are the moral and psychological consequences for a man who as a boy was raised to blow up anthills and shoot birds out of the sky, as he reports of his American childhood? What are the consequences for this man who would be a pacifist? The consequences are to live in a borderland of mind and spirit as well as of geography and to make of that inner conflict a redemptive art.

In "The Twelfth and Final Dream" of *Dreaming the End of War,* Sáenz writes: "I want to cross the river, but I know / I cannot swim—will drown trying / To reach that holy place."[6] The river is the Rio Grande and the Styx, and his loved ones call to him from the other side. The river is all that divides and defines him—anguish and aspiration, priesthood and secular life, straight and gay identity, Mexican and American identity, rage and the will for peace, man of the soil and man of the book, dreamer of nightmares and daydreams, student of the art of living and the art of writing, all of which lie closely together in his heart. I have written that Levertov had a great heart for the world that was realized in her poems. She hungered for a poetry that brought more world into consciousness, as she wrote in "O Taste and See," "The world is not / with us enough." There is plenty of world in Sáenz's life and lines, too much world for either poem or heart to contain. "Though I can take a word and make it rhyme, / I cannot shove the world into a couplet."

He has made his neighborhood show itself: "We have been fighting a war on this border / For hundreds of years. We have been fighting the war so long / That the war has become invisible as the desert sands we / Trample on."

> Nothing in the desert is
> Tame. Not the people, not the sand, not the winds, not
> The sun, not even the river that resembles a large ditch,
> That's laughed at by visitors and locals alike. Nothing
> In the desert has ever had anything resembling mercy
> On Mexicans attempting to leave their land, to become
> Something they weren't meant to be.

The poet is that becoming, however, enacting a sense of citizenship on the land and among the creatures of the land, harboring an allegiance to an impossible ideal:

> All the beautiful words destroy one another, until there is only
> One word left standing, *Resurrection*. The word sounds like
>
> The last column holding up the Acropolis, the name for the last
> Shovel digging up the dead: *wake, breathe, live.* But I know this is
>
> A dream that will never come to pass.[7]

The reverie of the poem holds as real—real as a shovel!—the idea of resurrection after faith in the idea has passed. This dance within one's own contradictions is what we are, and poems that can reveal and even revel in the struggle, both political and inward, enable us to rise, if not to transcend, in order to see and make seen what we are. Yes, Ben, the poem ascends.

• DEAR DENISE •

Al Young

Dear Angela [Yvonne Davis],
. . . Should you run into Yvonne, tell her that I love her also and equally. Tell her that I want to see her, up close. Tell her I'm not a possessive cat, never demanding, always cool, never get upset until my (our) face and freedom get involved. But make her understand that I want to hold her (chains and all) and run my tongue in that little gap between her two front teeth. (That should make her smile.)
(*Soledad Brother: The Prison Letters of George Jackson*, 1970)

Dear Denise,

Like me, you had a tooth-sweet gap. We loved each other's gaps. Sometimes it's stories we tell one another that bind us, that fill in gaps. One aunt used to call me the Howdy Doody Boy. The generation that grew up watching Buffalo Bob and Howdy Doody on early 1950s black-and-white TV is vanishing fast. You didn't get over here to America until 1948. I was nine. Your generation, my mother's generation, related to people and events long faded, snowed under, or lost to their children and grandchildren. Until I looked mindfully at my mother's birthday, I didn't realize how much I'd lost track of you in calendar time. You felt so close always to my own generation.

Generation—yes, that was certainly a byword of the Eisenhower era that grew and shaped me. *Generation*—this was the name, too, of the University of Michigan's campus inter-arts magazine and literary journal I coedited with Ann Doniger in the late 1950s. While my quiet circle of rebels strained hard to be cool, the temperature of the U.S.-Soviet Cold War was dropping from chilly to glacial. Sooner or later, we knew, one side was going to drop the Bomb. To keep hip, we lived to the hilt but outside the mainstream. Thayer Bice, one of our hip classmates, found work in a New York ad agency. Word has it that she coined the phrase "Pepsi Generation," as in the unduckable jingle: "Come aliiiiiive! / You're in / the Pepsi Generation!" It wouldn't be long before we could recognize the umbilicus that linked

Madison Avenue marketing to what we'd only seen as soul space. We thought we were underground. We thought we were what later came to be called off the grid. Eventually Salem cigarettes usurped the notorious image of Black Panther Huey Newton plopped in a fan-backed wicker chair, clutching a rifle at one side and a spear at the other. Salem's replacement for Huey was a bourgeois hippie with longish hair and an Ernie Kovacs mustache.

To make a new life over here with your Harvard-anointed American GI husband, Mitchell Goodman, you migrated from Britain to America. My family, like millions of others, migrated from the South to find work. My father, a World War II navy vet, settled us in Detroit, where he found work and labored for the rest of his life on the assembly line at General Motors' Chevrolet division. In the late 1940s, we moved into a neighborhood that was largely Jewish and working-class: Pingree near Twelfth, long before Twelfth Street was renamed Rosa Parks Boulevard.

A fool since age three for anything readable, I loved to nurse a lemon phosphate or loiter at the corner drugstore news and magazine rack and leaf through *Life, Look, Quick* (from which *Jet,* the popular African American pocket-sized magazine, borrowed its format), *Reader's Digest, Coronet, Saturday Evening Post, National Geographic,* and the *Police Gazette,* which always ran cover stories about Adolf Hitler's still being alive and hiding out in South America. Along with those I read *the Daily Worker,* the *National Guardian,* and *Mainstream,* the cultural voice of the Communist Party USA. At age eleven you went around London door-to-door, pushing the *Daily Worker* over there.

When I shared with Mother some of the radical viewpoints I'd picked up from my drugstore reading, she squeezed my shoulder, smiled, and said: "Every bit of what you're telling me is true, old boy, but you need to keep that to yourself, hear?" Like you, Denise, I've always stood for the underdog: the poor, the working poor, which currently covers much of our global 99 percent: the alienated, the excluded, the excommunicated, the voiceless, the helpless. Growing up in the inglorious McCarthy era, I observed and experienced firsthand the bitter, dark heart of U.S. politics.

By the time I got to Ann Arbor, in 1957, to study at the University of Michigan, my social views and opinions were such that they prompted the freshman English teaching assistant to ask me not to come to class. "You'll get an 'A,'" he told me. "I'll post the assignments. You write the papers and slip them under my office door. I have a wife and new baby, and I like this job. I just can't afford to have you bring up certain subjects in class." Poor guy. He told me all this in deep winter, on a walk around the Diag, the womb-center of campus. He presumed his office was wired. This was the glacial hello to higher learning given me in the inquisitional McCarthy era.

One decade later, tuned to *The Dick Cavett Show,* I watched the mother of Ronnie Dyson—a black, barely teenaged, one-hit singing star—speak live on-screen to celebrity anthropologist Margaret Mead. "Dr. Margaret," Mrs. Dyson said, "you were talking about the generation gap. I just want you to know I don't believe in no generation gap. When this boy of mine gets out of line, I just reach over and bop him one. See, this closes up that gap."

Gaps, like old-fashioned movie film frames, make, break and hold us together. I couldn't even begin to fill the gaps in our living friendship. This very letter, which already quivers to go its own way, I mostly write to see if our respective approaches to the mystical still mesh. Hasidic Judaism, like Islamic Sufism, like Gnostic Christianity, like Buddhism, like Jnana Yoga all fit together in ways that orthodox religious doctrines do not. I always thought you inherited your mysticism from the preachments and teachings of your father, the rabbi; a Russian-born Hasidic Jew who converted to Anglicanism. I picture you and your big sister, Olga, camped out on stuffed chairs and upholstered sofas in the library of your five-bedroom family home in Essex; watched over by proper, groaning bookshelves. If your mother isn't reading to you, your father is.

Whenever I think of you, the question of your homeschooling revisits me. While it is fashionable now, especially in the United States, home schooling must have been controversial in your native London. When I read that you were mostly home-taught and self-taught, it made me feel good, since I've always known that artists, writers especially, school themselves and never stop. Heroically Kenneth Rexroth, your one-time mentor, editor, and wannabe lover, was the autodidact's autodidact—and he never let us forget it.

What better way to acquire, experience, or reflect on a classical education? I always loved the highways and back roads our conversations traveled. All those turns and twists and no-detours personified our quiet, mostly joyful rapport. We've even talked about this. A major in liberal arts at Michigan, I still welcome opportunities to take what I've learned from one discipline and apply it to another. How might botany shed light on the intellectual history of medieval Europe? What does math have to do with anthropology? How does Russian differ from Spanish or Portuguese? How do folklore and Buddhism mix and match? After Sputnik got launched, this kind of education fizzled. The narrowed concern and outlook of specialization rolled in on the liberal arts like Soviet tanks in Hungary or Yankee U-2 planes over Russia. We agreed that specialists are killing us. What our species needs to survive are generalists: visionaries skilled in the arts of synthesis. Poets, among others. Early on, you fell in love with Samuel Taylor Coleridge, Lord Byron, the Shelleys, John Keats, and those poets we still group as the Romantics. You grounded yourself, too, in Victorian and contemporary lit, leaving few gaps unfilled.

I come from deep-down religious people who, with the delightful exception of Mother, steered clear of the Eastern meditation and yogic adventuring I took up in 1964 following a blissful encounter in April of that year with a Berkeley motorist. He responded to me, a carless hitchhiker, by taking me to where I needed to go and, with a handshake, treating me to a feast of *shaktipat,* a gracious awakening kundalini energy that kept me spiritually high and alert for weeks. I told you about it, then wrote it up in "I'll Remember April," the opening piece in *Things Ain't What They Used to Be* (1986), the third volume of my musical memoirs.

My mother, Mary Campbell, testing out one church after another (Baptist, Methodist, Congregationalist) in her lifetime, was drawn to the writings of Mary Baker Eddy. She ended up a Christian Scientist. At the hospital clinic in Mexico, where she'd gone for late-cancer laetrile treatments, she told me during one of my visits: "Here you are looking for God all over in India and the rest of the world. Don't you know I'm the one led you there? I always knew there was something better than all this crying and moaning and carrying on the Baptists do."

Nothing was changed, all was revealed otherwise; not that horror was not, not that the killings did not continue, not that I thought there was to be no more despair, but that as if transparent all disclosed an otherness that was blessed, that was bliss. As you wrote in "City Psalm," "I saw Paradise in the dust of the street." Back then, when we met—1966, 1967, 1968, 1969, on up through the 1970s, when the much misread '60s really took off, you and I still smoked. Once I started noticing flakes of tobacco entombed in the envelope seals of letters you sent, my heartbeat doubled. "Wow!" I thought. "This is where Denise took time to lick the glue. Am I the lucky one, or what?" The look of you, remembered from photographs, lit up the sky that shone and moved between the leaves of the trees your poems made. You floated into my heart and never took leave.

Just telling you this eases me back to a time when people actually wrote one another, spoke to one another in real time, and, between conversations, thought about each other. I was just entering the heartfelt, heady galaxy of poetry. You were one of its stars. One thing I'm going to have to get straight: the afternoon in Boston when several of us—you, Mitchell, Nick, and a couple of other guests—were gathered in your living room. I'm trying to remember the setup and sequence. The writer Tillie Olsen either knocked at your door directly, or someone walked out to see who was ringing your doorbell. In any case when you heard who was calling on you unannounced, you freaked. You were convinced that Tillie was an agent, an informer, a spy who worked for the FBI.

I knew Tillie from Stanford, where she, the author of *Tell Me a Riddle,* was regarded as a worrisome writer celebrity, a splinter in the sides of Wallace Stegner and Richard Scowcroft, who headed creative writing. I observed that before the 1950s American writers did not, by and large, go to college to become writers; they taught themselves the way you did. Creative writing as we now know it, as a specialized discipline, got off the ground with poet Paul Engle's Iowa Writers' Workshop at the University of Iowa. Stanford novelist-essayist Wallace Stegner launched and administered Stanford's program in creative writing for decades.

     Al Young

Officially still listed as Albert James Young, I spent 1966–67 as a Stegner Writing Fellow in fiction. I worked on *Snakes,* my first novel, which came out from Holt in 1970, a few months after Corinth Books brought out *Dancing,* my first poem collection, in the fall of 1969. I signed and sent you a copy, unaware then of the colossal role dance had played in your youth, when you studied so formally and hard to become the kind of ballerina your troubled sister, Olga, could endorse. From then on our paths crisscrossed and steadied.

Then you invited me to Boston, where I stayed with your family and addressed the poetry workshop you were teaching at MIT. I loved it that you were teaching poetry and literature there, just as I still get a big kick out of hearing Connecticut poet laureate Marilyn Nelson's stories about her teaching days at West Point. Poetry belongs everywhere. You set up readings for me at the Rhode Island School of Design, Providence, and also at Brown.

Back in East Boston one Saturday afternoon, Tillie Olsen had come unannounced to the door. Given all the tumult and fallout that comes with being a popular, politically outspoken celebrity, you had grown hypercritically leery and wary of everything around you. I remember how tired you were of one local Black Panther in particular whose byword and raging cry was "Off a pig, off a pig! Have you offed a pig yet?" "I can't stand it," you complained. I felt sorry for you and for him and the whole country, really. You knew that your phone was tapped, your mail intercepted, and your every move under surveillance. If day-to-day life in the 1950s had meant living with the prospect of nuclear attack, daily life in the late 1960s moved along with the understanding that the concentration camps for dissidents were already under construction. Not only couldn't anyone over thirty be trusted; you pretty much couldn't trust anyone.

You didn't trust Tillie. Who knows why. It wasn't even one of those reconstructed Stalinist or Trotskyite ideological collisions; it was just a plain old gut-level distrust you felt. After I said I would take responsibility for the danger her presence posed, you calmed down and let me go to the door. I greeted Tillie and her young driver and let them in. Seasonably, curiously, she was wearing rain gear, a sturdy trench coat. Her salt-and-pepper hair sparkled, and her pink, flushed skin, like her dancing gray eyes, glowed. Under your sway I could see a little devilishness on Tillie's smiling face as she spoke to me, you, Mitch, Nick, and the rest of us. But I could also see the tedious, angelic Tillie, too. Why had she chosen this moment to pay you a sudden visit? What had brought her to Boston? She never explained. By then, the early 1970s, in the blossom of feminist enfoldment, *Tell Me a Riddle* had become something of a cult sensation; Tillie was popular on the lecture and reading circuit. Her impromptu, chit-chat visit was brief. In no time she and her polite accomplice were out the door. Your glacial, unreceptive mood, I'm sure, sped her departure. "Strange, don't you think?" you said. "I still don't trust her."

Decades later you would apologize every chance you got to all of your writer friends, colleagues, and followers for your dogged, unstoppable devotion to ending what Vietnamese history books now call the American War in Vietnam, among other ugly conflicts and causes. Sandra Drake, a Stanford professor of English, once told me: "Denise has so much soul. Notice how all the people of color and people who've been wronged automatically gravitate towards Denise after they hear her read and speak."

Mexico is where your mother, Beatrice, went to live. You paid regular visits to her there. Mexico was also where you wrote "Scenes from the Life of the Peppertrees," a poem of yours that first endeared me to you. Although it had been reprinted from *Overland to the Islands,* a book I didn't yet know, your sonic, filmlike lyric jumped right out at me from the pages of *Evergreen Review,* the one with James Dean on the cover. At that time, 1957, my three teen heroes were jazz saxophonist Charlie Parker, dead at thirty-five; Welsh poet Dylan Thomas, who reached age thirty-nine; and acting sensation Dean, who made it to twenty-four. The message each of their rapid life passages conveyed for my bomb-fixated generation was striking: if as an artist you've got anything going, then you're obliged to self-implode and check out early. You weren't like that. For all the surrounding self-fixated, self-destructive writers you published with, you weren't like that.

Even then, when I got down to sorting out your literary affiliations, I came up puzzled. Sometimes you threw in with the so-called Black Mountain school (including, among others, Robert Duncan, Charles Olson, Paul Blackburn, Hilda Morley, Jonathan Williams, Joel Oppenheimer, Fielding Dawson, John Wieners, Ed Dorn, and Robert Creeley), or you didn't mind that critics threw you in with them. At other times you got lumped in with the Beats (such as Jack Kerouac, Allen Ginsberg, Lawrence Ferlinghetti, William Burroughs, Gregory Corso). Both schools laid claim to William Carlos Williams, with whom your affinity is clearcut. Such fickle labeling, however, never stopped you from writing about whatever you wished, and in your own style. The range of your interests and subjects impresses and inspires me yet. Rather than prattle on in the confessional mode, as most of your contemporaries did, you always took the shortest way inward, which was to look outward. The whole world, you understood, resided in you.

Pressed to describe you overall, I would have to call you devotional. Wherever the beam of your concern or curiosity fell, it illumined—deeply, warmly, sometimes burning toward obsession. As the Vietnam War intensified, I watched your commitment to peace and justice escalate. *Escalate:* a heavy buzzword that accurately captures the process of levying darker and darker punishments on a civilian populace that suffered poisoned crops, poisoned trees, poisoned water, countless hidden landmines, and seven million tons of dropped bombs. We burned down every hut in a village, routinely rounding up and murdering every man, woman, and child we could find. As you wrote in "What Were They Like?":

> . . . most were peasants; their life
> was in rice and bamboo.
> When peaceful clouds were reflected in the paddies
> and the water buffalo stepped surely along terraces,
> maybe fathers told their sons old tales.
> When bombs smashed those mirrors
> there was time only to scream.
> There is an echo yet
> of their speech which was like a song.
> It was reported their singing resembled
> the flight of moths in moonlight.
> Who can say? It is silent now.[1]

All this, my friend, at a time when journalists were allowed to report such events. They've since cut this out. If you were to pop back up on the scene right now, you'd have to travel out of America to find a picture of a dead American soldier or her coffin in any American news medium. That photo of the little girl running with flaming napalm at her neck—forget it. Truth has gone meanly underground since you left. We've talked about this. Did World War I with its poison gas set the precedent? Was it World War II? Buchenwald? Hiroshima? I wish you were here to help me measure the effects of predator drone strikes, extraordinary rendition, Abu Ghraib, waterboarding, Guantánamo, 9/11—and mercifully I can guess that you have no idea what I'm ranting about. Bless your heart again and again, your kindred heart.

Denise, could I ever get you to understand the earth-scorching magnitude of slaughter, cruelty, torture, hatred, and ignorance common to warfare, commerce, and politics today? When I listen on the radio to fellow émigré Detroiter and former U.S. poet laureate Philip Levine tell interviewer Bill Moyers how much he still loathes the brutality of American capitalism waged against the poor and working poor and America's racism, I actually have to smile. *Das Kapital.* Capitalism is still the fifty-thousand-pound specter that haunts the whole world—a life-sucking, soul-sucking Godzilla. You couldn't have stood it. And there's so much more you wouldn't understand. Not right away. You would have to grow into it, get with it, as the saying went in your time. Once, in a yogic text on the doctrine of reincarnation, I read that we get reborn as infants to grow into the shock of coming back. Physically, geographically, culturally, conceptually, politically—everything changes. We need to adjust gradually and grow into any place we revisit. This delicate memory of you and our friendship makes for a perfect example.

Sometimes, though, I imagine you as the reincarnation of Allegra Byron (1817–1822), Lord Byron and Claire Clairmont's pitiable love child, who died at age five of malaria and, I suspect, parental neglect in a convent orphanage in Ravenna.

Having learned at three to read and write, the child soaked up all the work of her illustrious, self-important father and his close friend Percy Bysshe Shelley. She wrote letters in polite Venetian Italian to her Papa and Mammina (the Countess Teresa Guiccioli, Byron's mistress), imploring them please to come see about her.

Why do I imagine you as little Allegra? I've always woven a multi-gifted you into that murky Romantic muddle, when Byron; Shelley and his future wife, Mary Wollstonecraft Godwin; her half-sister, Claire Clairmont; and John William Polidori—Byron's personal physician and opiate connection, who also authored *The Vampyre,* a seminal vampire story—met up in Switzerland by Claire's design. Boundaries of intimacy blurred. You could've been the nineteen-year-old Mary Shelley, who on a "who can write the scariest story" dare, went back to a rented house on Lake Geneva, sat down, and came up with *Frankenstein*. You describe something similarly daring in an interview:

> When I started writing explicitly Christian poems, I thought I'd lose part of my readership. But I haven't actually. I think interest in religion is a counterforce to the insane, rationalist optimism that surrounds the development of all this new technology. This optimism is a twentieth-century repeat of attitudes in the nineteenth century, when they thought that steam, electricity, and telephones were going to make for some kind of utopia. There's a lot of dependence on technology today, and a willful ignorance that it's messing up resources, may end up destroying life on this planet, and then we'll have to start over without it. Our ethical development does not match our technological development. This sense of spiritual hunger is something of a counterforce or unconscious reaction to all that technological euphoria.[2]

How could either of us forget 1968? It was the year that trapped everyone's attention all over the world. It was the year of the Tet Offensive, when the Vietcong swept across South Vietnam, and the year of the My Lai Massacre. It was the year Dr. Martin Luther King, Jr. was shot down in Memphis, the year Lyndon Johnson signed the Fair Housing Act, the year Robert F. Kennedy was shot down, the year university students rose up to cripple France, the year student protesters shut down Columbia University, the year Mexico City hosted the XIX Olympiad, which ended in tragedy. It was the year the Catonsville Nine broke into the Selective Service Center in Catonsville, Maryland, and burned draft cards; the year Richard Nixon rode into the presidency; the year Mao Zedong demonstrated to China's Communist Party and the world that he wasn't joking when he talked about a Cultural Revolution; the year of the People's Park, a 2.8-acre vacant lot on Haste Street just above Berkeley's Telegraph Avenue, which became the site of a fatal shooting when protesters decided that the university-owned property shouldn't be

Al Young

converted into a parking lot and UC playing field. Since this was the last of three semesters required for me to fulfill my degree for graduation, I was determined to survive.[3]

But 1969 jumped, too. You were in town. You found me. As the UC Berkeley visiting poet, you came looking for me. "No one in the English department knew you," you said. "How was I supposed to know you were enrolled in Spanish?" Quietly, privately, I loved the sound of those words. I always loved your voice. That had been my main idea: to sneak past departments of English and teach Spanish. *Quízas.* Perhaps. Why not? ¿Cómo no? That spring you invited me up to your rented flat. Remember?

I keep coming back to that dinner night in Berkeley. At the kitchen table, I gently asked you questions. I had no interview in mind; I was just curious and eager to separate my print version of you from the living you. You told me about Rexroth. You said he played the biggest role in getting you and Mitch from England to America. You also said that after you'd met him, you realized that he had ulterior motives, to say the least. Hearing that he had big designs on you made me uncomfortable. Rexroth had been another of my adolescent heroes whose influence has lasted. When I first arrived in San Francisco, I looked him up at his home address of 250 Scott Street in the phone directory and called him from a pay phone in North Beach. He said that normally he would ask me over for coffee or a glass of wine, but at the moment he was going through a bout of deep sorrow. His wife, Marthe, had just left him. Decades later I learned from Linda Hamalian's unblinking *Life of Kenneth Rexroth* that the great poet, essayist, and polymath had always been something of a philanderer and rogue. You told me, though, that once you let him know you weren't available, that you were devoted to your husband, Rexroth backed off. After that, you said, he continued to praise your work in his commentaries and reviews of the contemporary poetry scene. He was amazing that way, you explained. He would not let a personal disappointment or grudge get in the way of his literary judgments. Robert Creeley, you said, was in the habit of writing love letters to each of his friends' wives or girlfriends, maybe just to find out who would bite. He wrote several to you, then gave up.

As I had done the previous summer, I worked again in the summer of 1969 as a writing teacher for UC Berkeley's branch of the Economic Opportunity Program, working mostly with black Oakland and Berkeley youth. The magazine the kids had put together in the previous year had made such a big hit that our program had gotten extra funding. *Us!* That's the name the students chose for a publication that featured poetry, stories, drawings, commentary, and other contributions. All of this fell under the umbrella program known as the Great Society. The main idea was to keep the lid on the social pressure cooker that should have already exploded. The question everyone was asking as each spring ripened was "Are we going to have another long, hot summer?"

Knowing I'd begin teaching at Stanford as a Jones Lecturer, my wife, Arl, and I moved in the middle of that summer back from Berkeley to Palo Alto. It was the year of the televised U.S. moon landing. The news hit us in Pátzcuaro, in ancient Michoacán, a state still in the throes of protests by university students who had declared Michoacán a Marxist-Leninist state. The natives saw it as a televised event; few believed it had happened. We were on holiday, the kind Europeans enjoyed. None of this two-week stuff; we were down there for one month at least.

An affection for Mexico helped bond us as well. I lived there in spurts in the early 1960s: Mexico City, Oaxaca, Chapala, Ajijíc, Jocotepec, Guadalajara. I would work, save, and borrow until I had enough to Greyhound my way from Northern California to San Diego, where I'd board another Three Gold Star bus (Tres Estrellas de Oro was the name of the line) to get back into Mexico. Gringos had it good. At twelve pesos to the dollar, the peso waved a mighty welcome. Writing and reading were my addictions, and—like you after T. S. Eliot praised a poem you had the nerve to send him—I was practicing to get good enough to break into some kind of literary circle. My generation was too young for the Beats and too old for the hippies, who were just beginning to form and stir. I sent stuff out to little magazines everywhere. John Sinclair accepted poems of mine for his Detroit-based *Work.* Jerome Klinkowitz took a story of mine ("The Compensation Claimant in Sacred Idiom") for *Nexus,* his San Francisco–based journal. Len Fulton published a poem in *Dust.* Two Mexico-based publications accepted work of mine: *San Miguel Review,* an English-language émigré journal, and *El Corno Emplumado* (*The Plumed Horn*). Picture a feathered cornucopia spilling out goodies, an old-fashioned horn of plenty from a time when writing was still done with quills. For a magazine title, how weird is that? A lively, inspirational bilingual journal, *El Corno* billed itself as "A Magazine from Mexico City."

Brooklyn-born Margaret Randall and Sergio Mondragón, her Mexican husband, edited *El Corno Emplumado.* Both of them poets, both of them socially alert arts activists. Their multicultural trajectory skated the cutting edge. They published original work in Spanish and in English. Occasionally they strayed into Haitian or Ivory Coast French. Sometimes they ran facing-page translations; mostly they didn't. As you well know, it was exciting to show up in *El Corno* along with such luminaries as Nicolas Guillén, Julio Cortázar, Carlos Fuentes, René Depestre, Lawrence Ferlinghetti, Jack Hirshman, Anselm Hollo, James Baldwin, Jerome Rothenberg, Thomas Merton, Buckminster Fuller, Octavio Paz, Russell Banks, and Yevgeny Yevtuskenko.

You told me about a visit you'd paid to Meg and Sergio's months before Arl and I hit Mexico again that simmering summer with plans to see them, too. "I was turned off," you said, "by the way they lived with their children and guests. It was a bit too lax and chaotic for me. They're good people, though." I get your drift. I'll never know exactly what you meant. Here's my guess: You drew lines. You set

Al Young

boundaries, standards, goals. We loved what they stood for. They were hippies. You were hip.

Before long I was publishing in so many small press journals that I decided to start one of my own. I called the maiden issue *Love (Incorporating Hate)*. Subsequent issues were titled *Loveletter*. With the same caliber of nerve or naïveté that prompted you to send your work to Eliot, I wrote you. I asked if you had anything to contribute to my tiny journal. I also wrote Canadian poet George Bowering and jazz adventurer John Coltrane. Each of you came through. Bowering sent us "Time Magazine's Poem," and Impulse Records producer Bob Thiele sent Coltrane's poem "A Love Supreme." You sent two: "Initiation" and "Living," a timeless, reflective little gem, now considered one of your classics. Here is the last part of it:

> A red salamander
> so cold and so
> easy to catch, dreamily
>
> moves his delicate feet
> and long tail. I hold
> my hand open for him to go.
>
> Each minute the last minute.[4]

Of course I thrilled to see *Loveletter* credited on the acknowledgments page of *The Sorrow Dance,* your next collection from New Directions.

By the end the end of that busy summer, the whole zeitgeist of that era flashed into place. From time to time throughout our travels that summer, I paused to telephone Meg and Sergio in Mexico City. Someone polite always answered. A man sometimes; sometimes a woman. Always in Spanish I explained who I was, why I was calling, and how much I looked forward to meeting them. Always I was assured that my message would get delivered. As hip as I thought we were, it didn't occur to me to remember how many everyday people in Mexico were informants. Only after our plane set down in LA for a connecting flight did I realize what we'd flown and bussed ourselves into.

Waiting for me, waiting for Arl, as we stepped off the plane were two corny, trench-coated FBI agents. One took Arl into a room; the other escorted me to another room. They asked me to open my bags. Pretending to look for drugs, my agents examined every book and scrap of paper I'd packed, including copies of *El Corno Emplumado.* The flight was delayed for close to three hours while they put us through this. When we got to San Francisco and then home to Palo Alto, I contacted the American Civil Liberties Union. The ACLU told me the FBI couldn't arrest or threaten us, but they did have every right to detain us like they did. I learned that Meg had fled to Cuba. Sergio had gone to the United States. I had been talking on their phone line to agents, interlopers of some kind. A remote witness to the assassinations of John F. Kennedy, Malcolm X, RFK, and King, all of them killed between 1963 and 1968, I sadly understood. I knew the battle you were waging against imperial American privilege was going to get met hard. Nothing had changed since Mark Twain spoke up against it. I knew the police state practices George Orwell had dramatized so popularly in *1984* and *Animal Farm* were just as active then and there as they are here and now.

Denise, how disconcerting I find it to behold your face on a self-adhering U.S. postage stamp with no glue for me to lick. Your spirit refreshes me always. I love you, I love you, I love you.

East Boston
for Denise Levertov

Up in this warm, solid house of yours,
while you make breakfast, I stand sighing
at the window, breaths away from
this workingclass block, where trash cans
lined up in front of old buildings
look natural with sun shining down on them

If my heart seems to leap from my shirt
away away away from this instant it's
because the short drive in from Logan Airport
thru last night's minute of neighborhood
streetlight with children playing in it
is whisking me back thru my decades again . . .[5]

Al Young

• P.S. MIND THE GAP •

Aldon Lynn Nielsen

Though she would have written "gat-toothed." "Like me, you had a tooth-sweet gap," Al Young writes to Denise Levertov. "Gat-toothed," or "goat toothed," meaning to have a "lickerish" tooth, a sweet tooth, an idiom many of that generation in the United States learned from the musical *Guys and Dolls* and its song "More I Cannot Wish You." But here's where *gap* and *gat* close up the gap between them. A gat-toothed person is supposed in folklore, because of that "lickerish" tooth, to be wanton, lustful, more than simply sweet—in other words just like the gap-toothed Wife of Bath. "Gat-toothed was she," Chaucer writes, and the footnote to the edition of *Canterbury Tales* I've been carrying about with me for decades helpfully explains: "Gat-toothed, gap-toothed, by physiognomists supposed to indicate a bold, lascivious nature. Some mss. have *Gap-toothed.*"[1] Levertov had "gat-toothed." She had already been in the United States for years by the time she met a young Sudanese man named Abubakar during a trip she made to Eastern Europe. And yet her tongue still gave her away. She never lost that early, acquired Britishness, and her vocabulary marked her in conversation with younger people:

> My diction marks me
> untrue to my time;
> change it, I'd be
> untrue to myself.

Reaching Rijeka, which was once, as Levertov informs us, Fiume, now part of Croatia, she paused for drinks with five young Sudanese. They exchanged news of revolution. As she wrote in her poem "Staying Alive," Levertov presented Abubakar her Panther Party button, that image so familiar to my generation, the "Black Cat emerging / in power from behind bars," surrounded by the textual imperative "FREE ALL POLITICAL PRISONERS." I had several of those buttons. Levertov presented hers to Abubakar, who translated the slogan with his friends.

Abubakar, gat-toothed
like me. "They say it's lucky,"
I told him, "and means you will journey
very far."

She had already journeyed far; still she did not, on the evidence of her poem, tell the young man about the Wife of Bath or about the other connotations of that shared diastema. The George Jackson letter from which Young quotes was published the same year as Levertov's meeting with Abubakar, so in all likelihood, she had not yet read them, but, like the rest of us in those days, she would have been familiar with the image of Angela Davis, from the newspapers if not from those ubiquitous posters. What most speak of when recalling those images is the "bush," the impressive afro hair, but the gap in her front teeth was hard to miss. "Gat-toothed like me," Levertov might well have thought looking at those photos. Like Amiri Baraka, too, as it happens. All one need do is look at those photos to recognize how purely metaphorical was Jackson's imagined contact with that gap in Davis's smile. "That should make her smile," he writes in his letter to her, hoping to make her smile, to reveal the gap, as he revels in it. The space between the teeth; the space between tongue and teeth. It is a difference of tongues that Abubakar's friends must negotiate as they circle the panther button brought them by the poet from America. Levertov's own tongue marks the gap between her and her American compatriots. This is no disadvantage. "Caliban, push your tongue / heavy into the calyx": so closes *The Freeing of the Dust*. For Martin Heidegger, language was the house of being. For Levertov, "without a terrain in which, to which" she could belong, "language itself is my one home, my Jerusalem"

For Jackson, at home with his language in a prison house, there was an erotics of the letter that would permit his insinuation into Davis's smile, a poetics of inside and outside interpenetrated lingually. A lingual sound is pronounced with the aid of the tongue, particularly the tongue's tip. Jackson imagines Davis reading what would be on the tip of his tongue and smiling, revealing the gap he would worry. I was tempted for a moment toward an untoward conclusion about the politics, as well as the erotics, of the shared dental feature. Young, Baraka, Levertov, Davis— every one of them to the left. But then there is Condoleezza Rice, rightward-tending with a slight gap. Rice, like Davis, was from Birmingham, Alabama, of the bombed church and the murdered little girls. Yet the ideological gap between Rice and Davis far exceeded the gap of a few blocks between the Alabama homes of their youth. Hard to imagine a correspondence between Rice and Jackson. There was little correspondence between Rice and Levertov, aside from an early avocation for the arts and that powerfully proverbial gap. While Davis was a fugitive, Rice was a student in Denver. While Davis was a fugitive, Levertov was carrying news of America's revolutionaries to Europe. Davis was captured in October, by which time Levertov was back in the States. We shared the times, but there were gaps in that sharing. Levertov's diction marked her as someone from another time (and place); she would not be untrue to herself.

And so "gat-toothed," though too she may have written it that way so that American readers might feel the gap in history and etymology between themselves and their tongue, feel with their tongue the gaps in their language. Levertov did treasure the occasional fellow feeling. In part 4 of the same sequence that reports the meeting with Abubakar, "Staying Alive," just pages after the appearance of "gat-toothed," she incorporates the recollections of another British ex-pat: "(Bromige writes: 'I recall the muffin man too, and the naphtha lamps, I think they were, in the open-air market, High Rd. Kilburn, after early December dark. Now I sit up here on a California hillside. This difficulty of what resonance has the language, for you, for me,—I need to take up but the push and shove of events (that's a telling phrase of Merleau-Ponty's!) has me, and meanwhile I go on writing poems sometimes like shouting down a deep well.')" What Levertov makes of that well is fascinating:

> Those are the same lamps
> of my dream of Olga—the eel or cockle stand,
> she in the flare caught, a moment, her face
> painted, clownishly, whorishly. Suffering.
>
> "It's your own well.
> Go down
> into its depth."[2]

Levertov, inveterate reader and friend of William Carlos Williams, offers a friendly amendment to one of the central passages in *Paterson,* a passage in which Williams juxtaposes snatches of hectoring letters from Pound about Williams's reading to the diagram of a core sample, with its note to the effect that the same minerals may be found at similar depths in both Europe and America. The language she shares with Bromige, that she shares differently with Young, is her own well. "This difficulty of what resonance has the language"—that's not the way an American native speaker would ordinarily get such a thing said. But Bromige was from England by way of Scandinavia and Canada. His depths, which he is never out of, do not correspond exactly with Levertov's, despite their shared memories of wartime childhood. There is a gap. Structuralism, something Levertov didn't attend to closely, taught us that meaning erupts within, has its condition of possibility in those gaps. It's the gaps that generate our signifying. Levertov, Young, Bromige, each practices a poetics of the gap.

Generations are addressed, too, in Young's letter. He turns to an episode of *The Dick Cavett Show,* one that I also watched, to recall something that had broad currency back in the day. One evening featured a conversation with anthropologist Margaret Mead, author of *Coming of Age in Samoa.* Mead had studied with the same mentor as Zora Neale Hurston, Franz Boas. A black mother offered a riposte to Mead's take on the "generation gap," one of the most discussed phenomena of the time. In telling the tale, Young mentions the fact that this woman was the mother of Ronnie Dyson, described by Young as "a barely teen-aged, one-hit singing star." Of course that one hit was "Aquarius," from *Hair,* the show that changed Broadway forever for good or ill, and Dyson had the lead vocal. That's him singing the opening: "When the moon is in the seventh house / and Jupiter aligns with Mars." And while he may have seemed a one- or even two-hit wonder at the time of the Cavett taping, he was hardly finished. With "Why Can't I Touch You?" a song from his next Broadway show, *Salvation,* he was launched into our musical memories, and that was followed by songs such as "I Don't Wanna Cry," "When You Get Right Down to It," and my own favorite, "I Just Don't Want to Be Lonely." His mama raised him well. But she was there to tell Cavett and Mead just one thing, "I don't believe in no generation gap."

This was a common sentiment within the black community, as were several other nostrums supposedly distinguishing black from white. Preachers in many African American churches I visited back in the day were given to urging their younger congregants away from the bad example of the white hippies, even as Jimi Hendrix, Sly Stone, George Clinton, and hosts of others were leading a charge toward a blacker counterculture. In a time of black nationalism, many felt the urge to separate themselves from cultural phenomena seen as coming from the white community, and yet, as so many cultural nationalists came to learn, such separation did not come easily. At the Black Panthers' rally on the steps of the Lincoln Memorial, held in conjunction with the People's Constitutional Convention, again in 1970, I have never forgotten hearing a prominent member of the Panthers' national leadership opine that "black people don't need women's liberation because *our* women are already liberated," and yes, there were more scowls of disagreement from sisters in the crowd than fervent nods of approval from those in vocal agreement. Within a few short years, black womanists would be publishing stinging critiques of the assumptions implicit in some white feminist thought, while at the same time rejecting in equally stinging terms the paternalism of such phrases as "*our* women." It may have been common sense within black communities that the generation gap was a white thing, but that didn't stop there being any number of black hippies on hand in Washington, DC (even at that Panther rally), and most other parts of the country.

"Gaps, like old fashioned movie frames, make, break and hold us together," observes Young, and for him, the generational markers of time structure those

Aldon Lynn Nielsen

gaps. "My generation was too young for the Beats and too old for the Hippies," he notes, placing himself at the midpoint of a range stretching from my tail end of the Baby Boom back through his cohort to those who witnessed World War II as children and helped spark the revolution that came to be recognized as the New American Poetry. We'll always have 1968. As our parents' generations were ineluctably marked by the experiences of the Great Depression and the Second World War, those of us born just before that war or in the decade following it speak down into the depths of our well, though we speak with differences. If not exactly red diaper babies, both Levertov and Young were youthful propagandists for the Left, Levertov selling the *Daily Worker* door to door, Young reading that paper along with *Mainstream*. By the time of my newspaper-obsessed youth, few of us would be caught dead with the *Daily Worker,* but that was because most of us New Lefties regarded the CPUSA as a reactionary body only slightly preferable to the John Birch Society. Angela Davis was among the last of these boomers to align herself with the Communists, and that was in large part due to her philosophical training. The gap between the Frankfurt School thinkers she studied and Gus Hall was beyond parody. But we the younger still than Young had our underground papers and the Panther paper. It wasn't just Young's portion of the youth rebellion that was bomb-obsessed: witness Corso's *The Happy Birthday of Death* with its foldout poem "BOMB" in the shape of a mushroom cloud. And it was my end of the Baby Boom that erupted in applause at Ginsberg's performances of "Whom Bomb" (and note his 1984 appendix to that piece, dedicated to jazz greats Don Cherry and Elvin Jones). Those who saw the bomb come in their childhood, and those of us who were born with the bomb, will always say "the bomb," marking ourselves as untrue to new time, if true to ourselves.

And the times brought with them a level of wariness and paranoia. The story Young tells of Levertov's worries as she went deeper and deeper into political activism are characteristic of the postwar era. People who'd lived through McCarthyism in the United States could never rest secure in the security state. Any friend might be turned. While we did not learn to say "COINTELPRO" till after its activities had happened, we knew something was happening, even if we didn't know what it was. My end of the boom was plagued by narcs and informants. My high school was infiltrated by undercover officers fitting themselves in among the many children of military families who tended to transfer in and out at odd times of year. At SDS meetings I assumed (correctly, we later learned) the person loudly urging us to burn something was probably the informant. If Levertov was "hypercritically leery," she had good reason to be. At the group house I lived in when I left my parents' home, just north of DC's Dupont Circle, we knew perfectly well that the house phone was bugged. The building had previously been home to an SDS group, and the address was still of interest to the authorities even if the building itself was now occupied by poets and guitar strummers. (How could you tell them apart in those days? This was a time when the FBI had someone at every one of Baraka's poetry readings, buying books.) At least every two weeks, a pair of FBI agents would stop by our house to show us photos of fugitives: one was Angela Davis; another was Bill Ayres, who later opened his home to political candidate Barack Obama. While the one agent would show us their photos, the other would wander around our living room, dutifully making note of the return address on any piece of mail. We were all leery and hypercritical. Still we were not all leery and hypercritical in the same way.

On one aspect of our shared decades I have to differ with Young's account. From my vantage point writing as a post-Sputnik poet, the view of American education's decline and fall looks very different. Far from fizzling, like some of America's early attempts at rocket launches, the kind of education Young cherishes was in fact boosted by Sputnik's success. Once the Soviets had managed to put a bleeping (in the literal sense) thing into orbit, we had to invest heavily in public education, and I was one of the chief beneficiaries of this too short period in our education history. During my years in public schools, and all of my education up through the BA was in public schools, the United States was bent on providing top-quality, free education to its youth. We simply could not fall behind those Russians. This was not made universally available, it is true. We were still fighting to desegregate our schools and to equalize our opportunities. (That was among the central struggles for my cohort.) But we were fighting for equal access to one of the best educations tax dollars could buy. And this was not limited to what later generations have come to term the "STEM" subjects. Recent scholarship about the "cultural front" has demonstrated the breathtaking lengths to which U.S. foreign policy included strong arts initiatives. We were even sending poets to places such as Africa and Eastern Europe. And those of us who had student loans in those days will recall they were NDEA loans—the National Defense Education Act. Scholars were serving their nation by doing graduate work in medieval poetics. It is true that scholarship became more specialized in this time, but the great closing of the American mind did not happen when tenured radicals got jobs on campus; it happened when the tax-cutting mania was clamped down tight on America during the later generations, and it has stayed clamped down.

My seeing education history differently from the way Young sees it is a matter of the two of us looking through different ends of the proverbial telescope, the boomer telescope, if I can mix metaphors. (Or the boomer kaleidoscope, if I can mix them more psychedelically, which, given the topic, might be more appropriate.) Not surprisingly Levertov, Young, and I experienced the later twentieth-century revolutions in poetics somewhat differently as well. In part this has to do with that experience of education. Much as the 1930s generation of objectivists had cut their teeth on the first anthologies to include the Modernist rebels, by the time I was in junior and senior high school, the poetics of the New American

                                                           Aldon Lynn Nielsen

Poetry were beginning to make themselves felt in the curriculum. By the time I reached my senior year, Modernism was taken for granted. Close reading was what you did. The Beats were in Brentano's (along with the first wave of the Black Arts poets), and hippies were on the horizon. The first book of poems I purchased with my own cash was *The Dead Lecturer,* by LeRoi Jones; the first I'd persuaded my father to purchase for me was Allen Ginsberg's *Kaddish.* (My Baptist father checked with a Jewish woman at his office to find out what a "Kaddish" might be. Probably just as well that he didn't read the book itself.) Here are more gaps to mind. Jones's next collection, *Black Magic,* was the last volume bearing the moniker LeRoi Jones in isolation. His newer chapbooks already carried his new name, Amiri Baraka, and for the next decades, his names appeared gapped on the covers of his major collections: "LeRoi Jones / Amiri Baraka." Where the slash signed a progression into cultural nationalism, by the time of *The Autobiography of LeRoi Jones/Amiri Baraka,* the book's author had, like Davis, become a communist, albeit a communist of a different order from her.

Levertov was instrumental in making the revolution in poetics that was now part of my outside-the-classroom self-education. She was homeschooled. I schooled myself in her work, took her home, along with all those other poets I was discovering. The Beats brought me to the New York School. Jones was my gateway to Black Mountain, where Levertov had been before me. But as so often proves true, not all of the revolutionaries wholly approved of the children of their revolution. As early as 1961, Levertov expressed concern about the directions being taken by the poets coming just after her. This is part of a wider phenomenon in which we can see an early postmodernism and later departures into other modes of the postmodern. In issue number 11 of Jones and Diane di Prima's newsletter *Floating Bear,* Levertov published "An Argument" in response to Robert Kelly's Deep Image manifesto in *Trobar* number 2. The essay opens with a rhetorical move characteristic of such exercises. Just as so many have claimed that Modernism is more Romanticism, or that post-structuralism isn't really doing anything we were not already doing, Levertov writes: "An insistence on the need for 'deep image' seems to me unnecessary because all real poetry must always contain deep images. When the deep image is consciously sought, the unconscious of the literate modern poet seems to throw to the surface images which pass for deep because they are not strictly bound by rational preconceptions and because they resemble in a vague atmospheric way a whole body of other images made familiar to us in a half-century's literature."[3]

By the time I had begun to think about such matters for myself, it was no longer at all evident that all real poetry must contain deep images or indeed that it was necessary for a poem to contain images at all in order to qualify as real. While I would have my arguments with deep image, which was already giving way to other movements, its passing marked by the appearance of several quite good anthologies, the arguments launched from my end of the boom would differ from those of Levertov. In the end her final blast against this movement among poets who could have been her slightly younger siblings was a vague complaint about form. "Another result of an exclusive concentration on the deep image is a neglect of form," she writes, and in the end her complaint is that these poets "write in a literary idiom."[4] Is this not always the complaint? It certainly was lodged early and often against the original imagists, as it was used subsequently to dismiss all the offspring of projective verse.

Which would, of course, include Jones. During a Q&A after a panel that included readings by him and Gwendolyn Brooks, critics in the audience at one of the first conferences on African American writing, a conference sponsored by Berkeley Extension and held at Asilomar, seemed intent upon opposing the good Brooks to the bad Jones, inconsiderate of things formal. Levertov had expressed misgivings about the editor of *Floating Bear* well before his turn to the Black Arts. In a letter written to Robert Duncan the year prior to Levertov's essay on the deep image in *Floating Bear*, she complained that she had had a hard time writing to Creeley of late because of his interest in Jones's earlier magazine, *Yugen*, coedited with his wife, Hettie Cohen: "Creeley sent a beautiful poem called 'The Rose' in a recent letter. But I find it hard to write to him since I was shown a letter he had written to LeRoi Jones in praise of *Yugen*, a magazine I put in the same category with recent *Evergreens* except LeRoi is a nice fellow with terrible taste." It would seem Duncan, too, was souring on Jones. He served with Donald Allen, editor of the now-canonical *New American Poetry*, as adviser to the better-known Berkeley Poetry Conference organizers and had supported Jones for one of the prime spots at the conference as it was in the planning stages. As the conference approached, though, Duncan was changing his mind about Jones, in part based on his judgment of a reading in March 1965. "He read entirely hate the whites," Duncan told Levertov. "*Insincere* in the only meaning of that word that seems important to me."[5]

Today's readers looking at this letter and having in mind the popular image of the Baraka of the Black Arts era, perhaps thinking of poems like "Black Art," might not find this such an extreme judgment, but we need to keep in mind that the poetry Jones was reading on that tour was the poetry of the first book of his I read, *The Dead Lecturer*, at about the same time Duncan was writing his letter. Listening to the tape recordings of Jones's Asilomar reading later made available by Pacifica Radio reveals a yawning gap between what is audible in the performance and what Duncan is saying to Levertov about it. Eerily Duncan's dismissal of Jones, who was well on his way to becoming Baraka, seems to prefigure his later judgments of the antiwar politics of Levertov's own poetry. In one interview, at least as Levertov read the comments, Duncan accused her of "taking sadistic pleasure in the horrors" she'd depicted in "Life at War."[6] If it is cold comfort to recognize that

                                        Aldon Lynn Nielsen

what goes around, as we said in the 1960s, comes around, it is evident that however sincere each poet's evaluation may have been regarding Baraka, or regarding one another, there was an edge in the judgments that had to do with a grinding generation gap.

Some among the *New American Poetry* artists could be quite encouraging of radical movements in poetics that appeared in their wake. Creeley, for instance, no matter how intolerant he could be of others sometimes, no matter how inconsistent some of his critical views may appear to us in retrospect, did not seem to have the viscerally negative response to, say, the Language poets as Edward Dorn or Levertov did. Where Charles Olson had railed against the shining remnants of a regnant Western humanism in the wreckage of the Modernists, groups of poets began to appear in the 1970s who no longer adhered to the conception of the breath unit as an organizing principle for the poetic line, who directed a searing philosophical critique against the insistence upon the presence of the poet in the writing, who rejected the speech-based poetics of much that had gone just before. Worse than that, they read voluminously in something that wasn't even called philosophy but had sprung up in the United States under the rubric of "theory." Levertov, though long a champion of new poets of many schools, was having none of it.

By the late 1980s, Language poetry was already being lambasted as an academic thing even as it was just beginning to be spoken of in academia. Like Allen's *The New American Poetry,* Ron Silliman's landmark generational anthology, *In the American Tree,* included only one African American poet, Erica Hunt. In neither era was it the case that this absence from the anthologies marked an absence of black avant-garde writers. Rather it was an outward sign of the persisting gaps between the social spheres of black and white artists. In 1987 a book appeared, edited by Hank Lazer, titled *What Is a Poet?* The volume was the aftershock of a conference Lazer had organized at the University of Alabama in 1984, and it was one of the few such conferences to cast its nets so broadly as to catch big swimmers in the mainstream as well as some among the more noted of the recently radical inveighers against things as they were. At one point in the discussions, Charles Bernstein, in the summary Donna Hollenberg offers in her biography of Levertov, "claimed to defamiliarize language so as to resist historical forces and prevent language from being taken for granted. This practice was unacceptable to Levertov."[7] In the debate that Lazer tried to moderate, in which Bernstein, Levertov, Marjorie Perloff, and some of the others engaged, it was clear that defamiliarization was not the only thing unacceptable to Levertov. Root assumptions going back to the linguistic turn in philosophy early in the Modernist era, assumptions about the absolute mediation of human experience, roiled her sensibilities. My own highly mediated experience of such debates has taught me that opposition to this concept invariably leads to talk of pain and of infants. As Lazer's book indicates, Louis

Simpson had just launched this line of attack by asserting forcefully that "for poets experience occurs as a *primary* thing, without language in between."[8]

On my own first reading, while the males at the conference were going on about soldiers and getting shot at, I was wondering where this gap was, what was this "between" that language did not occupy between primary experience and . . . well, what exactly? The poet, in this construction, seems to have gotten somehow between himself. It is Levertov who introduces the suffering child: "If a child dying of cancer is suffering excruciating pain just as if it were a grown person who is able to reflect upon its pain, does that mean that it is not experiencing that pain? Bullshit!" It is not at all clear from the discussions that Levertov ever recognizes the conundrums set up by her and Simpson's objections. It is not at all clear why pain is thought to be a primary experience that is felt without reflection, occurs in an entirely preverbal environment, takes its place outside, or a nanosecond removed from, some central experiencing self. Levertov, like Simpson, seems to think that there is a gap between that which is primarily experienced and the subject doing the experiencing, but that this gap is not a space of mediation. She is unable ultimately to put words to what is felt prior to words, for the simple reason that she has never lived in any other than a signifying environment. Eventually Levertov backs her argument into a corner from which it is difficult to extricate it, insisting that language is a "non-static" but nevertheless "fixed set of rules."

She seems to mean no more than that while there are many languages, each language operates upon a consensual set of parameters. But if the rules are consensual, they cannot be fixed, because the consensus is itself constantly in flux. "Gat-toothed" and "gap-toothed" occupy the same language differently, producing significance out of their differences. She seems to be arguing against a sort of private language argument that was not in fact made by her interlocutors, and against that straw man, she charges arrogance: "I think it is arrogant and that's what I find pernicious about this viewpoint. It is making private property out of the public beach."[9] (Interesting analogy there—under California law, the beaches belong to the public, something of which Levertov would have been aware during her Stanford years, but there have been continuous legal struggles with wealthy owners of beachfront properties who attempt to deny the public access to their public beaches. Levertov would appear to align Language poets with privileged holders of real property, a seemingly unlikely alliance in the late 1980s.) Among the sadder facts gleaned from a reading of Hollenberg's superb biography of Levertov is the knowledge that the poet held these objections to the new poetries and new theories so strongly that she lobbied against Stanford's hiring of Perloff, concerned about the influence someone with her dangerous (though clearly not poststructuralist) views might bring to bear on the students in Palo Alto.

From his position midway between Levertov and my end of the Baby Boom, Young shared some but not all of Levertov's wariness, both in politics and in

Aldon Lynn Nielsen

poetics. He writes that when he tries to sort through her literary affiliations, he remains puzzled. His own life's affiliations may present similar puzzles to readers new to his work. Clearly closer to the Black Arts than Levertov could manage to be, Young was never uncritical. O. O. Gabugah, the persona he summons to introduce his *Collected Poems,* which fittingly includes works by Gabugah, became one of Young's vehicles for gentle critique. Gabugah's satirical slant on the race politics of Young's youth and our hard times outlives the moment of his original invention. I first encountered Gabugah and Young together. Not too long after completing my draft service and returning to school, I bought a copy of Young's third collection of poetry, a book I bought mostly on the strength of its great title, *Geography of the Near Past* (and I went back to the store and bought his second book, *The Song Turning Back into Itself,* for much the same reason). In that book I read a selection of the writings of Gabugah, introduced by Young. Young mentions that Gabugah had achieved publication of his work in the *Nation,* though I see that he found acceptance there some years after Levertov had finished her time as their poetry editor. I'm glad that Gabugah ("slave name" Franklin Delano Watson) survived the times and lived to introduce Young's collected self, and I was glad to have met him in the same book that includes Young's poem to Levertov, "East Boston." I'd like to think that Levertov liked to think of Gabugah and his off-kilter take on the times and languages he shared with his creator, Levertov, and the rest of us. Gabugah liked to play with and in the language. (See "What You Seize Is What You Get," a poem that found its satiric and deadly serious echo in Baraka's "What You See Ain't What You Goetz.")

If Levertov was a sometimes uneasy inhabitant of her later times, she was never self-satisfied. Young, referencing her continued self-education, says that she never left any gaps unfilled. But when it comes to things such as ideology and poetics, there is no end to the gaps. The gap is the condition of possibility of thought. Her diction marked the gap between her and us. We could hear the gap in her speaking. Time opened up between some of her words and ours, and it was in that time that we found her truth. She would not be untrue to herself. Hers were acts always "of passionate attention."[10] Our game wasn't cricket. Her game wasn't stickball. But that was a gap that made her smile. Young recalls "when the England you smiled in wasn't so new."[11] Levertov's New England was an open house. We didn't, don't, need her always to agree with us. We need the language that was her Jerusalem. As William Blake, one of Levertov's favorite poets, put it, "I will not cease from Mental Fight, / Nor shall my Sword sleep in my hand: / Till we have built Jerusalem."[12]

• THE ALMOST WILDERNESS •

Emily Warn

'm waiting for the kettle to boil in Denise's kitchen. It's mid-November and raining. The branches of her unruly pear tree in the front yard are outlined against the gray sky. At three-thirty it's already dusk. Looking over neighboring roofs and down to Lake Washington, I can barely distinguish lake water from the black forest rising behind it.

I pour boiling water into Denise's serviceable yellow teapot, wide enough to hold four cups, swirl it around the sides, and dump it into the sink. I put three tablespoons of English breakfast into the pot, refill it with water, and steep the tea until it is black and strong. I set it on a tray next to a sugar bowl, pitcher of milk, and a plate of cookies and carry it all into the living room, where Denise is sitting on the couch.

Brewing a perfect pot of tea was our secret pleasure; our first sip was conspiratorial, the second and third signals to begin a conversation. In between tea times, we found ways to remember them to stay connected. On one of her travels, Denise bought me a tiny book with illustrations and instructions for each step. I would search Seattle's bakeries and import shops for the most buttery shortbread to bring when we next visited. Her English upbringing meant she could outdrink me, insisting that I drink one more cup, eat one more cookie. I'd always accept even though I was buzzing from caffeine and from trying to keep up my half of the conversation.

On our way to a reading or concert, she would often offhandedly tell me about an insight she had after a dream or after something she'd read, or seen, or sensed: a woman fishing on a pier who symbolized in her mind a historic era; a dream of her parents climbing the stairs; an intuition of the dead seeing through her eyes. Only later when I read poems based on these insights did I realize she had confided something of great importance to her.

We were driving along a stretch of Lake Washington Boulevard, which begins at Seward Park near her home and parallels a bicycle path for five miles. Century-old sycamores are all that separates the boulevard from the bicycle path, and a row of aging cherry trees all that separates the path from the shore. The boulevard is a legacy of the Olmstead brothers' vision for Seattle of a series of greenways connecting all the city's parks.

Even if there were more direct ways to an event, Denise loved this circuitous route. She could see all the way across the lake and beyond to the Cascade Mountains or peer closer to shore where flocks of coots and scaups bobbed on swells and herons fished from harbor posts. At intervals we would pass fishing piers, city parks, marinas, and swimming areas. On that day we drove through heavy drizzle, the light damped, the mountains invisible. Denise turned to me and remarked, "I worry that William Carlos Williams would not like my recent poems." "Why?" I asked.

In settling here Denise turned not toward the American idiom and sensibility as her muse but to the cultural milieu of her childhood upbringing steeped in nineteenth-century British and Russian literature and in the eclectic Christianity of her Welsh mother and her Anglican father—a Yeshiva student in his youth who became a noted translator of the Zohar. "Dear 19th century!" she writes in "A Hundred a Day." "Give me refuge in your unconscious sanctuary for awhile."[1]

In the poems she wrote in Seattle during the last decade of her life, one hears echoes of Alfred Lord Tennyson and William Wordsworth as much as that of Ezra Pound or William Carlos Williams, her mentor. In their diction and inflections, in their rhythms and tropes, they often run counter to Williams's aesthetic belief that poetry should present the "direct treatment of the thing" and arise from listening to American speech: "It is there, in the mouths of the living, that the language is changing and giving new means for expanded possibilities in literary expression and, I add, basic structure—the most important of all."[2]

"I'm choosing," Denise said, and here I'm paraphrasing, "to use words and the phrasing I heard in my childhood. Though they might sound stilted to an American ear, they are pleasing to mine." Latinate and antiquated words and anthropomorphic figures of speech appear regularly in poems from her last three collections. For example, in "Settling," a poem about being welcomed to the Northwest, the sun is "restless," the mountain (Mount Rainier) is "tolerant in its steadfastness," the gray weather has been "foretold," not by people but "by all and sundry."[3]

Her poems' subject matter and aesthetic closely resemble nineteenth-century Romanticism in their resolute striving to discover a universal truth, or at least a cultural one, in her subjective experience of nature. Adopting this stance in the twentieth century was tricky at best given the predominant view among poets and theorists that universality and a true, unique self are socially constructed and therefore false. Yet in many of her poems about the natural world, it seems as if she could not help but be transported to that earlier time and find there not fixed truths but the materials for mythmaking. Encountering the Northwest landscape's grandeur, its protean light and weather, were for her comparable to when John

Ruskin first saw the Alps: "but all unawares / came face to face / with the sublime." Transforming her experience of the sublime into poetry was, as she writes later in this poem, "The Faithful Lover," to make the "seen, then re-seen, recognized, wrought in myth."

Denise first articulated her ideas about the role myth played in her poetry at a talk she gave to theologians and poets in 1967 at a conference on that subject. In preparing the talk, she looked through her work for a dominant theme and discovered that it was that of life as a pilgrimage. She defines a pilgrim's life as a journey that "leads from one state of being to another." Presciently the first time she uses the word *pilgrim* in a poem, she declares, "Leave your dark autumns, the roads / oppressed by drooping alder," and "follow your sunrise shadow to the west!"[4]

Soon after moving to Seattle, Denise traveled to Italy for a residency in Bellagio. From there she sent me an early draft of "Two Magnets." Among the antique presences of "broken gods" and "faded saints" of European history, Denise longs for her new home, a yearning that is "like a child interrupting, tugging at my mind, incongruous, persistent." The child in her wants to explore what is yet unknown, the trees and animal presences, the salmon "circling with muscular swiftness—tints of green, pink, blue, glowing mysteriously." And yet once back in the Northwest, Denise longs for "the worn stone of human centuries":

> Part of me lives under nettle-grown foundations.
> Part of me wanders west and west, and has reached
> the edge of the mist where salmon wait the day
> when something shall lift them and give them to deeper waters.

She has come to the edge to understand the "deeper waters" to which she will be delivered. "A boat is moving / toward me," she writes in "What Harbinger," the opening poem of *Sands of the Well*, "but who / is rowing and what / it brings I can't / yet see."[5]

Denise's corner of the Northwest landscape—its mountain, lake, moon, sky, and animal life—were the perfect emblem for her pilgrimage's end. It is as if her lifelong fidelity to attention had prepared a subject for her that made her spiritual questioning and poetic skill complementary ways of knowing. Throughout her life and work, she was fascinated by, in Robert Duncan's words, the idea of poetic form "as a way of 'knowing' the real . . . not only in order to participate in the universe but also to participate in self."[6]

If the landscape as a whole becomes a metaphorical space through which a poet-pilgrim journeys, then the gray heron is her companion along the way. Herons perched on posts or standing still in shore grass were common sights for Denise on her walks beside the lake. She could train her gaze on them as fixedly as they could watch for luckless fish. A pair of heron poems ("Heron I" and "Heron II") in *Evening Train*—their verisimilitude the envy of Northwest poets—illustrates how the analogies and symbolism of her mythmaking sometimes ruled a reader's response rather than leaving it open-ended.

In "Heron II," her line breaks, rhythms, and imagery flawlessly mimic that always astonishing moment when a gray heron lifts its gangly, almost prehistoric-looking body and flies. It

> rises from perfect stillness on wide wings,
> flies a few beats
> sideways
> trails his feet in the lake,
> and rises again to circle
> from marker to marker.[7]

Then the heron lands on a floating dock—figuratively with a thud—when Denise compares it to a prince coming down from a castle to walk among peasants in a village. The comparison makes for a lighthearted poem; nonetheless its trope might be amusing only to readers who know and treasure nineteenth-century Russian novels. More to the point, it seems lopsided, a weak counterpoint to the "direct treatment of the thing."

In "Heron I" she compares a heron to a saint and vivifies both. She names the heron Saint Simon, remembered for his single-minded devotion; the heron is "standing, standing, standing / upon his offshore pillar," unwavering in its absorption because of its hunger and thirst:

> Hunger,
> thirst, fulfillment
> are ripples that lap his surface;
> his patience absorbs them.
> Time does not pass, for him;
> it is the lake, and full, and still,
> and he has all of it, and wades to strike
> when he will upon the fish.[8]

The particularity of the perception and its imagery fuses Christian mythology and the natural world into an archetypal image of spiritual hunger. The desire to experience the absolute—or timelessness—is inseparable from the act of seeking it: "Time does not pass, for him." Her portrayal of the spiritual immersion necessary for revelation—the striking of the fish that lies hidden beneath the surface of a still lake—can be read as a Christian symbol and also as one that transcends it, arising as it does from its exacting likeness. The heron in its stillness becomes a resonant, irreducible presence, an animal spirit.

From an early age, Denise and her sister, Olga, had a sense of "having a definite and peculiar destiny" because of a felt kinship with two ancestors who were religious seers—a Christian one on their mother's side and a Jewish one their father's. Because of the strength of their intuited connection, Denise and Olga were certain those earlier lives "would be somehow unified and redeemed" in them. As she wrote in "The Sense of Pilgrimage," "One of them was Schneour Zalman, the founder of Habad Hasidism; the other, Angel Jones of Mold, a Welsh tailor whose apprentices came to learn Biblical interpretations from him while cutting and stitching. The presence in the imagination of such figures and their relation to oneself is a kind of personal mythology, and can function as a source of confidence and as an inspiration for the artist; but I am unsure of whether, or how, it may acquire sufficient universality to affect others: perhaps by causing the reader to seek, and to recognize, parallels in his own background."[9]

In many poems in her last books, Denise gazed back at her childhood to understand better the origins of and her confidence in her calling. In "From Below" she recalls being a young child whose sensations rather than thoughts drew her attention to gazing and wondering "about what rises / so far above me into the light." In "That Day" she recounts a rapturous vision, shared with her mother, of "a column / a defined body, not of light but of silver rain," moving across a lake and wrapping them in "its veil of silver." Their astonishment is compared in the poem to "Blake's inkwash vision / of 'The Spirit of God Moving upon the Face of the Waters.'"

Of all the childhood poems, "First Love" most explicitly locates her mythic and poetic origins in a particular experience. She is crawling on the ground at a family picnic when a flower growing in "a bare patch of that poor soil" arrests her attention:

> It looked at me, I looked
> back, delight
> filled me as if
> I, not the flower,
> were a flower and were brimful of rain.
> *And there was endlessness.*
> Perhaps through a lifetime what I've desired
> has always been to return
> to that endless giving and receiving, the wholeness
> of that attention,
> that once-in-a-lifetime
> secret communion.

Emily Warn

Her boundaryless (undifferentiated) communion with the flower is paradoxically also an experience of individuation—she knows herself to be and not be the flower, and just as paradoxically she senses her experience of timelessness occurs within the temporal—of her life and of human history:

> suddenly
> There was *Before I saw it,* the vague
> past, and *Now.* Forever. Nearby
> was the sandy sweep of the Roman Road,
> and where we sat the grass
> was thin.[10]

Thus her experience of the *all* at the picnic becomes literally and figuratively the sacred space and time from which she sets out, an initiate with new spiritual and cultural knowledge to guide her: "What I desired / has always been to return." In remembering this experience, Denise interestingly rejects her earlier conception of pilgrimage as "stages of a journey, moments of vision presaging the secret that will bring seeker to his goal, but which are quickly forgotten again, or hidden again in the imagination."[11]

Instead, in "First Love" she has come to understand that her vision was a "once-in-a lifetime" occurrence, a fact she reiterates in "Once Only" (surely a nod to Rainer Maria Rilke): "every initiation / did not begin / a series, a build-up: the marvelous / did happen in our lives, our stories / are not drab with absence: but don't / expect now to return for more." One can prepare to be "utterly present" to moments of oneness, but they are all, "now or never," beautiful but transitory, as life is. In "A New Flower," a companion poem written from the "new" perspective of life's end, she strips away a sunflower's petals to find

> A darker shade
> of the same spring green—a new flower
> on this fall day, revealed within
> the autumn of its own brief bloom.

I set the tray of tea and cookies on a coffee table within easy reach of Denise. Her sock monkey is propped on its pillow on a straight-backed chair. Behind me bookshelves are crammed with contemporary novels, art books, books of essays, and with Anton Chekhov, Charles Dickens, and other literature from her childhood. Many more bookshelves filled with poetry are upstairs, closer to where she revises her poems' drafts. In the past Denise has often jumped up, disappeared, and then returned with a book to make a point or share a passage. Now it takes a great effort for her to sit up.

Having our tea in the living room feels strange. The room is more like a parlor, reserved for visiting scholars, than the kitchen where we usually sip tea and talk—after we've pushed aside piles of mail and propped open books to make room for the teapot. A vase filled with flowers, common ones from her garden or Northwest floral varieties—tulips, sunflowers, daffodils, lilies—always sits in the window, which frames her beloved view of a narrow inlet of Lake Washington. From the table she could see four Lombardy poplars on the far shore rise in a shapely, formal European elegance against a tangle of firs, cedars, and maples, a dark-green forest, an "almost-wilderness," a remnant of the old growth forest that once covered the Northwest. Through the window Denise could watch the moon rise above it. As she wrote in "October Moonrise,"

> Moon, wisp of opal fire, then slowly
> revealed as orb arising,
> still half-hidden; the dark
> bulk of the wooded ridge
> defined by serrations of pine and fir against
> this glow.

The moonlight's glow becomes a path of "gold unalloyed" on the water, her observation sliding into a metaphor for spiritual seeking, one more example of how the city park and its harbor, its "woods, the lake, / the great-winged birds, the vast mountain at the horizon, / are Nature: *metonymy of the spirit's understanding*" (emphasis added), as in "The Almost-Island." She never names the elements of the Northwest landscape: Lake Washington is the lake, Mount Rainier the mountain, Seward Park her "almost-island." Her erasure creates an idealized Platonic landscape, its elements becoming in her poems likenesses of the forms of ultimate reality, of the forms behind the forms.

If nature in her poetry is a metonym for spiritual understanding, then the mountain stands for a divine presence hidden within yet not of this material world—at least she investigates through her poems whether this is true. She could see the mountain through her southern kitchen window and, of course, from many vantage points throughout the city. The mountain towers above it all, often hidden by Northwest weather, "a majestic presence become / one cloud among others, / humble vapor, barely discernible."[12]

Each mountain poem takes its shape in an "unending 'silent secret conversation'" that Denise holds with the mountain, a dialogue between her poet-pilgrim self and the divine, which is best characterized by Paul Celan's ideas. Alluding to Walter Benjamin's essay on Franz Kafka, Celan quotes the line "attention is the natural prayer of the soul." He continues, "The poem becomes . . . the poem of a persona who still perceives, still turns towards phenomena, addressing and questioning them. The poem becomes conversation. . . . Only the space of this conversation can establish what is addressed, can gather it into a 'you,' come by dint of being named and addressed, brings its otherness into the present."[13] In the mountain poems, she intensely focuses on directly grasping the mountain's physical form so that she can make visible its invisible presence.

In "Elusive" the mountain is there on the horizon, then not, a rhythm that the opening lines replicate:

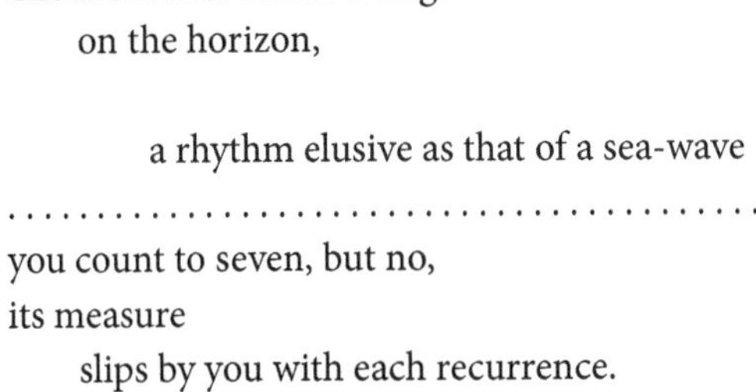

> The mountain comes and goes
>   on the horizon,
>
>   a rhythm elusive as that of a sea-wave
> . . . .
> you count to seven, but no,
> its measure
>   slips by you with each recurrence.

Appearing and disappearing, the massive mountain becomes fluid, a "sea-wave," flowing in time as Denise's perception of it flows in the poem, and yet its cadence is beyond measure. The poem's artistry actualizes what cannot be known—that the mountain is inescapably physical and yet unfixed, an ever-changing and so nonexistent essence.

The paradox of the real's becoming a way to see inwardly the nature of the absolute is also the subject of "Looking Through":

> palest blue,
> as if
> snow and rock,
> the whole great mass of mountain,
> were transparent
> and one could look
> through at more sky
> southward.
> Luminous mountain,
> real,
> unreal sky.

While Denise's mountain metaphysics cannot be exactly correlated with a single religion, some do take place within a Christian context. For example, in "*the mountain's daily speech is silence,"* the silence is that of God throughout the centuries. In "Effacement" insubstantial clouds cloak the mountain's immensity, turning it into the humble "archangel / walking with Tobias on dusty roads."

Halfway through our tea, our talk turns, as it usually does, to poetry. We discuss which books we're reading, poetry we've recently discovered that we like, and of course, our own work—what we're writing about and whether we're writing or struggling to write. That afternoon I boasted about setting up a new routine so I could be more disciplined about writing. She paused, looked at me intently, and replied matter-of-factly, "You know, Emily, I've never written according to a schedule."

On my way home along the lake, and many times afterward, I have thought of that remark. Denise didn't doggedly pursue poetry projects. She didn't force herself to write when there was nothing for her to say. Her poems arrived out of an intensity and delight in watching for the extraordinary in daily life. They were a sharing of "joy as if it were cake or water, / something ordinary, not rare at all."

Six weeks later Denise passed away. Her absence has become a presence for me. I see Saint Simon in every heron on Lake Washington. When I drive around a bend and suddenly see snow-covered rocky clefts in the clouds, it's her mountain and not Mount Rainier. I feel as if I've also glimpsed her, my sightings unpredictable and ephemeral, conspiratorial and companionable as our friendship: "next time," she writes in the last line of her last poem, "I'll move like cautious sunlight, open / the door by fractions, eavesdrop / peacefully."[14]

Donna K. Hollenberg

• PRIMARY WONDERS, PRIMARY JOYS •

Emily Warn and Denise Levertov

Soon after she moved to Seattle, Denise Levertov noticed a difference between the responses to nature in poets from the Northeast and those from the Northwest, her final home. Northeasterners are more attuned to a "humanly populated landscape," and their responses are mediated through other humans, she notes in a 1991 essay, whereas poets of the Northwest "often have a working, not only a recreational—relationship to wild nature." In their poems we are given more of "what is seen," with less emphasis on the poet's reaction to it, she continues, citing as an example Emily Warn's "Axis Mundi," written when she worked as a chain sawer in the natural parks. Levertov comments on Warn's "connectedness" with and "respect" for the wilderness—in this case in the form of the thick trunk of an alder tree situated in a steep ravine, which she and a friend felled, making a clearing in the rain.[1] Yet while this poem certainly evinces Warn's working knowledge of wild nature, as Levertov notes, it is written in the first-person plural, which she overlooks. In fact the titular "axis mundi," or central pillar, is the androgynous "we" of life and myth, as they are engaged in the surrounding landscape. To be fair, Levertov discusses a number of Northwest poets in her essay and thus may have highlighted the aspect of Warn's poem most relevant to her argument, but her omission suggests a lack of understanding of her friend's life as a lesbian, a lack Warn mentioned in an interview.[2] I want to explore the differences between their poetry from the perspective of this lack before turning to their strong mutual interest in nature and their immersion in the mysteries of religious faith.

Warn was first introduced to Levertov by Sam Hamill in the mid-1980s and then became her student at Stanford University in 1992, in the last class Levertov taught there, but she first read Levertov's poetry in high school in Detroit. As a teenager she remembered particularly "The Mutes" and "To Speak," both poems from Levertov's 1967 book, *The Sorrow Dance*. The first is about "the groans men use / passing a woman on the street," when they cannot express their feeling for her in words. Levertov calls such utterance "grief-language . . . language stricken, sickened, cast down," recognizing it as ill-expressed tribute stemming from unfulfilled lives.[3] The second dramatizes the capacity of speech to transform sorrow by moving it "from its / crouched place barring / the way to and from the soul's hall" out into the light, where it can be seen and recognized.[4] When we consider Warn's life at that time, these remembered poems are eerily predictive.

As Warn relates in the preface to *The Book of Esther* (1987), although she grew up in the home of her maternal grandparents in an Orthodox Jewish community in Detroit and was enchanted by Jewish ritual as a child, at age thirteen she felt "banished." By then she understood the role the rabbis had prepared her for: "to bear the pain of labor, to serve my husband, brother or son." The prospect of this role was so untenable that gradually she left her family and her faith, "joined the secular world," and began a spiritual journey that took her to distant parts of the country, to a Zen practice she found inseparable from the practice of poetry, and to an acknowledgement of her love for women. It was her fascination with the character Esther, both as she appears in the Torah and as Ishtar, the Babylonian goddess worshipped at that time in the same region, that allowed her to reclaim her connection with Judaism and to gain her mature voice as a poet and as a lesbian. Like herself in those years, Esther "was an outsider, someone who lives and survives on the fringes of a society that excludes her, and . . . tries to silence her." Significantly in the Torah's version of Esther's story, "the Hebrew God's name is never mentioned."[5]

In the early 1960s, Levertov also wrote "Song for Ishtar," in which, imagining the moon goddess as a sow who "grunts" in her throat and herself "a pig and a poet," she playfully breaks the taboo against selfishness felt by achieving women.[6] This poem and "Hypocrite Women," both published in *O Taste and See* (1964), protest the way women were seen and saw themselves in that prefeminist moment, although Levertov later disavowed the feminist label. (Her concern in that book was social involvement on a broader scale.) Warn's engagement with Esther is much deeper and more extensive than Levertov's. Not only is she the subject of an entire early book, but Warn also includes a section of poems about her in *The Novice Insomniac* (1996). In "Purim," from the earlier book, Esther is depicted as she who "wants to rise into the hearts / of all women ever herded by horses or whips" into "the hands of men who use women's bodies / as proof of their laws." She is "used to emptiness, / used to a broken world / used to the rhythm of transformation." Warn develops this heroic aspect of Esther in "Sounding the Good Name." In the poem's three stanzas, she first explains why Esther's name has lived five thousand years, attributing its longevity to each woman who had the courage to steal "the god from the stars to survive," even as she yearns for a time when she can "shake the stars with laughter." Then she turns to a specific, historical Esther, Etty Hillesum, a young Dutch Jewish woman who, rejecting offers to hide during the Holocaust, chose to serve fellow Jewish refugees in the transit camp Westerbork until she was sent to Auschwitz

                                                            Donna K. Hollenberg

and murdered. Hillesum's diaries have since become famous, not least for their record of her struggle to meet the evil of her situation with inner strength. In Warn's view she wished to be taken to the death camps so that her people could witness an inner mentality blind to an evil as incomprehensible as God.[7] This is the Esther who lives on in Warn or in anyone who, in Esther's name, continues to stand up for outsiders in the face of evil.

Levertov's parents rescued adolescent Jewish boys from Austria in the 1930s, and Levertov was deeply disturbed by the world's silence during and following the Holocaust. When that silence was broken by the widely publicized trial, in 1960–61, of Adolf Eichmann, she wrote her first overtly political poems, the sequence "During the Eichmann Trial," in response. Unlike Warn's focus on a heroic Esther, Levertov imagines the character of Adolf Eichmann, a Haman of sorts. She asserts our need to see and pity him (and the killer instinct in ourselves) before we can then feel the terror of his victims, a stance understandable following a period of pervasive psychic numbing. Levertov attempted to imagine evil in the context of universal complicity, but she did not confuse pity with forgiveness, and later in the decade, she became a revolutionary poet and social activist. Levertov's speaker in the Eichmann sequence is gender neutral, but in her 1970 abecediary, *Relearning the Alphabet,* she remembers being male-identified in "childhood dream-play"—"the knight or squire, not / the lady." Acknowledging the socially engendered passivity of many girls of her generation, she prefers to be "quester, petitioner, win or lose, not / she who was sought."[8] Levertov grew up to be feminine and sometimes aggressively heterosexual. In the 1980s she strongly objected to the view of some lesbian feminists who claimed heterosexual sex to be oppressive.

Warn shares Levertov's penchant for spiritual quest, but in *The Novice Insomniac,* many of her poems are elegiac as well as deeply drenched in a neo-Romantic sense of mystery. Unlike Levertov, whose father, a Jewish Christian and Anglican priest, was her spiritual guide until adulthood, Warn's Irish Catholic father, psychologically damaged during World War II, left the family when she was small.[9] Section 2 of this book is titled "Kaddish," after the Jewish prayer for the dead, and its title poem is dedicated to her father, whom she calls to across "a prairie of grief," unable to forget the searing pain of his departure. The book's impetus, Warn writes in "The Genesis of Insomnia" (defined as a state of vivid dreaming), is a desire for "oblivion," so that she may "build the rooms of God" unnoticed. In her essay in this volume, Warn mentions Levertov's lifelong attachment to the English Romantic poets of her childhood, whose vision she carried with her to the United States and whose speech rhythms she returned to in her later years. They are present behind Warn's poems in this book as well. While Levertov was a devotee of John Keats— his "Ode to a Nightingale" was the first and only poem she knew by heart—Keats's "Darkling I listen" is also present in Warn's hallucinatory dream state. In fact, throughout *The Novice Insomniac,* the poet darkles—that is, she lies concealed in the dark, waiting for her dreams to shine. They do throughout but especially in the last two sections of the book, "Bravura" and "Solitary Date Orchard." The latter has as its epigraph Abraham Heschel's statement that "wonder," a "state of maladjustment to words and notions," is "a prerequisite for an authentic awareness of that which is."

This statement prepares us for "New World Parrot," a deft, comic narrative poem about a female-inspired shift in power. The scene is a group of women, "some / brushing against, some kissing / each other," who are gathered for a birthday party in the garden around a locust tree, in which a "lost parrot" perches, unknown to them. When a young man asks from across the street if anyone has seen his lost bird, at first they "shake their heads no, / laughing in unison." Then one woman locates the parrot, which now "swoops" into their midst, "landing / on a woman's shoulder," until the man, who is sitting with them now, entices it back to him with its favorite food, telling them "from the beginning / how the parrot flew / from its cage" to join them.[10] Warn's accolade to the power of storytelling reminds me of Levertov's six-part early poem "Claritas," from *O Taste and See* (1964), in which she imagines the artist as an "All-Day Bird," a "whitethroated sparrow," who strives "to make his notes / ever more precise, closer / to what he knows." The fine distinctions he makes, often in shadow, "falling between note and note," lead him ultimately to an ecstatic illumination expressed as pure sound that reminds me of Ralph Vaughan Williams's tone poem "The Lark Ascending." Here is the ending of "Claritas":

> Sun
> Light.
> Light
> light light light.[11]

Warn and Levertov renewed and extended their friendship in the 1990s, when both wrote poems that could be read as examples of "natural supernaturalism," as M. H. Abrams described the reformulation, in an increasingly secular world, of the classic triangle of God, mind, and nature to a two-term system of human consciousness transacting with nature.[12] Warn's poems "Beyond" and "Topos," from "Highway Suite," the fourth section of *The Novice Insomniac,* are examples of this reconstituted triangle. "Beyond" is a four-part poem, set at a lake "amidst acres of wheat" in the heat of summer. Here the poet hears "seagulls cry" and sees "geese land" and a "lone sandhill crane" settle before it is cool enough to walk back at night behind a bristling porcupine. The poem begins and ends with stanzas of three-stepped lines (à la William Carlos Williams) arranged around two core stanzas in solid blocks. In the first of these, Warn writes,

                                                    Donna K. Hollenberg

The horizon, not the sky,
draws me, the place where
the land's openness, and the sky's
endlessness meet. The sky shuffles
its tints and clouds. The land rustles.
The horizon stays put, a defining line
that recedes whenever I set out
to reach the notched boulder
on the farthest ridge.[13]

At the literal level, in "Beyond" Warn describes being on the prairie, but this stanza also perfectly conveys what Mircea Eliade calls "a boundary situation," central to religious experience, in which humankind becomes "conscious of [its] place in the universe."[14] That horizon is a "defining line" where sacred and profane meet. Similarly Warn's poem "Topos" conveys a sense of the numinous within the place in which she walks, this time a "meadow in spring sunlight" amid "shadowy oak groves." She details the flora and fauna she passes—cicada, manzanita, pheasants, deer, yellow mustard, even horses—with loving precision, but her deeper motif is "held breath," a way of expressing awe. As she puts it in the poem's second stanza, "A rhythm begins, a loping forward / along the rim of coastal hills," and we feel that for her, walking is a way of meditation in the Buddhist sense, a "tao." In fact, despite the ancient Greek root of her title, she repeats the words "I will pass the way" in the final stanza.[15] Whether centered in ancient Chinese thought or Western, the operative axis in this poem is more vertical than horizontal.

Soon after she moved to Seattle, Levertov was received into the Roman Catholic Church, the culmination of a gradual return to Christian faith begun in the 1980s. In the course of this return, she wrote a number of important poems about exemplary Christian subjects, such as "The Showings: Lady Julian of Norwich, 1342–1416," published in her 1987 book, *Breathing the Water.* Always a nature poet, she continued to write poems we could call examples of natural supernaturalism, like the examples of "mountain metaphysics" and the heron poems Warn cites in her essay included here. Levertov's short poem "Venerable Optimist" combines both facets of this stage in her life. It honors the priest Father Philip Kelly, a family friend of Joan Hallisey, with whom Levertov often attended church in Boston.[16] Levertov regarded Kelly as a free spirit able, like Warn, to see in the dark. In her tribute to him, he sees the dark "as a ragged garment": "Through its rents and moth-holes / the silver light came pouring."[17] Levertov's "Primary Wonder," the final poem in *Sands of the Well* (1996), the last book she published during her lifetime, can also be read in conjunction with Warn's poetry in its deep awareness that the "quiet mystery" prevails, even as many world problems remain unsolved. As Levertov faces death, she praises the "Creator, Hallowed One," for sustaining "anything, anything at all."[18]

Levertov encouraged Warn to investigate the Catholic side of her heritage from her father, which she has yet to do, and she did not live to read Warn's 2008 book, *Shadow Architect*. Yet I'm certain she would have lauded Warn's focus on the twenty-two letters of the Hebrew alphabet in this book; its depth of scholarship and feeling for Jewish tradition would have reminded her of her own father's Hasidic background. (Warn's most important source text is by Rabbi Yitzchak Ginsburgh, a distinguished Hasid.) In the preface Warn writes that the book is her "midrash," her interpretation of the Torah, and that the letters "became . . . doorways into one strand of that tradition," the "hermeneutic conversation known as the Kabbalah." Its structure, a collaborative spiritual journey with poems devoted to each letter accompanied by drawings by Pacific Northwest visual artist Dennis Evans, would also have resonated with Levertov, who collaborated with the photographers Mary Randlett and Peter MacAfee Brown in two poetic sequences. Warn organizes her spiritual journey into three sections. In the first section, poems about the first nine letters, she tells a "linear story": one "shoulders the yoke of *alef* and sets out to invent a self." The second section, about the next nine letters, comprises poems about a "series of trials" rather than a straightforward sequence. The last four poems "present the insights of a realized adept," and as part of the finale, the *tav,* she chose "to loosely translate an eighth-century midrash . . . from the Aleph-Beit of Rabbi Akivah."

The title of Warn's book, *Shadow Architect,* is taken from the fourteenth letter, *nun,* which means "fish" in Aramaic (the language of Jesus) and "kingdom" in Hebrew or "the heir to the throne." It is associated with David, the progenitor of the Kingdom of Israel, Ginsburgh tells us, and in Warn's poems more particularly with "Bezalel, the artisan of the Tabernacle, G-d's house," during the sojourn of the Israelites in the wilderness. The name Bezalel means "'in the shadow of G-d'" and the verb "to shadow" means "to emulate." So did Bezalel, through the knowledge of the power of the letters and their permutations, emulate G-d in the act of Creation, whose ultimate purpose is that all Creation become a 'house' for G-d.'" In Warn's poems about this letter, "The Shadow Architect," "The Tabernacle," and "The Shadow Architect's Studio," she focuses first on the ephemeral quality of this "portable temple of words," which has "no purpose // other than to house the Name." Then, as she fashions letters "into a tree that sighs, that stays put yet moves, / reaching to its limits," she is filled with hope.[19] I am reminded of Levertov's 1968 poetic sequence, "A Tree Telling of Orpheus," about the transformational power of song, its ability to enable us to remember and to "see more."[20] For Warn as for Levertov, "the mystery of making is not a secret hidden within / but a series of moves, a sequence of steps." Finally, in a prose poem about the mundane contents of the shadow architect's studio, Warn ponders the strangeness of a portable temple "for ten words engraved on stone which claim language is more holy than image, that Logos precedes cosmos," and she imagines the bartering that

                                              Donna K. Hollenberg

took place not only for "the finest yarns and most precious metals" but also for "the hours of Bezalel."[21]

Ginsburgh tells us that *nun* "corresponds in Torah to the image of falling" and that, "in particular, humility is the vessel necessary for receiving true insight into G-d's will." This quality permeates the final section of Warn's book, "Instruction for Lighting Fires," which represents the last stage of this journey. The last poem in the book, "Prophecy," is breathtakingly beautiful. It begins by dramatizing a corresponding insight to the earlier image of falling, the intuition that the "experience of Divinity and true unification is . . . essentially a downward flow. . . . You draw down Divinity to effect the absolute refinement and ascent of Worlds."[22] In a long opening stanza about the naked birth of a human being, Warn repeats the word *without* twenty-five times in fifteen lines, inviting her readers, through a catalog of lack, to exhale deeply, to empty themselves. Then, in a shorter stanza, where most of the lines begin with *and,* she describes our desire for "what cannot be had in this world" but we seek anyway, developing "skill" and acquiring "silver / and fields and vineyards and glory / and honor and everything else God has created here."

Next, in several shorter stanzas, she points out that when one "departs from this world," one is empty once more, "whether one is a pauper or king." For, as it is written in Ecclesiastes, "No man rules the life breath." Her poem then turns once more, as she asks why "we toil *as surely as sparks / fly upward*" to fill ourselves when "our appetites can never be sated."[23] I am reminded here of Celan's depiction of an "*Atemwende,* a turning of breath," experienced when he was attempting to reach an "inhabitable distance," which "by attention to things and beings" felt "close to utopia."[24] Warn offers an answer to her question about desire and apparently fruitless work in her final stanza, where quoting Isaiah, she finds consolation in the form of "words in your mouth," which she interprets as the ability to "stand before death happy to have labored / in the Name, as it is written."[25]

Perhaps we can read Levertov's "Moments of Joy," published posthumously in *The Great Unknowing* (1999), as a complement to Warn's "Prophecy." In this short narrative poem about finding God, Levertov employs as metaphor the excitement felt by the grown children of a devoted scholar, who is often apart from them while they sleep, when they awaken to find him sitting, "sleepless," at the foot of their beds, "clearly there to protect / as he had always done." When such an awakening occurs, "the child springs up and flings / arms about him, / . . . taking him by surprise, / and exclaims, 'Abba!'—the old, intimate name / from the days of infancy."[26] Jesuit theologian Karl Rahner, who emphasizes that divinity seeks visibility and a full human response, has called this "the abba experience of intimacy with God," and in Levertov's poem "the old scholar, the father, / is deeply glad to be found," matching the child's joy in finding him.[27] Both Levertov and Warn, each in her own way, have expressed in their poetry this joyful sense of divine grace.

• DENISE LEVERTOV •
Craft and Conscience

Eavan Boland

Like so many other readers, I admire and cherish Denise Levertov's work. Her poems, her images, and above all her distinctive, astringent poetic voice are always present to me. I feel fortunate to have known her somewhat, to have followed her into the workplace at Stanford, where I succeeded her as a professor of English and creative writing, and to have read with her there. Our few conversations are clear and fondly remembered by me. In every way she seems to me a defining poet of the twentieth century, one whose stature grows as the years pass.

But my attitude to her work, nonetheless, is made complex by some of the turns and swerves in her achievement. Nor am I troubled by this. The gift of a great poet, it seems to me, is not simply to be part of reading, remembrance, and judgment, but also to provoke argument in all those secret territories of comprehension. Or maybe simply to join in and enhance an argument that already exists. So when you think of that poet, you not only read them, you also argue with them. Going back and forth. Adding and taking away points. Making and retracting statements as if the poet was still actually there. Which of course, in a certain sense, they are.

When I first met Denise, such an argument was only just forming in my mind. I met her in the mid-1980s in a conflict-driven Ireland. I was beginning to write poems that looked more closely at my own Irish national tradition, contesting it more often than not. And I was beginning to write prose as well. It was a time when language, thought, and every kind of expression—political, cultural, poetic—was in a constant state of revision in the country. An unsettled time. An exciting one.

And yet not one I could immediately relate to Denise's politics or poetry. I knew before I met her that she had been an activist at the time of the Vietnam war. I also understood, simply by reading American literature and commentary, that the Vietnam War had summoned fresh commitments and critical doubts from all kinds of American writers. That it had become a cause for protest.

But the Northern Irish violence, then at its height, was not a cause—not to me, and not to any other Irish writer I knew. It was a complicated array of attitudes, events, historical markers, and neighborly inheritance. I saw it as less a singular situation than an outcome of many. What it summoned therefore was not the collective exercise of conscience but the poise of private judgment and the endless need—at least it seemed so to me—to protect a poetic self from public consciousness. A decade earlier, at the age of twenty-nine, I was already sure of this. I had written an article for the *Irish Times* called "The Weasel's Tooth." There was a need, I wrote there, "to take, in a time of crisis, a cold, reasonable and self-accusing look at oneself, at past beliefs, past mistakes. I must add, indeed insist, that is not simply a personal, but an entirely private assertion of my instinct of where the writer must look in Ireland now. For within that very privacy—that lack, to use a colloquialism, of safety in numbers—lies, I believe, the last chances of writers now in Ireland to liberate themselves from the myths, the hallucinations of cultural unity, the imaginative anti-patriotism which has maimed Irish writing, even as it has, I believe also, mauled Irish politics."[1]

I met Levertov at this pivotal moment. We were introduced in a small house in Dublin, where she was staying with a friend. She was due to give a reading that evening in Buswells Hotel in the center of the city and then travel on to Waterford. I had known of her and had admired her work for many years. In person she immediately appeared to me as a woman of great charm, with a glancing wit that had an undercurrent of merriment. She also seemed to me then, as she does now in memory, somehow displaced. With her English birth, American citizenship, and Russian inheritance, she could have been one of those European exiles at a café table on a summer evening, the mere sight of whom is a historic summary in itself.

My main impression of Denise then is the same as I have now. She was and is a peerless lyric poet. The source for this may well be in those displacements I just mentioned. Her lyric poems are never exactly like anyone else's. Her travels and estrangements had formulated for her a migrant sensibility. Her influences were mixed. Her attachment to William Carlos Williams convinced her of the value of a willful demotic. On the other hand, her beginnings as a poet in the England of the 1940s, in the aftermath of Dylan Thomas and George Barker, left a watermark of musical noise under the conversational ease of her later poems. She is both throwaway and heraldic in her best work. In those iconic poems, she easily persuades the reader to enter a world that begins with small talk and ends with rigor and challenge. In her poem "From the Roof," in her 1961 volume *The Jacob's Ladder*, there is just such a shift on view with a woman gathering in the washing to a whisper of the River Styx:

> my arms full of playful rebellious linen, a freighter
> going down-river two blocks away, outward bound,
> the green wolf-eyes of the Harborside Terminal
> glittering on the Jersey shore,

and a train somewhere under ground bringing you towards me
to our new living-place from which we can see

a river and its traffic (the Hudson and the
hidden river, who can say which it is we see, we see
something of both).

Despite my admiration for her lyric gift, however, this essay constitutes an argument with Denise that has never quite been resolved. Two years ago, in 2013, I wrote the introduction to her magisterial *Collected Poems* brought out by New Directions. There in a certain sense I could lay my dissent aside in sheer admiration for the force and continuity of a powerful vision. But my argument with her is part of a broader argument with poetry itself, and so it returns here in a particular form. Nor is it lightly based. It goes to the heart of her writing and beliefs—also to my own. It questions not only the effect of her poetic journey from England to the United States, from being a British to an American poet, but also her interpretation of the poet's stance. Above all my argument seeks to focus on her unique possession of the civic poem, her insistent redefinition of the settled responsibility of the twentieth-century poet. Though I have disagreements with some of what she said, and a little of what she wrote, I reiterate here what I said at the beginning. To be able to engage with any poet in this way is a true gift, one that speaks to their resilience and substance.

I have a clear memory of Levertov that, even today, recalls for me her strength, her difference, and her candor. It was February 1995. I was in Stanford, at a dinner that centered around my visit there—a visit that culminated in my appointment to Denise's old job. I had arrived from snowy upstate New York, invited to come to Stanford as a part of a search of which I hadn't been any part. I had given a reading earlier in the afternoon and was glad to look up and see Denise in the audience. Later that evening there was a dinner, which she also attended.

It was late. The dinner was almost over. Denise was sitting near me and reminiscing about her experience teaching the Wallace Stegner workshop. She had taught it for ten years and was fondly respected by the poets and her colleagues for her compassion, her idiosyncratic way with the selections, and the sterling witness she gave as a poet. Now she had decided to leave, partly, it seemed, for health reasons.

This was only our third meeting in a decade. I found her conversation, as I had before, graceful and also laced with a tonic wit. This time, however, she was speaking not about her history as a poet but about her experience as a poet-teacher. Despite the obvious goodwill of her conversation, her comments seemed unfamiliar to me and somehow out of reach. I had taught workshops, but not this one. The topic faltered. The conversation came to an end.

We were eating in the Faculty Club at Stanford. The small private dining rooms there gave on narrow corridors and then turned abruptly toward the glass-doored exit. When dinner was over, I came out and saw Denise hesitating, looking back from the end of the corridor. She came back toward me as if to make a final point. *Of course you must make your own workshop,* she said. *It's just that I believe in community.*

The remark seemed to me both moving and unsettling. It was gracious, yet I felt an immediate distance from it. In case this might seem an overinterpretation of a simple comment on teaching, I should explain my reaction: Denise seemed to me then, as she does now, an exemplary poet. But also one whose work and witness describe an arc from individual statement to communal testament. The problem for me lay in the further end of that arc. The more her work—especially some of her later work—moved toward communal witness, the more difficulty I was likely to have with it. I struggled with that estimate later, but I always circled back.

The reason I struggled with this topic came from my own fault lines. Often indeed I worried I was transposing these onto her work. I came from a small country where the public and communal poem had, at least in my view, a questionable history. In fact the Irish nineteenth century is barnacled with patriotic oratory, with lofty statements in rhymed stanzas, where the outcome was an acid bath of rhetoric in which poetic voice was all too often dissolved.

As a beginning poet, I was sure the way forward was to challenge the communal voice. It seemed right to test it with the private voice. I was convinced that an Irish poet—which was my only compass of identity back then—should only return to public statement when it had been abraded by these private perspectives. But that conviction was far more a gradual realization that a sudden insight. At first, as a schoolgirl boarding in a convent at the edge of the sea, I had to find my way through William Butler Yeats, looking closely at the places where his lyric subject fractured and his voice strengthened. At the age of sixteen, I could only unwind those poems, piece by piece, wondering and guessing as I went. And too often changing my mind about almost everything.

In that very year, 1960, my first at boarding school, Denise published a poem in the United States, in the magazine *Poetry.* In less than fifty lines, it stated and restated her relation to history and the public sphere, weighing them in a marvelous series of propositions about place and displacement. Looking back now, this poem –"A Map of the Western Part of the County of Essex in England"—seems to me to clear a new space, to mark a bright pause in American poetry. This, after all, was the age of Robert Lowell, of Elizabeth Bishop's estrangements, of John Berryman's painful soliloquies. Even when history was summoned, the summons was most often delivered by elegy. Now here was Denise's poem, claiming her origins even as she admitted the loss of them.

Something forgotten for twenty years: though my fathers
and mothers came from Cordova and Vitepsk and Caernarvon,
and though I am a citizen of the United States and less a
stranger here than anywhere else, perhaps,
I am Essex-born:
Cranbrook Wash called me into its dark tunnel, the little streams of
Valentines heard my resolves,
Roding held my head above water when I thought it was
drowning me; in Hainault only a haze of thin trees
stood between the red doubledecker buses and the boar-hunt,
the spirit of merciful Phillipa glimmered there.

This free and bold tone shows Levertov at her best. The speed of the shift from
pastoral to magical, from the named rivers to the "haze of thin trees" that is all that
separates her from the heraldic past, is itself a marvel of lyricism. The shift continues from the image of the fourteenth-century Phillipa, daughter of the Duke of
Bedford, and the other gleams of the past in this small corner of England. But the
poem moves toward dispossession rather than possession, as so many of the best
poems by Levertov do:

All the Ivans dreaming of their villages
all the Marias dreaming of their walled cities,
picking up fragments of New World slowly,
not knowing how to put them together nor how to join
image with image, now I know how it was with you.[2]

However powerful this poem, it has often seemed to me to be subtly at odds with
Levertov's kinship with community. Certainly, community is mentioned. The geo-
graphical territory of Essex is provided in the title and as the subject. And yet a
plangent loneliness comes from the lines: a self that has not been gathered into the
usual categories of place or identity and, for that reason, is free to roam through the
big adventures of naming rivers and redefining exile. Not a communal voice, then;
at least not in this poem. This does not seem to me to be exactly the same poet
who came back down the corridor to me at Stanford saying, *it's just that I believe in
community.* It seems a more doubting voice, recognizing the possessions of place
only in the moment of dispossession. Is there a disconnect here? Or is it simply
that as time went on, something shifted in Levertov's vision? Indeed the struggle between community and privacy, between conscience and imagination, was
to define Levertov in a way that separates her from other twentieth-century poets.

It is not always possible to track the shift by which a poet turns from one ethos
to another. But there is no doubt that at a certain moment, Denise turned toward

Eavan Boland

the public poem, seeing it as a transport for the poet's responsibility and not simply as an expression of the poet's imagination. In an address to the International Meeting of Writers in Sofia, Bulgaria, in 1980, she expands this, suggesting that the role of the poet itself carries the obligation to give witness, to bring a message to others, to harness the powers of art to the purposes of communication: "To struggle for justice, we must have a world to struggle in. We must develop all the renewable sources of energy, and like the ancient tribal peoples (whose wisdom we have ignored on all the continents while we trampled upon their sacred places and attempted, at various epochs of history, to destroy them altogether) we must recognize again that the Earth is our Mother. If poets cannot understand this, who will? And if we do understand it, then indeed, we have a role to play, a task to perform: we must use our poet's imagination and our gift of language to bring these realizations to others."[3]

I had a personal experience of Denise's attachment to the public poem. We read together in 1994 at the Cuirt Festival in Galway. As we crossed the Corrib River on the way to the arts center where the event was to take place, she explained to me she would start her reading with a reproach about the litter situation in the city. That seemed to me both endearing and characteristic, however unsettling to the visiting dignitaries and local politicians. It simply proved a concern with the communal and the commonweal, which was one of the most generous aspects of her personality. And to signal a concern for a historic city rather than an intrusive attitude.

Her attitude to the public poem and who should write it, however, was more abrasive. It came up in a brief conversation we had before the reading. She touched briefly on those eminent American poets, and there were several, who would not join her in the 1970s in protesting the Vietnam War. We were sitting on uncomfortable benches in a small back room of the center where we would read. She was looking back to a lost America. The occasions of the war and the commitment to public protest were long over. But her sense of betrayal was in the present, and her regret and even irritation that some poets would not ally themselves to her project of protest poetry lingered.

There was a confidence and insistence about these remarks that stayed with me. They made it clear she was an intelligence, a sensibility, a conscience, and a creator without a single shred of doubt; that the ethical and aesthetic were fused in and by her imagination. In her world the private and public poem had ceded their boundaries to one another. She was loath to unbind them.

And yet in the 1970s, in interviews and conversations, letters and poems she was careful to weave together the roots of activism with the agency of craft, often in original and compelling ways. In one interview she answered a question about Ronald Reagan's policy toward Nicaragua, and his statement that he needed the "support of the American people" to continue it. Levertov responded that "if there are enough demonstrations of concern anticipating the possible invasion of Nicaragua and protesting the already existing intervention, it sounds, from what he said, that they may actually be a deterrent. I'd like to think that poetry, political or otherwise, contributes to that deterrent. Poetry is and should be part of resistance movements."[4]

In a speech for an antiwar rally at the University of Massachusetts Amherst, on April 15, 1970, she made a broad statement of commitment:

> With others of my generation, I moved along to organizing "Writers-and-Artists-Protest-the-War-in-Vietnam" ads in *The New York Times,* in emulation of the French intellectuals' protests about Algeria. Rallies and demonstrations became more and more frequent; veterans destroyed their honorable discharge papers, and we took them to the White House in a little coffin; we organized poetry readings and art exhibits and anthologies, and showed slides of napalmed children. We moved into the support and encouragement of draft resistance. And the war dragged on and at home poverty continued and racism intensified. And the demonstrations got bigger and bigger, but they still were one-issue efforts—Stop the War in Vietnam. And at last a better understanding of the futility of this one-issue campaign began to get through my thick head and some other thick heads.[5]

And yet in a certain sense, these remarks, though quotable, are misleading. They highlight the activist, the agitator, the community builder, the consensus seeker. But Denise was also a scrupulous and loving commentator on poetic craft. She wrote and conversed on the breath, the line, the image, the cadence. These elements were always present to her. In one letter I received from her at Stanford, at the beginning of my time there, she chastised me kindly for reading my own poems without enough attention to breath.

In fact never once did she lose sight of craft and the necessity for it. Her letters to Robert Duncan in the 1950s and '60s glow with accounts of her own poetic growth. But the craft-conscious poet and the activist—the letters make this clear—could occasionally be in conflict. With the onset of the Vietnam War, Duncan rejected her public stance with increasing impatience. "The poet's role," in Duncan's view, "is not to oppose evil, but to imagine it."[6] Duncan could live with and admire Levertov the poet. It was Citizen Levertov that finally exasperated him into a bitter silence.

For me Levertov's stance as activist and poet—as the writer who said that "we have a role to play, a task to perform"—remains an important challenge to the settled categories of both craft and vocation. I have often thought how poignant a contrast she makes to that other migrant from England, Anne Bradstreet. Whereas

Eavan Boland

Bradstreet left a public culture of poetry in the seventeenth century and found herself in the private adventures of home and faith in the New England colony, Denise had done almost the opposite. She left England in the 1940s, when the political poetry of an earlier decade had burned itself out, and found a new politic in the New World.

But the politic she found was remade by herself. Over a lifetime of activism, it widened to include not just responsibility but obligation. Not just inscription but prescription. Her statements, as I have quoted them, both trouble and provoke me into the rich inner arguments I so value. From a very young age, I had seen the necessity to keep the activist and the poet at a safe distance from one another. It was something I learned in the culture I came from. And to a certain extent, I learned it hard.

Looking back, I can see there really was no choice for a young Irish poet, especially a woman: it was necessary to process those decisions early. And I did so: as a student I would travel home from Trinity College on a winter evening, walking down past Merrion Square, the old Georgian neighborhood of the nineteenth-century Anglo-Irish professional classes. There I often stood under the window of Speranza, or Jane Wilde, as she was known later. Speranza, to give her the nom de guerre by which she was known, had been born in the early nineteenth century. She went on to be better known as Oscar Wilde's mother. But in 1848, as a young woman, she made a stand with her openly seditious poems for the *Nation*, the main patriotic journal of the day. One of those poems was called "Jacta Alea Est": "The Die Is Cast." It was a call to arms, an invitation to Irish insurrection. All on her own, Speranza managed to get the magazine closed down.

My suspicion of the public poem came from my vantage point as a reader of poets such as Speranza. The nineteenth-century Irish canon bristles with public poets, swept into oratory and polemic by the injustices of the day. With a few exceptions—Samuel Ferguson and James Clarence Mangan come to mind—the poems are grindingly self-reflexive and steeped in rhetoric. The poet belongs to the cause, the cause to the nation, and the poem is engulfed by the process.

It took time for me to see that clearly. The siren song of the Irish public poem stirred me as a teenager, although never again afterward. I grew out of it quickly, keeping my attention on Yeats, whose ingenious weaving of the public world and private revelation was exemplary. Yet I can still see myself, looking up at that bright and geometric shape on winter nights. Those Georgian windows, with their sashes and panes, were models of grace and carriers of colony. For all that, and despite the ambiguities, there was a moment when my teenage self envied a writing life in which doubt played no part.

My admiration, my envy hardly lasted a season. As I stood under that window in the freezing cold, my own island was only eight years away from the Northern crisis. Out of that furnace came many things. For a poet—I am speaking for myself here—what most clearly emerged was the need for a disciplined language. Also a clear-sighted view of the role of the poet and a permanent suspicion—at least in my case—of the public poem.

Rightly or wrongly, I looked for that suspicion in Denise. I failed to find it in the work that began to register her commitment and protest in the '60s. Given the situation in Ireland, I looked eagerly and early to her poems of protest on the Vietnam War. In 1967 she published *The Sorrow Dance,* which contained the sequence "Life at War." Now, having seen the entirety of her work, in *Collected Poems* I am no longer sure whether the suspicion I looked for could or should have been a legitimate expectation.

By 1968 Levertov had radicalized her idea of poetry and the poet. Until then she had been, as I mentioned before, a signature lyric writer. In that guise she is the poet who gathers "washing as if it were flowers" into her arms in "From the Roof." She can voice "the ache of marriage." She can make a free-handed cityscape in a poem such as "February Evening in New York," where she takes risks with cadence and image to evoke the fluid blues of an urban winter evening:

> As the stores close, a winter light
>> opens air to iris blue,
>> glint of frost through the smoke
>> grains of mica, salt of the sidewalk.[7]

The difficulty for her reader—and I think this difficulty will persist, and maybe should—is in finding a connection between the author of these poems and the one for whom conscience colors the aesthetic. By 1968 it is not so much the poem that is changing in Levertov's mind but the concept of the poet. Years later, in an essay called "Paradox and Equilibrium," published in *New and Selected Essays,* she advocates the integral possibility of social vision and aesthetic statement:

> To suppose that art (of any kind—literary, visual, theatrical, etc.) can be politically and socially "engaged" and still possess its aesthetic integrity is to concede to art an unrestricted, multifarious nature that includes hortatory, and consequently even the (morally) utile. Pure poetry, diatribe, and passionate exhortation meet in the prophets. But the modern artist who wants at once to show truth and urge action must confront the fact that violent and horrific images are commonplace in the age of "live coverage" and instant replays. How can it serve to record, in words or pictures, "man's inhumanity to man"—and to the earth and all that is in it—when people have developed such protective shells of numbness? There is only one way—the way of aesthetic power.[8]

Eavan Boland

There are questions here. Did those two poets—the activist and lyricist—break with each other? Does Levertov's work run the risk of fracturing around her war poems? Or is the risk just to the retention of her audience rather than to her aesthetic? We are lucky to have a revealing correspondence between her and Duncan, edited by Albert Gelpi and Robert Bertholf. It shows the growth of a moral vision that, although she never states so openly, comes almost to the threshold of disowning her earlier, private lyric self.

In her 1967 essay "The Poet in the World," she defended her position: "People are always asking me how I can reconcile poetry and political action, poetry and the talk of revolution. Don't you feel, they say to me, that you and other poets are betraying your work as poets when you spend time participating in sit-ins, marching in the streets, helping to write leaflets etc. My answer is no; precisely because I am a poet, I know, and those other poets who do likewise know, that we must fulfill the poet's total involvement in life in this aspect also."[9] There is a certain vagueness here. Allen Tate's old and sound propositions return to mind: "For what is the poet responsible? He is responsible for the virtue proper to him as a poet, for his special arete: for the mastery of a disciplined language which will not shun the full report of the reality conveyed to him by his awareness."[10]

In the best of her antiwar poems, Levertov's language can be unsettling in its collective intent. Even in a poem such as "Tenebrae"—for which I have enormous admiration—this comes up. The poem moves through its reproaches about the war, through its sustained rebuke of the sensibilities and distractions that are shutting it out. Sometimes the poet's voice makes an uneasy angle to the pronoun. There is a colonization of the third-person plural that can seem almost didactic. The poem finishes with the lines, "And at their ears the sound / of the war. They are / not listening, not listening."[11]

Duncan, in his letters to Levertov—which by 1968 were becoming increasingly acerbic—was particularly harsh about this final line. His language seems to me to miss the real moral intent and power of "Tenebrae." But it is still valuable to look back and see that for certain readers at that time the moral emphasis in the poem looked like a betrayal of aesthetic commitment: "If we were to read this protest of 'they are not listening' with the possibility that the message of the poem does have content as a dream has content—then we would read that following the opening lines, it is the poem itself that is not listening, that has turned to the vanity that all moralizing is in order to evade the imminent content of the announced theme."[12]

These issues recur in the poems from "Life at War," the final grouping in *The Sorrow Dance.* In the title piece, the need to turn the poem, and the poet, from lyric inquiry to public address forces Levertov once again into an oracular relation to the third-person singular. She has no choice but to assume a community of feeling:

> We have breathed the grits of it in, all our lives,
>   our lungs are pocked with it,
>   the mucous membrane of our dreams
>   coated with it, the imagination
>   filmed over with the gray filth of it.[13]

What seems to me especially striking here is the imposition the public stance makes on the poem. Language, tone, and even overall structure are affected. The poem, encased in rhetoric and pronoun, has less space to breath or move.

The question, the doubt, the hesitation about the purpose of the poem is not just the reader's. By now it is shared by the poet. It's plain in Levertov's letters to Duncan at the height of the Vietnam war that she herself is starting to doubt anything that appears to her purely aesthetic. Did this mean that in the face of war, she was willing to yield a private lyric self to an ethical program of witness, believing that only in this way could she make common cause with the common wrong?

When writing the Introduction to the *Collected Poems* I began to discover unexpected reactions in myself to all this. I found myself formulating different answers than the ones I once would have put forward. I began to believe that the rupture between the private Levertov of the early lyrical poems and the later political poet was more apparent than real. I saw real signs of continuance that I had missed in earlier readings. Looked at closely, the poet of witness is in the early poems—the poet who sees the underworld river through the Hudson in "On the Roof—just as the lyric observer is present, turning sequins into shrapnel in "Tenebrae."

In a later poem by Levertov, from *Sands of the Well* the lyric poet and poet of witness come together so strongly as to convince me they had never really been at odds. The poem is called "Uncertain Oneiromancy" and seems to me one of the finest she wrote. I heard it first that evening in Galway when we read together in 1994. Its presence and power were immediately obvious.

When the poem opens the speaker is describing a dream, although that fact only becomes obvious some way down the page. The opening line—"I spent the entire night leading a blind man"—is ambiguous. It merely suggests that the speaker has been through some ordeal, guiding someone who can't see. The second line fills in the location. This blind man has been led through "an immense museum." And the reason for this quickly becomes plain. He has been taken into, and led through the building for his own safety. He has been guided through this great, but still badly defined enclosure so that he could avoid the danger of the open streets outside—"all the swift/chaotic traffic."

"Uncertain Oneiromancy" isn't a long poem. It accomplishes its dark and inward-turning narrative in twenty five lines. By now six have occurred and the

Eavan Boland

scene is set. An unknown speaker has spent the hours of darkness guiding a man who has lost his sight through an institution specifically established for those who can see. But the poem at this point has little time for its own ironies and hurries on.

> I persuaded him
> to allow my guidance, through to the other
> distant doors, though once inside, labyrinthine corridors,
> steps, jutting chests and chairs and stone arches
> bewildered him as I named them at each swerve,
> and were hard for me to maneuver him
> around and between. As he could perceive nothing,
> I too saw only the obstacles, the objects
> with sharp corners: not one painting, not one carved
> credenza or limestone martyr.

The sightless man, the poem tells us, has been brought there for his own safety yet the unexpected has happened. The museum turns out to be surprisingly dangerous. In order to protect him from colliding with corners and angles, the speaker has to keep warning him about "jutting chests and chairs and stone angles." So absorbing is this task, that the speaker—and this is important to the poem—becomes beauty-blind. All she can see are the hazards to a man she brought here as a protection from traffic. Now in a traffic of their own, she misses the power of the objects around her. So busy is she guiding him, warning him, taking his arm and steering him here and slightly pushing him there, that she sees nothing else. Or as the speaker puts it "not one painting, not one carved / credenza or limestone martyr."

As the poem moves on, the old convention of the blind poet is reversed. It is not, after all, the poet who is blind. The poet, the speaker, can see. It is the man she is guiding who is blind. But then, as the poem comes to its powerful conclusion, the poet and the speaker, the blind man and his guide begin to shimmer and dissolve and the whole, mighty argument about vision and faith cracks open in a few lines.

> . . . I stood looking after him,
> watching as the street enfolded him, wondering
> if he would make it, and after I woke, wondering still
> what in me he was, and who
> the *I* was who took that long short-cut with him
> through room after room of beauty his blindness
> hid from me as if it had never been.[14]

Ironies fold into mysteries here, and both become the possession of any open-hearted reader of this piece. Who is the blind man? Don't we learn at the end that he is a fraction, not just of suffering, but of the poet also? And what exactly is this museum? A place where beauty can be visualized, yes. That much is obvious. But a place of unexpected dangers also. And who is this speaker, so aware of danger and yet—at the end—so wistful for the beauty she has forfeited through a single ethical action?

"Uncertain Oneiromancy" is a political poem. It is also an essay in the power and mystery of imagination. Its folded ironies, the suppressed eroticism it canvasses in its flat-voiced narrative, its mapping of the powerful and the powerless, and the unresolved allegories of art and suffering within it compel the reader toward the poem's meaning. Its strength lies in the questions it raises and the absolute refusal of the speaker to go beyond her own limits of narration.

This is not a poem of easy vision or available meaning. It arranges the contraries of ethical and imaginative experience and leaves them to become the reader's own. It also reverses and ironizes the dream convention, allowing the sighted woman to lead the blind man and finally blending the two in an image of mystery and insight. It is an ars poetica made all the more poignant because it is written by a public poet who once contested the private voice and now finds sustenance and truth in it.

In Levertov's case she could have answered any or all my challenges with this single poem. It proves the strength of her lyric voice as well as her subtle understanding of the relation of imagination to the ethical dilemma. In order to return to that poise, she made a signature journey through the public poem and undertook a volatile interpretation of poetic responsibility. I may not always agree with every direction she took. But to be able to ask questions of her work that I know it can always answer is a rare gift indeed.

Eavan Boland

• ENDING IN ABANDON •
Eavan Boland and Denise Levertov

Michael Thurston

In her graceful and gracious argument with Denise Levertov, Eavan Boland mentions their shared link to Stanford, where Levertov taught for part of each year between 1982 and 1993 and where Boland has taught since 1996. While Stanford itself might offer some clue to substantive links between the two poets, the nature of each poet's appointment at the university is perhaps more telling. During the last few years of her time on the Stanford faculty, Levertov lived for most of the year in Seattle, where she also taught part-time at the University of Washington. Similarly Boland divides her time between Stanford, where she directs the creative writing program, and Dublin. Perhaps we see here some indication of the peripatetic aspects of the poetic vocation in general, but it seems to me that the circumstances of these two poets' academic employment actually testifies to a deeper shared history of displacement and mobility. Born in Ilford, Essex (UK), Levertov immigrated to the United States in 1948, lived for some years in Massachusetts, and then settled, if that is the right word, on the West Coast (in two locations, separated by more than eight hundred miles). Daughter of a diplomat, Boland was born in Dublin, spent part of her childhood in London, and has lived and taught on both coasts and in the middle of North America (at the University of Iowa). Cosmopolitanism and the ache for home find their way into both Levertov's and Boland's poems, and they share other interests as well. Both, for example, address political issues and political life in their work; each is sometimes explicitly activist, each is sometimes more skeptical. What is striking, however, is not the similarity of subject—whether exile or politics—but the crucial difference between Levertov's and Boland's poetic representations of the world, the self, and the relationship between the two.

In her argument Boland characterizes this difference in terms of the personal versus the public poem, the arena of the lyric "I" versus the agora of the politically constituted collective. Boland's elaboration of the argument is apt, deft, and generous. In this essay I'd like to offer another way to frame the difference, one that, I hope, complements Boland's, for what is made clearly visible to me when I read these poets side by side is the fact that where Levertov's poetics—whether lyrical or political—is premised on the power of words to effect presence, Boland's is aware, always, of profound and ineluctable absence.

Since Boland addresses Levertov's "A Map of the Western Part of the County of Essex in England," published in her 1961 volume, *The Jacob's Ladder,* I'll adduce that poem as well. In it Levertov famously writes, "though I am a citizen of the United States and less / a stranger here than anywhere else, perhaps, / I am Essex born." The line captures at once the poet's sense (a dozen years after immigrating to the United States) of displacement (to acknowledge oneself "less a stranger here than anywhere" is by no means the same thing as to claim roots) and of the possibility of emplacement through memory. More than the simple assertion of her Essex nativity, it is Levertov's enumeration of sensed specifics that represents the landscape of her childhood. Levertov's syntax grants these recollected features agency: "Cranbrook Wash called me," "Stanford Rivers lost me," "Wanstead drew me." The places inhabited in the past, especially in the formative years of childhood, ground the speaker in a world replete with personal significance. But the poem is up to something more complicated than this as well, for along with those grounding features of Ilford and its environs, Levertov also recalls longing, when she actually inhabited that place, to be elsewhere. Only now that she is in "a far country" does she remember "the first river, the first / field," so the poem emphasizes the grounding power not of the place when one is in it but in the place as remade in memory.[1] The closing lines, with their catalog of discovered building materials, posit a clear relationship between the poetic vocation, with words and lines rather than bricks and lumber, and the rebuilding in imagination of the place in and with which one constructs an identity.

Boland's "An Irish Childhood in England: 1951" offers a similar cocktail of nostalgia and memory, but the dominant note in her poem is the exile's sense of estrangement rather than the re-creation of home in memory and poetic figure. Indeed where Levertov builds up the Essex she has left behind through the accumulation of experiential detail, Boland brings the same elements to bear in order to evoke loss. Her specifics—the big hips and navy skirts of ticket-takers on the London bus, "Ration-book pudding. / Bowls of dripping"—have agency like Levertov's, but they bring home to the child just how far from home she is. More than this, it is the present, the vantage point from which the poem's speaker remembers her Irish childhood, that is more effectively evoked; Boland devotes two stanzas in the middle of the poem to that present, a warm and humid night animated by the atmospheric energy of a coming storm. Like Levertov's speaker Boland's remembers longing for a place other than the one she occupied, but unlike "A Map of the Western County of Essex," "An Irish Childhood in England" names the longed-for place as the Ireland left behind. Distance from her Ilford home enables Levertov to re-create it; distance from her childhood in England enables Boland to re-create not so much it as the absences that constituted it. But amid these differences,

                                                                                    Michael Thurston

the poems share a crucial tendency toward a vocational conclusion. The act of memory for Levertov yields the building materials that figure her poetic work; a new structure can be built from the lived details thus recovered. For Boland recalling her experience of exile enables her to sharpen her sense of what nostalgia really was; it shifts, over the course of the poem, from the vague "love for what I'd never known I had" to the precise "space between the words that I had by heart / and all the other speech that always was / becoming the language of the country that // I came to." The key loss for Boland is her native "language," the "I amn't" that an English teacher condemns by saying, "You're not in Ireland now."[2] While Levertov assumes and performs the representation of presence, Boland understands that she can only limn absence, but both offer the building materials of poetry as the means for working through the conditions of displacement and nostalgia.

Typical of Boland's work along these lines, and interesting in comparison to Levertov's "Map of the Western County of Essex," is "Distances," in which the husband's departure, the couple's absence from the seaside town imagined in detail, and, finally, those details' failure to satisfy all emphasize absence. The key to the poem is the song the speaker hears on the radio and that the husband identifies as he leaves: "I Wish I Was in Carrickfergus." To wish oneself somewhere is, of course, implicitly to acknowledge that one is not there. Boland goes on to describe in compelling detail the fuchsias and market of the coastal Northern Ireland town, but she does so under the shadow of "emigrant grief." Away from it and wishing one were in Carrickfergus, the town is replete with temptations to appetite ("tacky apples"), comfort ("linen for sale"), and vision (a "hill / of spectacles"). The speaker realizes, though, that if she and her husband really *were* in Carrickfergus, the reality of presence would fail the standard of the distantly imagined. The afternoon would be "scentless" in spite of the fuchsias, the handkerchiefs would fail to absorb tears, the apples would be "mush inside the crisp sugar shell," and the spectacles would be "out of focus." More than this, even the disappointments of reality would be incommunicable; the speaker imagines the couple "longing to be able / to tell each other."[3]

The opposition I'm sketching is too broad to capture either poet's nuanced treatment of things and subjects and the relationships among these, but it holds in general, whether the shared topic is spring or children, politics or poetry itself. This blunt opposition between Levertov's confidence about presence and Boland's realization of absence might only earn a shrug; when we sharpen it on specific instances in the two careers, it takes on some significance. Both poets care about what is disclosed in moments of keen perception, whether these are experienced in person or in the poem. Levertov's poems tend to disclose noumenal presence. Though "O Taste and See" begins in denial—"The world is / not with us enough"— the poem undoes its own opening assertion. Obeying the injunction of a "subway Bible poster" to "taste and see," the poem evokes all that comes into being through imagination (and, through the figure of "imagination's tongue," all that can be spoken). The poem comes down heavily on the side of plenitude and being, so that even the nothingness of death becomes flesh. As we read the catalog of things in their thingness and acts that bring them to and into us, the line ending right there at the top of the page comes to seem more and more important. While the sentence says, "The world is not with us enough," the first line avers simply that "the world is."[4] As "Distances" suggests, and as many other of her poems show, Boland, though happy enough to register sights and flavors, ultimately finds the savor of negation and glimpses what Wallace Stevens calls "the nothing that is."[5] Even moments of intense communion—with her baby daughter, say, in "Night Feed" (from the 1982 sequence "Domestic Interior")—move through what is ("This is the best that I can be, / Housewife / To this nursery / Where you hold on, / Dear Life") to where the ladders end: "the long fall from grace."[6] In the same sequence's "Endings," the achieved act of perception yields the key and repeated insight:

> If I lean
> I can see
> what it is the branches end in:
>
> The leaf.
> The reach.
> The blossom. The abandon.[7]

Tastes great versus less filling.

This difference in disposition might be of only passing interest were it not for the way it informs the political consciousness of these two politically conscious poets, the ground for Boland's own argumentative engagement with Levertov. Boland mentions the "confidence and insistence" in Levertov's comments about the public poem and the poet's political responsibility. These seem, to me, to be of a piece with Levertov's ontological confidence and insistence. What I mean here is neither that assumptions about presence are more political than assumptions of absence nor that assumptions of presence necessarily give rise to one set of political commitments while assumptions of absence necessarily give rise to another. I do, though, want to suggest that a poetics like Levertov's, one dedicated to the proposition that the world's plenitude can be known and made manifest in poetic language, yields a political poetry whose confidence and insistence (even when cast, as a lot of public poetry is, in the voice of the lyric "I") sound like the Irish public poem that is Boland's bête noire, while a poetic stance predicated on language's insufficiencies and incapacities yields a political poetry characterized (like Boland's) by skepticism, cautious discipline, and what Boland calls "deep and permanent suspicion."

Michael Thurston

To give a better sense of what I mean, let me compare a representative political poem of Levertov's and one of Boland's best explorations of her own political poetic vision. "Life at War" is among the most powerful poems in Levertov's 1967 volume, *The Sorrow Dance.* It is a poem of emphatic witness, one undergirded by the assumption that what can be seen can be shown and spoken, that what is shown and spoken will effect change. The body is at the heart of the poem; Levertov casts the Vietnam War as a kind of pollution that harms the body ("our lungs are pocked with it"). She trains her keen eye on bodies broken in acts of war:

> to the scheduled breaking open of breasts whose milk
> runs out over the entrails of still-alive babies,
> transformation of witnessing eyes to pulp-fragments,
> implosion of skinned penises into carcass-gulleys.

These are things to which humanity turns "without surprise, with mere regret," typical and repeated violences, the "disasters of war" sketched by Francisco Goya two hundred years ago and described by Homer millennia before that. But Levertov uses her hard-won craft to refresh the horrors. The bodies broken here are, first, those of women and children, vulnerable and unprotected noncombatants. The violence is intimate, aimed at the soft tissues of breasts and guts. The focus on mothers and babies renders this as violence against regeneration. To see such things is to risk vision; eyes that witness these acts are themselves destroyed. And, as if implicitly following Sigmund Freud's lead by linking eye-violence to castration, the metonymic chain brings us at last to those impotent flayed penises. "These acts are done / to our own flesh," she writes. The poem insists on the brute reality of "burned human flesh" the smell of which rises from Vietnam even as the poet writes the lines.

In doing so it assumes (and in writing so Levertov assumes) that language can make that reality present to the reader (a stand-in for the witness whose eyes are at risk within the poem). Indeed Levertov is explicit about this assumption. The human capacities for language and imagination are precisely what the war threatens and what must be mobilized to bring about its end. Humans are creative beings. Our "language imagines" qualities antithetical to war: *mercy, / lovingkindness.* We see each other as made in the image of the divine. Repeated (more than that: "scheduled") violence coats "the mucous membrane of our dreams," films the imagination with "grey filth." The great horror of war is that it corrupts our capacity for compassion. But just as the horrors are perpetrated upon bodies and felt upon the pulses, the poem can remind us—by making these things present to us—that it is in the body, too, that we know joy and love. This knowledge is a "husky phlegm" in all we say, a "presence" that makes our nerves twitch.[8] The poem, like Levertov's political and poetic vision generally, is predicated upon presence. Dread and bitterness are lumps of dough in our bellies; the war is grit in the lungs, film on the skin; violence breaks bodies in ways that break the eyes of those who witness the violence; compassion is a twitch in the skin and phlegm in the throat. Language, crafted by the poet for just this purpose, presents to us our best selves and our worst actions. Love calls us to a life of peace. Such assumptions seem likely enough to produce not only confidence and insistence but also, perhaps, the sort of stridency of which Duncan accuses Levertov in the two poets' painful correspondence of the war years.

Boland's poetry is, I would argue, no less political than Levertov's. Its political manner, though, is cautious and doubtful where Levertov's is certain and sure, and I would locate the ground for Boland's attitudes not only in her reaction to the Irish public poem and its consequences on the ground in Belfast, Derry, and Omagh, but also in her own guiding assumption that what the poem can limn is not what is but what is not. All of this is apparent in "The Journey," a poem as driven to witness as is "Life at War," but one underwritten by and written out of skepticism about seeing, showing, speaking, and poetry's power to make any difference at all.

"The Journey" begins in medias res (and midsentence): "And then the dark fell and 'there has never,' / I said, 'been a poem to an antibiotic.'" While poets, male ones according to the single pronominal reference to them, waste their time dreaming up "hyssop dipped / in the wild blood of the unblemished lamb," the merits of sulfa go unsung. These poets' rush past the realities of the "infant souls weeping at the entrance-way" pointed out in the poem's epigraph (from the sixth book of the *Aeneid*) in their search for "the obvious // emblem" has dire consequences both for poetry and for its ability to respond to its world: "every day the language gets less // for the task and we are less with the language." The explicit foil for Boland's meditation on witness is this male and martial poetry whose myopic gaze misses obvious suffering, but the poem more subtly and thoroughly mounts a critique of precisely the poetry of witness that it seems, at first, to call for.

It does so through a dream vision in which Boland's speaker is instructed by Sappho, who shows up when the speaker is drowsy and receptive. This poetic predecessor leads the speaker on a descent that, though it unfolds over three stanzas and repeats the word *down* five times, still arrives at a place that seems at once the speaker's world and the underworld of myth: "beside a river in what seemed to be / an oppressive suburb of the dawn." There the speaker is claimed by Sappho—"you . . . stand beside me as my own daughter"—and absorbs a complex lesson on poetry's duty to "the silences in which are our beginnings." Sappho at first simply reveals a vision to Boland's persona: "Behold the children of the plague." Across the river the speaker sees shadowy women and children, victims, Sappho tells her, of precisely those diseases—"Cholera, typhus, croup, diphtheria"—that once "racketed / in every backstreet and alley of old Europe" but have been tamed (at

                                                            Michael Thurston

least in Europe) by the antibiotics that male poets have failed to celebrate. When the speaker recoils from the vision, Sappho urges her to overcome the distancing, historicizing view that would define the women by their work, class, or dress and to identify instead with their shared motherhood:

> But these are women who went out like you
> when dusk became a dark sweet with leaves,
> recovering the day, stooping, picking up
> teddy bears and rag dolls and tricycles and buckets—
>
> love's archaeology.[9]

This has happened; this is what humanity is capable of; this is the link that binds you to what you see. The general mechanics of the moment are similar to those at work in Levertov's "Life at War." Boland's vision of an alternative, silenced (and gendered) history resonates with the poetry whose silencing incensed the speaker at the beginning of "The Journey" and suggests the alternative poetic project she might undertake, a poetry that would, like Levertov's, bear witness to this history of women's suffering. Patricia Haberstroh has written that this is exactly what happens. Boland's speaker, she argues, "identifies with the anxiety of grieving women who must confront the terror of their children's death," and when the speaker whispers, "let me at least be their witness," Sappho encourages her.[10] This reading nicely aligns the poem not only with Levertov but also with much contemporary poetry on themes of history and suffering (and indeed with certain projects Boland has outlined for her work in her published prose).[11] But where Levertov's assumptions of presence and efficacy underwrite a confidence in poetry's capacity to effect change, Boland's assumptions take the work in a different direction. Her speaker explicitly offers to take up the mantle of witness, but Sappho's response seems less to encourage a poetry of witness than to indicate stark limits to poetry's witnessing capacity. "What you have seen is beyond speech," she says, "beyond song," which is to say that the vision Sappho has revealed to the speaker is beyond poetry, even a poetry whose primary aim is to "be their witness."

What follows, though, is not an abdication of poetic responsibility (Sappho has, after all, shown the poet this vision for a reason, and she goes on in the next stanza to "adopt" the speaker as her poetic descendant) but is instead a chastened and precise sense of poetic responsibility within poetry's limited capacities to respond. Boland is "chastened" and "precise" (especially considered against Levertov's confidence and insistence), a result of her skepticism, her awareness of poetry's inability simply to represent. Sappho shows Boland's speaker that poetry is limited in its capacity to respond to untold generations of maternal and familial suffering but that it must act within those limits. The limits, I would argue, are twofold in the poem. First suffering cannot be represented adequately. Where Levertov calls up graphic detail in an attempt to involve the reader's body in reaction to the violence wrought on the represented bodies, Boland opts for the suggestive image of suckling shadows, a refraction of what cannot be shown. If the suffering that brought women and children to this threshold of the underworld is unspeakable, this is nevertheless a generative silence, one in which women poets from Sappho to Boland "have an origin like water." While this vision of suffering is "beyond speech, / beyond song," it is, Sappho says, "not beyond love." But love lies outside the field of the poem. So the work of the poet might, in fact, be a call to change in the extraliterary (the political) world.

While it cannot be contained in the verbal construct that would bear witness, the suffering gestured at within the poem can be remembered ("remember it, you will remember it," Sappho tells the speaker) in the practices of "love's archaeology," in actions of caring that reenact these mothers' love. This seems, on the surface, not so dissimilar from Levertov's concluding gesture in "Life at War," where the knowledge of love and joy might be activated by the bodily knowledge of our capacity to kill, where the deft certainties of "living at peace" should result from the nervy presence of our violent tendencies. But here is where the second limit comes into play, for the acts that make common cause with history's victims are, for Boland, not the politics of a peace movement motivated by images of mothers and children elsewhere but are instead the practices of care undertaken for those at hand. To remember, after all, is at once to recall or hold in the mind and to reassemble, recollect. "Love's archaeology" for Boland is the exploration of a midden close to home, the gathering of bits and pieces. There is a modesty in the political ambition she sets up for poetry here, but that chastened ambition is in line at once with the poet's own resistance to the "public poem" whose dangers she sketches in her essay on Levertov and with the attuned awareness to absence that I am suggesting is key to Boland's vision.

I have dwelled here on what separates these two poets, but I will close with what I see as a strength they share. Where each explores and enacts the political in her own way, each is perhaps at her best when close attention to things in the world discloses an essential truth. Boland would shy from calling this essence noumenal; I am less sure that Levertov, with her philosophical confidence in hardwon craft, would cavil at the term. James Breslin describes the poems of a volume such as *The Jacob's Ladder* as performing a kind of "magical realism" in which Levertov's close attention to what she observes transforms it.[12] Think of the poem "The Tulips," whose short-lined stanzas demonstrate Levertov's transformation of all she has learned from William Carlos Williams and Robert Creeley as well as the transformation of the title flowers. We are first presented with the things themselves: "Red tulips / living into their death / flushed with a wild blue." When the observing eye is sufficiently patient, sufficiently passionate, hues that a more

Michael Thurston

superficial gaze might miss become visible. This is good, true, and valuable enough as an insight, but the poem goes on to work the image through a set of metaphoric condensations—all caught in progress rather than presented in stasis—so that the flowers are first wings, then ears, then rabbits. The gaze captures change and movement; it renders the tulips as dynamic as William Wordsworth's daffodils, but it locates the wind in the flowers rather than reporting on the wind's action on the flowers. It is only when we shift to another stanza, another viewpoint, that the wind itself becomes an agent, "shaking the loose pane," and when, in this draft, the tulips' petals fall, their sound distills the nature of the flowers and of the wind and of the witness: "that sound one / listens for."[13]

Sometimes both Levertov and Boland turn their exquisite lyric attention on an object to do the work of the ars poetica, attending (often through the image of another mode of art) to art itself and what its purposes might be. I'll close with two poems that have been linked in my mind since I first read them as emblematic of each poet's obliquely self-referring gaze. In "The Stonecarver's Poem," Levertov inspects a hand and reads from it a text about creation. She constructs the lines in this poem to hold multiple possible meanings in suspension. The first stanza—"Hand of man / hewed from / the mottle rock"—can, for example, be read so "hewed" describes the hand or the action performed by the hand, allowing the opening and controlling image to be at once sculpted and the sculptor's. The hand, whether carving or carved, suggests the human relationship with the divine by recalling Adam "almost touching" the hand of God, and this lineage reminds us of the further link between creation and Creation. The human imagination is a version of the divine creative will. The oscillation between possible readings continues throughout the short poem, so that it either is or makes the closing lines' "smallest inviolate / stone violet."[14] More than an implicit claim for the sacred power of art, then, the poem is both an exploration and an enactment of the rise of meaning from material, the inextricability of the artist's will and the medium's message.

Boland's "Bright-Cut Irish Silver" mines a vein of gender politics in a similar "object lesson": "I take it down / from time to time, to feel / the smooth path of silver meet the cicatrix of skill." The speaker reads evidence of engraving on the object as "scars," and she elaborates for the artisanal "aptitude for injuring" a markedly patriarchal lineage ("passed on from father to son, to the father / of the next son"). But things cut multiple ways in Boland's poem just as they do in Levertov's, for the phrase that concludes the opening stanza—"cicatrix of skill"—can mean at once the scar skill has left on the object or the scar that skill itself is. The question opened in this manner at the beginning of the poem is refined, if not answered, at the end. The "gift" of art that is imagined in terms of wounding is brought, through a set of parallel constructions in the penultimate two stanzas, into the poet's hands. "Cold potency," at once the object the speaker holds and the scarred and scarring skill that fashioned it, belongs, by the end of the poem, as much to the poet as to the engraver.[15] And the poem itself demonstrates this in its insistent and self-referring sound patterning. Notice the dense alternation of hard palatals and sibilants in "the smooth path of silver meet the cicatrix of skill," the liquid consonants in "injuring / earth while inferring it in curves and surfaces." These enact as they describe the lapidary skill "for wounding," in language as in silver.

Time and chance bring to the poet's hands the "cold potency" with which she fashions a verbal object, an object lesson. The specific curves and surfaces in which each poet infers her aptitude for injuring depend upon the places she has lived in and left behind; the poets she studies; the circumstances she feels compelled to face, to name, to absorb; the predisposition to see and to say what is or what is not, nothing that is not there or the nothing that is. Denise Levertov and Eavan Boland construe quite differently the responsibility poetry bears for, in, and to the demands of its moment. Each, however (and this is a key bond between them—more important, even, than Stanford), takes seriously the proposition that poetry is responsible, and each poet's searching and self-conscious exploration of that responsibility is its own complex and continually renewing gift.

Michael Thurston

NOTES

Wordsmiths in the Idea Factory

1. Kropotkin, *Mutual Aid,* 20.
2. Levertov, "Untaught Teacher," 157.
3. Reznikoff, "Talk," 97.
4. Williams, "Sort of a Song," 55.
5. Pasternak, *I Remember,* 62.
6. Levertov, preface to *To Stay Alive,* 105.
7. Levertov, "Untaught Teacher," 164.

Working Poets

1. Thackeray, *Pendennis,* 152.
2. Nelson, *Our Last First Poets,* 159.
3. Ibid., 17.
4. Raab, *Writers and Their Notebooks,* 138–39.
5. Since the writing of this essay, Pawlak has published four poetry collections: *Jefferson's New Age Salon: Mashups and Matchups* (Cervena Burva Press, 2010); *Go to the Pine: Quoddy Journals 2005–2010* (Plein Air Editions/Bootstrap Press, 2012); *Natural Histories* (Cervena Press, 2015) and *Renaissance: New and Selected Poems and Poetic Journals 2005–2015* (Hanging Loose Press, 2016).
6. Pawlak, *Buffalo Sequence,* 15.
7. Pawlak, *Special Handling,* 11–21.
8. Pawlak, *Official Versions,* 13–65

The Sudden Angel Affrighted Me

1. Waskow, *Godwrestling,* 15.
2. Levertov, *Stream and Sapphire,* viii.
3. Bertholf and Gelpi, *Letters of Duncan and Levertov,* xvi.
4. Levertov, "Poetry, Prophecy, Survival," in *New and Selected Essays,* 146.
5. Levertov, *Tesserae,* 7, 11.
6. Levertov, *Collected Poems,* 112, 767, 825, 345, 177.
7. Levertov, *Poet in the World,* 124.
8. For a more detailed account of their conflict, see "Opening the Gates of the Imagination," my review of the Duncan/Levertov letters in *Poetry Flash,* 296–97.
9. "Poetry, Prophecy, and Survival," in Levertov, *New and Selected Essays,* 146.
10. Levertov, *Collected Poems,* 342, 678, 756.
11. Bertholf and Gelpi, *Letters of Duncan and Levertov,* 669.

12. Levertov, *Collected Poems*, 677, 678.

13. Levertov, *New and Selected Essays*, 148.

14. Levertov, *Collected Poems*, 967

15. Levertov, *Stream and the Sapphire*, viii.

16. Levertov, *Collected Poems*, 735.

17. Ibid., 967.

18. Frye, *Words with Power*, 70.

19. Levertov, *Collected Poems*, 295.

20. Rabbi Burt Jacobson, founder of Kehilla Community Synagogue in Berkeley, also taught and guided me toward this view of faith.

21. Levertov, *Collected Poems*, 778, 855, 976.

Engagement, Inquiry, Faith

1. "I remember discussing the problem—the problem of the lack of peace poems—with some poet friends, Robert Hass and David Shaddock." Levertov, *New and Selected Essays*, 154.

2. Ibid., 15.

3. Levertov, *Collected Poems*, 363, 364.

4. Shaddock, "Denise Levertov," 135–36.

5. Levertov, *Collected Poems*, 432, 966.

6. Hallisey, "Denise Levertov's 'Illustrious Ancestors,'" 5.

7. Brooker, *Conversations*, 60.

8. Smith, "Songs of Experience," 181.

9. Levertov, preface to *To Stay Alive*, vii–ix.

10. Levertov, *Poet in the World*, 253.

11. Levertov, introduction to Shaddock, *Dreams*, xi.

12. Shaddock, *Dreams*, 65.

13. Levertov, *O Taste and See*, 15.

14. Hallisey, "Denise Levertov's 'Illustrious Ancestors,'" 8.

15. Shaddock, *In This Place*, II, n.p.

16. Levertov, Collected Poems, 67.

17. Ibid., 825.

18. Shaddock, *In This Place*, VIII, n.p.

19. Pacernik, *Meaning and Memory*, 69–70.

20. Shaddock, *In This Place*, XIII, n.p.

21. Levertov, *New and Selected Essays*, 250, 263, 258, 255.

22. Levertov, *Collected Poems*, 67.

23. Ibid., 89.

24. Levertov, *New and Selected Essays*, 257.

25. Dunbar, "Denise Levertov: 'The Sense of Pilgrimage,'" 23.

26. Levertov, *Collected Poems*, 836.

27. Levertov, *New and Selected Essays*, 253–54.

28. Levertov, *Collected Poems*, 956, 1001, 855.

29. Levertov, *New and Selected Essays*, 27; Shaddock, "Denise Levertov," 135–36.

30. Palmer, *Active Boundaries*, 22.

31. Shaddock, "Great Blue Heron in Boynton Beach," 42.

"Denise and Me"

1. Levertov, *Collected Poems*, 673.

2. Ibid., 980.

"Nothing / like a real bridge"

1. In her memoir, *True*, Armantrout recalls its title as "Morning," but this early poem has not been published.

2. This may be an understatement. See DuPlessis's analysis of Armantrout's poem "Tone" (1978), which reappeared in the epoch-defining anthology *In the American Tree* (2002). Rachel Blau Duplessis, "One Perfect Limousine," in *A Wild Salience: The Writing of Rae Armantrout*, ed. Tom Beckett. Cleveland : Burning Press, 1999, 39.

3. DuPlessis, "One Perfect Limousine," 39.

4. Armantrout, "Poetic Statement," 24.

5. Heidegger, *Being and Time*, 174.

6. "Poetic Statement: Cheshire Poetics," 25.

7. Armantrout, "Poetic Statement," 25.

8. "Cheshire Poetics," 25.

9. Armantrout, *Extremities*, 25.

10. "Poetic Statement: Cheshire Poetics."

11. Armantrout, "Poetic Statement," 24.

12. Perelman, "Exactly," 158.

13. Armantrout, *Collected Prose*, 48, 41; Armantrout, "Poetic Statement," 26.

14. Matthew Arnold, "To a Friend," in *The Poems of Matthew Arnold* (London: Oxford University Press, 1909), 40.

15. Oppen letter to June Oppen Degnan, August 5, 1967. quoted in Rifkin, "That We Can Somehow Add Each to Each Other?," 715.

16. Armantrout, "Poetic Statement," 124.

17. Armantrout, "Poetic Statement," 25.

18. Perelman, "Exactly," 155.

19. Armantrout, "Poetic Statement," 25.

20. Levertov, *Collected Poems*, 291–22.

21. Oppen, *Selected Letters*, 388.

22. Levertov, *Collected Poems*, 328, 322, 292, 322.

23. "One Perfect Limousine," in *A Wild Salience: The Writing of Rae Armantrout*, ed. Tom Beckett.

24. My reading should make clear that I respectfully disagree with DuPlessis's influential early reading of this sequence and its "quest," suggesting as she did that Levertov "rediscovers the authentic self" in the work by adhering to mythic structures rather than critiquing them. This appears still to be the accepted reading; see Rifkin, "That We Can Somehow Add Each to Each Other," 732.

25. Levertov, *Poet in the World*, 112.

26. Oppen, "Mind's Own Place," 32.

27. I quote from the poem "Technologies," which Oppen wrote in anger at Levertov and which opens *This in Which*, and from the essay he wrote "at her"—"The Mind's Own Place." Much of their quarrel can be found in Rifkin; I would only disagree with the way she sets

out the dates of the fight, making it look as though Levertov made the initial attack in a review when that was not the case.

28. Jackson, "Common Time," 20.

29. Ibid., 25.

30. Levertov, *Poet in the World,* 49. Emphasis added.

31. Quoted in Rifkin, "That We Can Somehow Add Each to Each Other?," 718.

32. Levertov, *Collected Poems,* 326.

33. Eliot, *Complete Poems and Plays,* 117–45.

34. Levertov, *Collected Poems,* 321, 323.

35. Hollenberg, *Poet's Revolution,* 144.

36. Levertov, *Collected Poems,* 65.

37. Armantrout, *Veil,* 71.

38. Armantrout, *True,* 119.

39. Derrida, "White Mythology," 211, 210.

40. Armantrout, *Veil,* 126.

41. Hejinian, "Interview with Rae Armantrout," 19.

42. Armantrout, *Veil,* 138.

43. Armantrout, *Versed,* 8.

44. Armantrout, *True,* 98.

45. Levertov, *Poet in the World,* 53, 4, 53.

46. Armantrout, "'My Poetry Isn't Built on Hope,'" 106.

47. Armantrout, *Veil,* 126.

48. Armantrout, *Money Shot,* 30.

49. See Derrida, "Violence and Metaphysics," for his explanation of deconstruction's hermeneutics of the question.

50. Armantrout, *Veil,* 91.

51. Levertov, *Collected Poems,* 327.

52. Armantrout, "'My Poetry Isn't Built on Hope,'" 106, 109.

53. Levertov, *Poet in the World,* 115.

54. Armantrout, *Versed,* 5.

55. Dickinson, *Complete Poems,* 87.

56. Hopkins, *God's Grandeur,* 15.

57. Armantrout, *Money Shot,* 27.

58. Stewart, "What Praise Poems Are For," 236.

59. *Journal,* July 1852.

60. Armantrout, *Versed,* 69, 89, 93, 13.

61. Armantrout, *Collected Prose,* 35.

62. Ibid., 36.

63. Armantrout, *Veil,* 58.

64. Ibid., 60.

65. Armantrout, "'My Poetry Isn't Built on Hope,'" 113.

Interview with Bruce Weigl

1. This interview took place on January 20, 2012.

2. One of the many "Little Mermaid" movies made.

3. Levertov, *Collected Poems,* 990.

4. Weigl, *Unraveling Strangeness,* 4.

5. Eliade, *Sacred and the Profane,* 166.

6. Weigl, *Archeology of the Circle,* 117–18.

7. Ibid., 135.

8. Weigl, *Circle of Hanh,* 7.

9. Levertov, *Collected Poems,* 880.

10. Weigl, *Declension in the Village,* 70.

Generations of Poets

1. "Life at War," in *Collected Poems,* 341.

2. Levertov, *Collected Poems,* 186, 341, 213–14.

3. Weigl, *Song of Napalm,* 44.

4. Weigl, *Romance,* 20.

5. versedaily.org. Accessed July 28, 2017.

6. Weigl, *Abundance of Nothing,* 24–25.

Poet's Ear, Poet's Voice

1. Denise Levertov to Susan Eisenberg, November 22, 1994, from the private collection of Susan Eisenberg.

2. DL to SE, May 31, 1982.

3. "Hanging in, Solo" and "Asbestos"; "Through the Ceiling, Maiden Voyage" and "Companion."

4. DL to SE, January 7, 1989.

The Expansive View

1. Eisenberg, *It's A Good Thing,* 42, 46, 44, 60.

2. Eisenberg, *Pioneering,* 5, 32, 3.

3. Eisenberg, *Blind Spot,* 3, 21, 26, 38, 66, 76.

4. Eisenberg, *Perpetual Care,* 7, 38, 32, 11.

5. Eisenberg, "Poems about Gaza Jews," 127.

The Integrity of Words

1. Denise Levertov to Betty Kray, summer 1966, ms. at 92Y Unterberg Poetry Center, NYC.

From Denise Levertov to Kathleen Norris

1. Norris, *Little Girls,* 40–41.

2. Levertov, *Collected Poems,* 262.

3. Norris, *Little Girls,* 15–16.

4. Ibid., 42.

5. Levertov, *New and Selected Essays,* 241.

6. Levertov, *Poet in the World,* 47.

7. Ibid., 97–98.

8. Norris, "Finding a Place for Poets in the Church," 1054.

9. Norris, "Monks, Meaning, and Metaphor," 47.

10. Norris, "What I Took Home from the Cloister," 11.

11. Levertov, *New and Selected Essays*, 249, 250.

12. Levertov, *Collected Poems*, 908.

13. Norris, "Monks, Meaning, and Metaphor," 47.

14. Norris, "What I Took Home from the Cloister," 12.

15. Levertov, *Collected Poems*, 775.

16. Lacey, "'To Meditate a Saving Strategy,'" 24.

17. Dunbar, "Sense of Pilgrimage," 22.

18. *Collected Poems*, quoted material from p. 961.

19. Levertov, *Collected Poems*, 961, 908, 114.

20. Levertov, *New and Selected Essays*, 257.

21. Norris, *Journey*, 128.

Dear, Dear Denise

1. Levertov, *Collected Poems*, 157.

2. Sáenz, *Elegies in Blue*, 67.

Dear Ben, Dear Denise . . .

1. Levertov, *Collected Poems*, 369.

2. Ibid., 673.

3. Quoted in Hawes and Kelly, *Cambridge Companion*, 144.

4. "Notes on Organic Form," in *The Poet in the World* (New York: New Directions, 1973), 13.

5. Levertov, *Collected Poems*, 370.

6. *Dreaming the End of War* (Port Townsend, Wash.: Copper Canyon Press, 2006).

7. Sáenz, *Dreaming*, 66, 39, 22, 23.

Dear Denise

1. Levertov, *Collected Poems*, 262, 342.

2. Levertov, interview, in O'Connell, *At the Field's End*, 35.

3. I left the University of Michigan in January 1960, in the first semester of my senior year, and moved to Berkeley. After a period of working at various jobs, traveling, and writing, in 1968 I went back to school at UC Berkeley. I attended Cal for three semesters (1968–69), completing with honors the BA in Spanish literature and language.

4. Levertov, *Collected Poems*, 270.

5. Young, *Geography*, 39.

P.S. Mind the Gap

1. "General Prologue to the Canterbury Tales," in *The Works of Geoffrey Chaucer*, ed. F. W. Robinson (London: Oxford University Press, 1968), 21.

2. Levertov, *Collected Poems*, 357, 383, 383, 508, 356, 389.

3. Levertov, Interview, in *Floating Bear*, July 11, 1961, 1115–17.

4. Levertov, "Argument," 115, 116.

5. Denise Levertov to Robert Duncan, May 18, 1965, in *The Letters of Robert Duncan and Denise Levertov*, eds. Robert Bertholf and Albert Gelpi (Palo Alto: Stanford University Press, 2004), 493.

6. Bertholf and Gelpi, *Letters of Duncan and Levertov,* 234, 492, 711.

7. Hollenberg, *Poet's Revolution,* 354–55.

8. Louis Simpson, "The Character of a Poet," in Hank Lazer, *What Is a Poet?* (Tuscaloosa: University of Alabama Press, 1984), 16.

9. Lazer, *What Is a Poet?,* 210, 211, 221.

10. Levertov, *Collected Poems,* 357.

11. Young, *Heaven,* 136.

12. Blake, *Milton,* 62.

The Almost Wilderness

1. Levertov, *Collected Poems,* 984.

2. Williams, "Poem as a Field," in *Selected Essays,* 291.

3. *Collected Poems,* 853

4. "Meditation and Voices," in *Collected Poems,* 32.

5. Levertov, *Collected Poems,* 853, 860, 32, 858, 915.

6. Duncan, "Ideas of the Meaning of Form," in *Selected Prose,* 35.

7. Levertov, *Collected Poems,* 856.

8. Ibid., 855.

9. Levertov, *Poet in the World,* 70.

10. Levertov, *Collected Poems,* 985, 981.

11. Levertov, *Poet in the World,* 63.

12. Levertov, *Collected Poems,* 1003, 988, 857, 900, 855.

13. Celan, "Meridian," in *Selected Prose,* 50.

14. Levertov, *Collected Poems,* 853, 896, 855, 1004, 1012.

Primary Wonders, Primary Joys

1. Levertov, *New and Selected Essays,* 5, 10.

2. In a 2002 interview with me, Warn said that Levertov "accepted her woman partner but was uncomfortable with it." Unless otherwise indicated, the autobiographical information here is from this source.

3. Levertov, *Collected Poems,* 252.

4. Ibid., 258.

5. Warn, *Book of Esther,* viii.

6. Levertov, *Collected Poems,* 183.

7. Warn, *Book of Esther,* 27, 5.

8. Levertov, *Collected Poems,* 325.

9. Levertov's mother, also pious and an amateur painter, was her artistic guide.

10. Warn, *Novice Insomniac,* 19, 7, 100, 107.

11. Levertov, *Collected Poems,* 201–2.

12. Abrams, *Natural Supernaturalism.*

13. Warn, *Novice Insomniac,* 60.

14. Eliade, *Images and Symbols,* 34.

15. Warn, *Novice Insomniac,* 66.

16. I am grateful to Joan Hallisey for this information.

17. Levertov, *Collected Poems,* 873.

18. Ibid., 976.

19. Warn, *Shadow Architect*, xi, xiii, 7, 86, 87.

20. Levertov, *Collected Poems*, 317.

21. Warn, *Shadow Architect*, 87, 89.

22. Ginsburgh, *Alef-Beit*, 208, 213, 18.

23. Warn, *Shadow Architect*, 135, 136.

24. Celan, "Meridian," in *Collected Prose*, 52.

25. Warn, *Shadow Architect*, 136.

26. Levertov, *Collected Poems*, 1010–11.

27. Rahner, *Everyday Faith*, 98; Levertov, *Collected Poems*, 1011. Levertov owned a copy of Rahner's book.

Denise Levertov

1. Boland, "Weasel's Tooth."

2. Levertov, *Collected Poems*, 165, 145–46.

3. Levertov, *Light*, 184.

4. Brooker, *Conversations*, 42.

5. Levertov, *Poet in the World*, 121.

6. Bertholf and Gelpi, *Letters of Duncan and Levertov*, 669.

7. Levertov, *Collected Poems*, 105.

8. Levertov, *New and Selected Essays*, 139.

9. Ibid., 136.

10. Tate, *Essays*, 17.

11. Levertov, *Collected Poems*, 344.

12. Bertholf and Gelpi, *Letters of Duncan and Levertov*, 666.

13. Levertov, *Collected Poems*, 340.

14. Ibid., 915–16.

Ending in Abandon

1. Levertov, *Collected Poems*, 145.

2. Boland, *Outside History*, 106–7.

3. Ibid., 69.

4. Levertov, *Collected Poems*, 213–14.

5. Stevens, *Collected Poetry*, 8.

6. Boland, *Outside History*, 140.

7. Ibid., 147.

8. Levertov, *Collected Poems*, 340–41.

9. Boland, *Outside History*, 182–84.

10. Haberstroh, *Women Creating Women*, 81.

11. A notable anthology devoted to those themes is, for example, Forché, *Against Forgetting*. See Boland's essays in *Object Lessons*, especially "Outside History" (123–53).

12. Breslin, *From Modern to Contemporary*, 163.

13. Levertov, *Collected Poems*, 167–68.

14. Ibid., 217.

15. Boland, *Outside History*, 29.

Abrams, M. H. *Natural Supernaturalism: Tradition and Revolution in Romantic Literature.* New York: Norton, 1971.

Armantrout, Rae. *Collected Prose.* San Diego: Singing Horse, 2007.

——. *Extremities.* Berkeley, Cal.: Figures, 1978.

——. *Money Shot.* Middletown, Conn.: Wesleyan University Press, 2011.

——. "'My Poetry Isn't Built on Hope': An Interview with Tom Beckett." In Beckett, *Wild Salience,* 104–14.

——. "Poetic Statement: Cheshire Poetics." In *American Women Poets in the Twenty-First Century: Where Lyric Meets Language,* edited by Claudia Rankine and Juliana Spahr, 24–26. Middletown, Conn.: Wesleyan University Press, 2002.

——. *True.* Berkeley, Cal.: Atelos, 1998.

——. *Veil: New and Selected Poems.* Middletown, Conn.: Wesleyan University Press, 2001.

——. *Versed.* Middletown, Conn.: Wesleyan University Press, 2009.

Beckett, Tom, ed. *A Wild Salience: The Writing of Rae Armantrout.* Cleveland: Burning, 1999.

Bertholf, Robert J., and Albert Gelpi, eds. *The Letters of Robert Duncan and Denise Levertov.* Stanford: Stanford University Press, 2004.

Blake, William. *Milton: A Poem by William Blake.* Boulder and New York: Shambala/Random House, 1978.

Boland, Eavan. *Object Lessons: The Life of the Woman and the Poet in Our Time.* New York: Norton, 1995.

——. *Outside History: Selected Poems, 1980–1990.* New York: Norton, 1990.

——. "The Weasel's Tooth." *Irish Times,* June 7, 1974, p. 7.

Breslin, James. *From Modern to Contemporary: American Poetry, 1945–1965.* Chicago: University of Chicago Press, 1984.

Brooker, Jewel Spears, ed. *Conversations with Denise Levertov.* Jackson: University Press of Mississippi, 1998.

Celan, Paul. *Collected Prose.* Trans. Rosemarie Waldrop. Riverdale-on-Hudson, New York: Sheep Meadow, 1986.

Chaucer, Geoffrey. *The Complete Poetry and Prose of Geoffrey Chaucer.* Edited by John H. Fisher. New York: Holt, Rinehart & Winston, 1977.

Derrida, Jacques. "Violence and Metaphor." In *Writing and Difference,* 84–132. University of Chicago Press, 1978.

——. "White Mythology: Metaphor in the Text of Philosophy." In *Margins of Philosophy,* trans. Alan Bass, 207–72. Hemel Hempstead: Harvester Wheatsheaf, 1982.

Dickinson, Emily. *The Complete Poems of Emily Dickinson.* Edited by Thomas H. Johnson. London: Faber & Faber, 1975.

Dunbar, Judith. "Denise Levertov: 'The Sense of Pilgrimage.'" *America* 178 (1998): 22–25.

Duncan, Robert. *A Selected Prose*. Edited by Robert J. Bertholf. New York: New Directions, 1995.

——. "'One Perfect Limousine.'" In Beckett, *Wild Salience,* 37–46.

Eisenberg, Susan. *Blind Spot*. Omaha, Neb.: Blackwaters, 2006.

——. *It's a Good Thing I'm Not Macho: A Cycle of Poems*. Boston: Whetstone, 1984.

——. *Perpetual Care*. Boston: Third Rail, 2016.

——. *Pioneering: Poems from the Construction Site*. Ithaca, New York: Cornell University Press, 1998.

——. "Poems About Gaza Jews." *Virginia Quarterly Review* 92, no. 1 (2016): 127.

——. *We'll Call You If We Need You: Experiences of Women Working in Construction*. Ithaca, New York: Cornell University Press, 1998.

Eliade, Mircea. *Images and Symbols: Studies in Religious Symbolism.* trans. by Philip Mairet. N.J.: Princeton University Press, 1991.

——. *The Sacred and the Profane: The Nature of Religion*. Trans. Willard R. Trask. New York: Harcourt Brace, 1957.

Eliot, T. S. *The Complete Poems and Plays*. New York: Harcourt, Brace & World, 1962.

Forché, Carolyn, ed. *Against Forgetting: Twentieth-Century Poetry of Witness*. New York: Norton, 1993.

Frye, Northrop. *Words with Power*. Edited by Michael Dolzani. Toronto: University of Toronto Press, 2008.

Ginsburgh, Rabbi Yitzchak. *The Alef-Beit: Jewish Thought through the Hebrew Letters*. Northvale, N.J.: Aronson, 1991.

Greene, Dana. *Denise Levertov: A Poet's Life*. Urbana: University of Illinois Press, 2012.

Haberstroh, Patricia, *Women Creating Women: Contemporary Irish Women Poets*. Syracuse: Syracuse University Press, 1996.

Hallisey, Joan. "Denise Levertov's 'Illustrious Ancestors': The Hassidic Influence." *Melus* 9, no. 4 (1982): 5–11.

Hawes, Marjorie, and John Kelly, eds. *The Cambridge Companion to W. B. Yeats*. London: Cambridge University Press, 2006.

Hejinian, Lyn. "An Interview with Rae Armantrout." In Beckett, *Wild Salience,* 12–26.

Hollenberg, Donna. *A Poet's Revolution: The Life of Denise Levertov*. Berkeley: University of California Press, 2013.

Hopkins, Gerard Manley. *God's Grandeur and Other Poems*. New York: Dover, 1995.

Howe, Florence, ed. *No More Masks: An Anthology of Twentieth-Century American Women Poets*. New York: Harper Perennial, 1993.

Jackson, Richard. "A Common Time: The Poetry of Denise Levertov." *Sagetrieb* 5, no. 2 (1986): 5–46.

Kropotkin, Peter. *Mutual Aid: A Factor of Evolution*. London: Heinemann, 1902.

Lacey, Paul. "'To Meditate a Saving Strategy': Denise Levertov's Religious Poetry." *Renascence* 50, nos. 1–2 (1997–1998): 17–32.

Lazer, Hank, Ed. *What Is a Poet?* Tuscaloosa: University of Alabama Press, 1987.

Levertov, Denise. "An Argument." In *The Floating Bear: A Newsletter: Numbers 1–37, 1961–1969,* edited by Diane di Prima and LeRoi Jones, 545. La Jolla, Cal.: McGilvery, 1973.

——. *Collected Poems*. New York: New Directions, 2013.

——. *New and Selected Essays*. New York: New Directions, 1992.

——. *The Poet in the World*. New York: New Directions, 1973.

——. Preface to *To Stay Alive*. In *Poems 1968–1972*, 105–7. New York: New Directions, 1987.

——. *The Stream and the Sapphire*. New York: New Directions, 1997.

——. *O Taste and See*. New York: New Directions, 1964.

——. "The Untaught Teacher." In Levertov, *Poet in the World*, 149–99.

MacGowan, Christopher, ed. *The Letters of Denise Levertov and William Carlos Williams*. New York: New Directions, 1998.

Nelson, Cary. *Our Last First Poets: Vision and History in Contemporary American Poetry*. Chicago: University of Illinois Press, 1981.

Norris, Kathleen. "Finding a Place for Poets in the Church." *Christian Century*, November 19, 1986, 1053–54.

——. *Journey: New and Selected Poems 1969–1999*. Pittsburgh: University of Pittsburgh Press, 2001.

——. *Little Girls in Church*. Pittsburgh: University of Pittsburgh Press, 1995.

——. "Monks, Meaning and Metaphor." *Critic* 49, no. 3 (1995): 38–47.

——. "What I Took Home from the Cloister." *U.S. Catholic*, October 1997, 9–12.

O'Connell, Nicholas, ed. *At the Field's End: Interviews with 22 Pacific Northwest Writers*. Seattle: University of Washington Press, 1998.

Oppen, George. "Technologies. In *The Collected Poems of George Oppen*, 93–94. New York: New Directions, 1975.

——. "The Mind's Own Place." In *George Oppen: Selected Prose, Daybooks, and Papers*, edited by Stephen Cope, 29–37. Berkeley: University of California Press, 2007.

——. *Selected Letters of George Oppen*. Edited by Rachel Blau DuPlessis. Durham, N.C.: Duke University Press, 1990.

Pacernik, Gary. *Meaning and Memory: Interviews with Fourteen Jewish Poets*. Columbus: Ohio State University Press, 2001.

Palmer, Michael. *Active Boundaries: Selected Essays and Talks*. New York: New Directions, 2008.

Pasternak, Boris. *I Remember*. New York, Pantheon, 1959.

Pawlak, Mark. *The Buffalo Sequence*. Port Townsend, Wash.: Copper Canyon, 1977.

——. *Special Handling: Newspaper Poems New and Selected*. Brooklyn: Hanging Loose, 1993.

——. *Official Versions*. Brooklyn: Hanging Loose, 2006.

Perelman, Bob. "Exactly: The Poetry of Rae Armantrout." In Beckett, *Wild Salience*, 155–64.

Raab, Diana M., ed. *Writers and Their Notebooks*, Columbia: University of South Carolina Press, 2010.

Rahner, Karl. *Everyday Faith*. London: Herder & Herder, 1968.

Reznikoff, Charles. "A Talk with L. S. Dembo." In *Charles Reznikoff: Man and Poet*, edited by Milton Hindus, 102–15. Orono, Maine: National Poetry Foundation, 1984.

Rifkin, Libbie. "'That We Can Somehow Add Each to Each Other?': George Oppen between Denise Levertov and Rachel Blau DuPlessis." *Contemporary Literature* 51, no. 4 (2010): 703–33.

Sáenz, Ben. *Dreaming the End of War*. Port Townsend, Wash.: Copper Canyon, 2006.

——. *Elegies in Blue*. El Paso, Tex.: Cinco Punta, 2002.

Shaddock, David. "Denise Levertov: A Remembrance and an Appreciation." *Poetry International* 3 (1999): 135–36.

———. *Dreams Are Another Set of Muscles*. Sausalito, Cal.: In Between Books, 1987.

———. "A Great Blue Heron in Boynton Beach." In *From the Well of Living Waters*, edited by L. Weiss, 40. Oakland, Cal.: Kehilla Synagogue, 2011.

———. *In This Place Where* Something's Missing *Lives*. N.p.: Alileah, 1990.

Smith, Lorrie, "Songs of Experience: Denise Levertov's Political Poetry." In *Denise Levertov: Selected Criticism*, edited by Albert Gelpi, 177–200. Ann Arbor: University of Michigan Press, 1993.

Stewart, Susan. "What Praise Poems Are For." *PMLA* 120, no. 1 (2005): 235–45.

Stevens, Wallace. *Collected Poetry and Prose*. New York: Library of America, 1997.

Tate, Allen. *Essays of Four Decades*. Chicago: Swallow, 1968.

Thackeray, William Makepeace. *The History of Pendennis: His Fortunes and Misfortunes, His Friends and His Greatest Enemy*. London: Black, 1903.

Warn, Emily. *The Book of Esther*. Seattle: Jugum, 1987.

———. *The Novice Insomniac*. Port Townsend, Wash.: Copper Canyon, 1996.

———. *Shadow Architect*. Port Townsend, Wash.: Copper Canyon, 2008.

Waskow, Arthur. *Godwrestling—Round 2: Ancient Wisdom, Future Paths*. Woodstock, Vt.: Jewish Lights, 1996.

Weigl, Bruce. *The Abundance of Nothing: Poems*. Evanston, Ill.: TriQuarterly Books/Northwestern University Press, 2012.

———. *Archeology of the Circle: New and Selected Poems*. New York: Grove, 1999.

———. *The Circle of Hanh: A Memoir*. New York: Grove, 2000.

———. *Declension in the Village of Chung Luong: New Poems*. Keene, N.Y.: Ausable, 2006.

———. *A Romance*. University of Pittsburgh Press, 1979.

———. *Song of Napalm: Poems*. New York: Grove/Atlantic, 1988.

———. *The Unraveling Strangeness*. New York: Grove, 2002.

Williams, William Carlos. "Poem as a Field.of Action." In *Selected Essays*, 230. New York: New Directions, 1954.

———. "A Sort of a Song." In *The Collected Poems of William Carlos Williams*, vol. 2, edited by Christopher MacGowan, 55. New York: New Directions, 1962.

Young, Al. *Geography of the Near Past*. New York: Holt, Rinehart & Winston, 1976.

———. *Heaven: Collected Poems 1956–1990*. Berkeley, Cal.: Creative Arts, 1992.

CONTRIBUTORS

RAE ARMANTROUT has published twelve books of poetry, most recently *Itself* (2015). *Versed* (2009) received the Pulitzer Prize and the National Book Critics Circle Award. *Partly,* a volume of new and selected poems, was published in 2016. Armantrout was a fellow at the Rockefeller Center in Bellagio, Italy, in 2014.

EAVAN BOLAND is the author of seventeen books of poetry, most recently *A Woman without A Country* (2014), as well as several books of prose, most recently *A Journey with Two Maps: Becoming a Woman Poet* (2014). She is the Bella Mabury and Eloise Mabury Knapp Professor in the Humanities at Stanford University. She wrote the introduction to *The Collected Poems of Denise Levertov* (New Directions, 2013).

MARTHA COLLINS is the author of seven books of poetry, most recently *Day unto Day* (2014). She has also published four collections of cotranslated Vietnamese poetry. She founded the creative writing program at University of Massachusetts Boston and served as Pauline Delaney Professor of Creative Writing at Oberlin College, where she continues to serve as editor at large for *Field* magazine. Her eighth book of poems, *Admit One: An American Scrapbook,* was published in 2016.

ALISON HAWTHORNE DEMING is the author of four books of prose, most recently *Zoologies: On Animals and Human Spirit* (2014), and four books of poetry, most recently *Rope* (2009). She has also edited two anthologies. Deming has received many awards, including two National Endowment for the Arts Fellowships. She is Agnese Nelms Haury Chair of Environment and Social Justice and professor of creative writing at the University of Arizona.

SUSAN EISENBERG, a multidisciplinary artist and educator, is the author of five poetry collections, most recently *Stanley's Girl* (2016), and the nonfiction book *We'll Call You When We Need You: Experiences of Women Working Construction* (1998). She is currently a resident artist and scholar at the Women's Studies Research Center, Brandeis University.

REGINALD GIBBONS is the author of nine books of poetry, among them *Creatures of a Day* (2008), a finalist for the National Book Award, as well as a novel and several volumes of translations. His most recent prose work is *How Poems Think* (2015). He was the editor of *TriQuarterly* magazine for many years and is now the Frances Hooper Professor of Arts and Humanities at Northwestern University.

DONNA K. HOLLENBERG, professor emerita of English at the University of Connecticut, is the author most recently of *A Poet's Revolution: The Life of Denise Levertov* (2013). She has also published three earlier books about the poet H.D. as well as many essays about twentieth-century poetry and fiction in the United States and Canada.

ROMANA HUK is author or editor of three books, most recently *Stevie Smith: Between the Lines* (2005). She has also published many essays on contemporary poetry and poetics in the United States, United Kingdom, Ireland, and France. She is editor in chief of *Religion and Literature,* which is housed in the Department of English at Notre Dame, where she has taught since 2002. Her current book project is "Rewrit[ing] the Word 'God': In the Arc of Postmodern Theory, Theology, and Poetry."

PAUL LACEY, professor emeritus of English at Earlham College, is the coeditor of Denise Levertov's *Collected Poems* (2013). He is also widely known through his writing in connection with the American Friends Service Committee, where he was clerk of their board of directors.

ALDON LYNN NIELSEN, the George and Barbara Kelly Professor of American Literature at the Pennsylvania State University, is the author of eight books of poetry, most recently *Tray* (2015). He has also published five critical works, most recently *Integral Music* (2004), and has coedited two volumes of innovative poetry by black writers. He is the recipient of the Josephine Miles Award, the Darwin Turner Award, and other honors.

KATHLEEN NORRIS is the author of *Journey: New and Selected Poems* (2001) and three books of prose, most recently *Dakota: A Spiritual Geography* (2001). She recently completed a term as the Robert J. Randall Distinguished Professor in Christian Culture at Providence College in Rhode Island.

MARK PAWLAK is the author of eight poetry collections and the editor of six anthologies. His latest book is *Natural Histories* (2015). For many years Pawlak has been an editor of *Hanging Loose,* one of the oldest independent literary journals and presses in the country. He is the director of academic support programs at the University of Massachusetts Boston.

PEGGY ROSENTHAL writes widely on poetry as a spiritual resource. Her books include *Praying through Poetry: Hope for Violent Times* (2003). For New Directions she compiled and edited *Making Peace* (2008), a selection of Levertov's poems. She blogs regularly for the journal *Image.*

BEN SÁENZ, professor of creative writing at the University of Texas, El Paso, is a poet, novelist, artist, and writer of children's books. He has published seven novels, four children's books, and five collections of poetry, most recently *The Book of What Remains* (2011). Among his awards are the American Book Award and the Lannan Poetry Fellowship.

PETER DALE SCOTT, a former Canadian diplomat and English professor at the University of California, Berkeley, is the author of ten books of prose, most recently *The American Deep State* (2014), and six books of poetry, most recently *Tilting Point* (2012). He was awarded the Lannan Poetry Award in 2002.

DAVID SHADDOCK, poet, playwright, and psychotherapist, is the author of three collections of poetry, most recently *Dreams Are Another Set of Muscles* (1987). He has also written a play and two nonfiction books on relationships and couples therapy. His poems have won the *Ruah Magazine* Power of Poetry Award and the International Peace Poem Prize among other honors.

MICHAEL THURSTON, the William R. Kenan, Jr. Professor of English at Smith College, is the author of three books, most recently (with Nigel Alderman) *Reading Postwar British and Irish Poetry* (2014), as well as numerous essays. He is a contributing editor for the *Massachusetts Review*.

EMILY WARN has published five books of poetry, most recently *Shadow Architect* (2008). Her essays and poems have appeared widely in a variety of American journals.

BRUCE WEIGL is the author of fourteen books of poetry and a memoir. *The Abundance of Nothing* was a finalist for the 2013 Pulitzer Prize in poetry, and most recently he published *The Secret of Hoa Sen* (2014), a collection of poems that he translated from Vietnamese with the author, Nguyen Phan Qye Mai. He is currently translating a book with Nguyen Ba Chung of 108 poems about war and peace from Vietnam's beginnings in the tenth century. Weigl is Distinguished Professor of Arts and Humanities and faculty liaison for veterans services at the Lorain County Community College.

AL YOUNG is the author of twenty-two books, including poetry, fiction, essays, anthologies, and musical memoirs. His most recent book of poems is *Something about the Blues* (2008). Young served as California's poet laureate from 2005 to 2008. Other honors include two American Book Awards and, most recently, the 2011 Thomas Wolfe Award. Young is Distinguished Professor in the MFA in Writing Program at the California College for the Arts in San Francisco.

INDEX

All works cited are by Levertov unless otherwise noted.

Abrams, M. H., 176
Abubakar, 153–54
Abundance of Nothing, The (Weigl), 86, 87
"Advent 1966," 26–27
"Agnus Dei," 27–28, 29
Alexander, Juanita, 119
Allen, Donald, 160
"All Shook Up" (Pawlak), 20, 21
American Women Poets in the Twenty-First Century: Where Lyric Meets Language (anthology), 54
"Annunciation," 45
Aquinas, Thomas, 32–33
"Argument, An," 159
Ariel (Plath), 6
Armantrout, Rae, 53–70
"Ascension," 113
"Ascension" (Norris), 109–10, 113, 117
"At the Justice Department November 15, 1969," 86
"Autobiography: Urn Burial" (Armantrout), 65
"Avenue C" (Kinnell), 11
"Axis Mundi" (Warn), 173
Ayres, Bill, 158

Baal Shem Tov, Israel, 38
Baraheni, Reza, 93
Baraka, Amiri, 154, 159, 160–61, 163. *See also* Jones, LeRoi
Basho, 16
Beat poets, 146
Beckett, Tom, 54
Before Columbus Foundation, 120
Being and Time (Heidegger), 54

Benttinen, Ted, 1
Berenson, Lori, 100
Berkeley, University of California, 25, 35–36, 49–50
Bernstein, Charles, 161
Berrigan, Daniel, 37
"Beyond" (Warn), 176–77
Bice, Thayer, 141
"Birthmark: The Pretext" (Armantrout), 65
Blackburn, Paul, 7, 8
Black Mountain poets, 30, 35, 47, 58, 146, 159
Blake, William, 163
Blind Spot (Eisenberg), 100–102
Bly, Robert, 124, 138
Boas, Franz, 156
"Body and Blood" (Norris), 116
Body Rags (Kinnell), 11
Bohmer, Roger, 1
Boland, Eavan, 193–202
"Bomb as Jesus" (Shaddock), 40
Book of Esther, The (Warn), 174
Book of Nightmares, A (Kinnell), 11
Book of What Remains, The (Sáenz), 121
Boston Five, 36
Bowering, George, 151
Bradstreet, Anne, 186–87
Branch Will Not Break, The (Wright), 105
Brandeis University, 88
Breathing the Water, 177
Breslin, James, 200
"Bright-Cut Irish Silver" (Boland), 201–2
Bromige, David, 155
Brooks, Ernie, 1
Brooks, Gwendolyn, 160

CPSIA information can be obtained
at www.ICGtesting.com
Printed in the USA
BVHW03*0454250518
517205BV00001B/1/P